W9-DFS-165

HARVARD EAST ASIAN MONOGRAPHS

79

MERCHANTS, MANDARINS, AND MODERN ENTERPRISE IN LATE CH'ING CHINA

MERCHANTS, MANDARINS, AND MODERN ENTERPRISE IN LATE CH'ING CHINA

by

Wellington K. K. Chan

Published by

East Asian Research Center

Harvard University

Distributed by
Harvard University Press
Cambridge, Massachusetts
and
London, England
1977

The East Asian Research Center at Harvard University administers research projects designed to further scholarly understanding of China, Japan, Korea, Vietnam, Inner Asia, and adjacent areas. These studies have been assisted by grants from the Ford Foundation.

Library of Congress Cataloging in Publication Data

Chan, Wellington K K
Merchants, mandarins, and modern enterprise in late Ch'ing China.

(Harvard East Asian monographs ; 79)
Bibliography: p.
Includes index.
A revision of the author's thesis, Harvard University.
1. Merchants–China–History. 2. Business enterprises–China–History. 3. China–Commerce–History. 4. China–Industries–History. I. Title. II. Series.
HF3776.C45 1977 380'.1'0951 76-30743
ISBN 0-674-56915-6

To my mother
and to the memory of my father

FOREWORD

The modern Chinese merchant class is best exemplified in Professor Wellington Chan's home town, Hong Kong. It is no accident that the modern type of Chinese businessman appeared in the late nineteenth century first in British colonies like Hong Kong and Singapore, where an imperial civil service cultivated law and order and due process in the interests of trade. Dr. Chan's study recounts what happened in the old Ch'ing empire when it finally tried to accommodate itself to the rise of modern commerce and industry. The mandarins, as of old, sought at first to make use of the merchants and their new activities, but by degrees some officials found it more expedient to become themselves entrepreneurs. Meanwhile the growth of Chinese trade and industry in treaty ports and provincial centers prompted Peking to try to patronize, superintend, and control these new developments. The effort did not succeed, and government control of the merchant class was not reasserted finally until two generations later, in the People's Republic.

This is an absorbing story, on the frontier where the international trading world met the growing commercialization of the Chinese subcontinent at the turn of the century. Dr. Chan's background has prepared him to analyze the issues and protagonists with exemplary insight. After schooling in Swatow, China, and Hong Kong, where his family had been in business for several generations, he took his BA at Yale in 1963, his B.Litt. at Oxford in 1965 and his Ph.D. at Harvard in 1972. Meantime he had taught for two years, 1968-1970, at Chung Chi College in the Chinese University of Hong Kong. A grant from the American Council of Learned Societies helped him to recast and amplify his dissertation to make the present volume. Wellington Chan now teaches history at Occidental College.

John K. Fairbank

CONTENTS

TABLES

ACKNOWLEDGEMENTS

This study began as a Ph.D. dissertation under John K. Fairbank, to whom I am most indebted for intellectual stimulation and research guidance throughout the various stages of writing and rewriting of this manuscript. I have also imposed on several friends and colleagues for critiques and comments. Marianne Bastid, Samuel Chu, Albert Feuerwerker, Stephen MacKinnon, Tom Rawski, and Edward Rhoads responded with numerous suggestions, all of which I treasured and appreciated, even when I could not follow them through. I should also like to thank Arthur Wright and Kwang-Ching Liu, who first introduced me to Chinese history and who continue to show interest in my work.

I also appreciate the unfailing kindness of the librarians and staffs of the several libraries where I carried on my research: the Harvard-Yenching Library, the Hoover Institution, the Fung Ping Shan Library, and the Chung Chi College Library in Hong Kong, the Toyo Bunko in Tokyo and the Institute of Modern History, Academia Sinica, in Nan-kang. I am also grateful to the East Asian Research Center at Harvard and the Institute of Southeast Asian Studies in Singapore for providing space and hospitality for the revision of this manuscript. The latter institution kindly published a somewhat modified version of Chapter I in its *Occasional Papers* series under the title of "Politics and Industrialization in Late Imperial China."

Financial support for this study has come from several Harvard-Yenching Institute graduate fellowships, a grant for one year from the American Council of Learned Societies, two summer grants from the Haynes Foundation, and a summer fellowship from the East Asian Research Center at Harvard. Without the generosity of these institutions, this work would not have been possible.

Finally, I wish to acknowledge my thanks to Mary Arnold and Peggy Lee, for admirably typing out the various versions; to Andrew

Rolle and Florence Trefethen, for saving me from many infelicities of style; to Dwight Perkins, for sponsoring the publication of this study; and especially to Priscilla Ho Chan, for years of her patience, understanding, and encouragement.

W. K. K. C.

Los Angeles, California
August, 1976

Chapter One

INTRODUCTION

It is still fashionable among reputable scholars to assume that orthodox Confucian ideology was unmitigatedly anti-mercantile, and that it subjected generations of Chinese merchants (*shang-jen*) to social disesteem, excessive state control, and exploitation. Relying upon this premise, critics and apologists alike have concluded that China's failure to establish a modern economy stemmed from her anti-mercantile ideology.

There is no dispute that, until the last twenty years or so, China's economic indexes registered no signs of progressive growth toward a modern economy. In 1933—a year for which there are sufficient statistical data—75 percent of her work force tilled the land and produced some 65 percent of the total net domestic product. By contrast, the comparable figures for Japan declined from 83 percent and 46 percent in 1879 to 46 percent and 20 percent in 1938. In 1933, the Chinese modern sector, that is, manufacturing, trading, mining, utilities, banking, and transport, accounted for only 12.6 percent of the net domestic product.[1]

The causes for such a failure in economic development are not readily apparent. To attribute it to an anti-mercantile ideology can only provide simplistic answers.[2] First, the generic word *shang* in such Chinese terms as *shang-jen* (merchant) and *ching-shang* (to engage in mercantile activities) is far broader in scope than the English terms "merchant" and "mercantile" indicate. To speak of *ching-shang* is to speak essentially of the whole non-agricultural economy, just as *shang-jen* can include traders, brokers, manufacturers, bankers, financiers, and managers in the service and transport industries. Although the Chinese non-agricultural sector on the whole grew slowly, there were nevertheless periods of great expansion and achievements in several fields.[3]

Second, one must make a distinction between the actual social practices under which traditional Chinese merchants operated and the Confucian social theory to which everyone subscribed. Beginning with the Sung dynasty (960–1275), credit facilities, trade, and the handicraft industry had developed into a complex network of inter-regional activities by merchants and officials that operated under the cover of correct ideology.

Third, the nature as well as the impacts of Confucian values on traditional Chinese society are still a matter of much debate. Preference for one's relatives, frugality, and economic self-sufficiency—to name just a few of these values—are not necessarily hindrances to economic modernization. Moreover, the Chinese tradition has been remarkably free of taboos against usury and the social betterment of the individual.

Fourth, the state did not control most of the domestic market and its factories. Many of these were in private hands, often with official collaboration. Under the Ch'ing, only salt, copper, silk, and porcelain were monopolized by the state, while many other major items of trade and industry, such as tea, sugar, grain, cotton spinning and weaving, and so forth, were almost completely privately owned and managed. Nor did the state supervise its monopolies effectively. The Japanese historian Saeki Tomi has estimated that half the salt consumed during the entire Ch'ing dynasty was sold by smugglers.[4] Yet salt was the most important of these monopolies.

Another explanation for China's slow economic development has been to point to her negligible level of net investment prior to 1949, which suggests that the Chinese, being too poor to save, had no capital to invest. One recent study, however, has demonstrated how the traditional economy was able to keep pace with a manifold increase of population by means of opening up new land and improving grain yield.[5] Another study observes that the images of a crisis-prone and poverty-stricken China have been distorted by projecting back into the nineteenth century those economic conditions prevailing between 1920 and 1949. British travelers who covered large areas of China's interior before 1870 described a world bustling with economic activity and enjoying a level of wealth comparable if not superior to that of contemporary

England.[6] A third study argues that the total potential "surplus" was about 37 percent of China's net domestic product.[7] Communist China's recent record of large capital formation without resorting to borrowing from other countries represents a successful tapping of these surplus funds.

But if each of these factors—values, social practices, state control, and potential capital—by itself did not constitute an insurmountable obstacle to economic modernization, the concatenation of these and other factors apparently did. To take the case of the availability of potential capital, how can one explain that so little was invested in the national economy of the late Ch'ing? One may cite a weight of tradition that encouraged even those who were not well-to-do to consume conspicuously on festive occasions. But to single out this trait without reference to others is meaningless, since one could, with equal reason, seek an explanation emphasizing frugality to the exclusion of other characteristics. One should ask more searching questions. Was there any incentive to save? Did the government encourage saving, and why? What sort of banking and other credit institutions were available to help savings? Were there sufficient investment opportunities?

The presence of incentive was obvious in the case of the railway's "Rights Recovery" movement when thousands of Chinese saw the need to raise capital among themselves in order to buy out foreign ownership and control. Here, nationalism versus imperialism provided the incentive. Railways, if located along busy commercial routes, were also appreciated as profitable ventures. The desire to build an economically powerful state in order to confront Western encroachment also forced the state to encourage private investments. It set up new organizational frameworks such as *kuan-tu shang-pan* (government-supervised merchant management) and *kuan-shang ho-pan* (officials' and merchants' joint management) as joint-stock companies to invite public subscription of capital. Credit facilities, however, remained traditional; meanwhile the state's tenacity in asserting control over most of these new enterprises caused private investors to feel resentment and distrust. The result was a vicious circle: as fewer private funds were poured in, the state had to turn to whatever public revenue it could find. This in turn led supervising officials to become even more insistent about the need for state control.

On the other hand, because of the lack of an efficient tax system, the government could not generate any sizeable revenue surpluses to do the job well. Unlike the tax system of Meiji Japan, which successfully skimmed off the surplus from the agrarian sector to pay for her initial industrialization, the late Ch'ing's tax structure was full of informal regulations varying according to local peculiarities. It had no systematic way of dealing with increased income as the national economy grew. It is estimated that a mere 2.4 percent of the net national product (versus Japan's 12 percent or higher in around 1880) was all the Chinese government received in taxes in 1908.[8]

This brief illustration cannot of course tell the full story. It should, however, hint at the vast number of opportunities and constraints that history and the environment offered to influence capital investment in late Ch'ing China. And what was true for capital formation was also true for the far larger issues of economic modernization.

This study will attempt to give equal weight to both the historical and environmental forces that shaped China's first modern[9] industrial enterprises founded during the last forty years of the Ch'ing dynasty. While specifically economic considerations also influenced these late Ch'ing efforts, they were often sacrificed in the interests of politics. After all, the Chinese political and intellectual leaders did not turn their attention to industrialization until they realized that economic weakness led to political weakness, and political weakness led to Western encroachment. Thus obsessed by the knowledge that wealth begot power, these early promoters of modern enterprise did not appreciate industrialization on economic terms. They did not understand that society and its whole way of life must make a decisive break with tradition; that other sectors of the economy, such as credit facilities, capital formation, the tax system, marketing, and farming practices, must make corresponding changes so that they could all add up to form a modern economic infrastructure in which industry was only one of several integral parts. Instead, patriotic men sought to use industry to augment the nation's strength; while less scrupulous officials sought to control it to increase their own political power base.

This does not mean, however, that the late Ch'ing elite were unwilling to come to terms with economic modernization. They held vigorous debates on its merits and dangers; they raised new questions about the role of the merchant in Chinese society; they created new economic institutions and improved old ones in hopes of adapting Western models into viable Chinese enterprises. As a result, new patterns in official and merchant relationships emerged on both personal and institutional levels, while an influx of official and gentry elements gradually altered the merchant class's composition and social status. In contrast to the picture of institutional ossification painted by some social critics, this study will show that the late Ch'ing's economic and social institutions and the men who ran them demonstrated much flexibility and an ingenious capacity for change.[10]

Yet the motivations and incentives which led to a reappraisal of what should have been major economic issues were politically inspired. The interactions between merchants and mandarins became the most important influence affecting the Chinese pattern of industrial development. The first major theme of this study, therefore, is the participation of merchants in modern enterprise and their problems with official supervision. As far as research materials permit, this issue will be examined from the perspective of the merchant. A second major theme, related to the first, is the problem of conflict and competition between the central and provincial governments over the control and direction of modern industry. In late Ch'ing China, this contest was very real and contributed significantly to China's failure to achieve industrialization.

Peking versus the Provinces

The theme of regional power and provincial interests has a long and lively history in China. Although the throne and bureaucracy claimed almost monopolistic power, the various dynasties ran a very light government where the prerogatives of central authority were delicately balanced against the rights of local initiative. Beneath the facade that the emperor was at the cosmic pivot and ruled all things, there was much decentralization into the hands of the local gentry elite. This was the secret of success of the Chinese imperial system. Today the Chinese Communist regime's retreat from the Russian style of centralization practiced during the 1950s represents an instinctive effort to preserve that historical balance.

During the second half of the Ch'ing dynasty, endemic peasant rebellions from the White Lotus to the Boxers continually eroded that balance. The central government survived the mid-century Taiping challenge only after provincially based armies rallied to its support. Thus, when the Chinese political leaders sought industrialization as a way of combating Western imperialism, the weakened center issued the call but could not lead the campaign. Having lost control over burgeoning local taxes, the central government had no surplus revenue that could be diverted to industrial projects. Money, talent, and initiative went to the provinces, since senior governors-general—Li Hung-chang, Chang Chih-tung, and Yuan Shih-k'ai—dominated modern enterprises from their regional bases.

Peking's attempts to control these developments were weak and unsystematic at first. After 1900, as part of the national government's drive for general reforms, a national policy of commerce and industry emerged, based largely on drastic institutional overhauls. Commercial and industrial affairs were delegated to a new ministry; soon thereafter railways and other types of communication were singled out to be managed by another new ministry. At the local and provincial levels, the central government established a national network of industrial and commercial promotion bureaus, authorized commercial schools and technical workshops, and encouraged merchant leaders to set up chambers of commerce according to uniform rules it had drawn up. Peking hoped these new institutions would provide it with direct access to local communities and serve as counterweights against the dominance of provincial authorities.

Other reform measures included the codification of commercial laws, the registration of companies and corporations, and the promulgation of a system of awards by official ranks and even nobility titles for economic promotion and achievements.

Many of these activities directed by the central government were distrusted by the provincial authorities. Competing interests on several of these programs led to conflicts between the two parties. Other programs received only token compliance. In the end, the national government failed to exert authority.

Yet, if industrialization was to succeed, the nation needed to agree on pulling all its resources into one common effort. Only a strong central government was able to make efficient allocation of scarce capital and other resources, to formulate a uniform set of administrative rules, and to determine an integrated plan for which industry was to have first priority so that successive industries could effectively build on those that came before. China by 1911 had several large modern industries in textiles, mining, iron foundries, shipping, and railways. But they were widely scattered, controlled by competing regional leaders. There was no industrialization on either a national or regional scale, since these modern enterprises were not functionally integrated, and there was no modern economic infrastructure—for example, modern credit and marketing facilities—to support their growth.

Japanese efforts during a comparable stage of development were vastly different. Several *han* governments had established modern industrial enterprises during the late Tokugawa. But after the 1868 Restoration, the Meiji leaders very quickly succeeded in overcoming former *han* loyalties, so that the central government not only became heir to these earlier efforts, but also led the nation uncontested to new centralized economic direction and programs.[11]

Merchants versus Mandarins

Competition for control also characterized the relations between Chinese officials and merchants. Soon after 1870, Li Hung-chang became the first senior official openly to solicit merchant participation in modern enterprise. Li realized that state revenues were insufficient to provide the required capital for the wide range of industry he envisaged for China. In order to draw in the merchants, he promised them merchant management and profitable returns in exchange for overall official supervision. With few exceptions, the more traditional merchants were unresponsive, while the compradors, with their acquaintance of Western commercial—though not industrial—management, responded enthusiastically. The latter provided both money and expertise, and successfully launched three major modern enterprises before the end of the 1870s. But as the official supervisors began to interfere with the business decisions of their companies, the compradors and other private investors became increasingly disenchanted. As a result, they withheld new investments and forced the official supervisors, who by then had become managers, to depend more and more on the limited amounts of state revenue as well as their own personal wealth.

At the same time, official promoters tried to reverse the trend by promises of more equitable partnerships under the slogan of *kuan-shang ho-pan* (officials' and merchants' joint management). Chang Chih-tung promoted several textile companies during the 1890s and 1900s under such a format. He had little success, mainly because Chang would not even trust his official managers, much less the merchant partners. As a result, most of modern industry failed through bureaucratic waste, inefficiency, and a lack of capital.

However, the influx of capital and direct managerial involvement brought about subtle but drastic changes not only in the nature of these modern enterprises, but also in the attitudes and values among the scholar-officials. While most of the new companies were run like additional government bureaus, leading to stagnation and outright failure, some became highly successful ventures as their official owner-managers adopted entrepreneurial directions and practices.

On the social level, the merchants' status and class composition underwent significant changes as many active and retired officials assumed managerial functions. Several of them continued to conceal their ownership or involvement. But even they were quick to prepare their sons for careers in trade and industry. A case in point was Governor Nieh Ch'i-kuei who, as a son-in-law of Tseng Kuo-fen and himself a member of an impeccable scholar-gentry family, professed no direct interest in the Hua-hsin Spinning and Weaving Mill. Yet he became an official-entrepreneur by supervising this and other mills. He then sent his two sons into full-time modern industrial management.

These developments reflected two major trends. First, a new social stratum of official-entrepreneurs and gentry-merchants was emerging from the old gentry class. Second, this new group was firmly committed to economic modernization.

From about 1900, these two trends also contributed to the growth of *shang-pan* (merchant management) industry with such official-entrepreneurs as Chang Chien and Chou Hsueh-hsi eschewing formal government sponsorship to organize their own companies. As "merchant" or private enterprises, these had full official protection but a minimum of official control, for they often belonged to the very officials who made government policies on commerce and industry. But there was no major expansion of successful industries of this type because they continued to rely on government loans and the personal wealth of a small côterie of official and gentry members. As a group, these "merchant" companies had fairly efficient managements, overcame the more stultifying kind of state control, but were still restricted by a limited source of capital.

One type of *shang-pan* enterprise that emerged at this time offered the promise of drawing upon the capital resources of a large segment of the population yet challenging the state's rights of supervision. This was the provincial railway company. In 1905 and 1906, a virtual ground swell of patriotic sentiment erupted in

Kwangtung, demanding that the railway construction rights the government had given to American and Belgian companies be returned. Led by Canton gentry and merchant leaders, this Rights Recovery Movement appealed to the common people to subscribe capital in order to build and run their own railways without foreign or state interference. In 1907, a similar movement gained strength in Chekiang and Kiangsu.

Thus transformed into political undertakings, these campaigns to found *shang-pan* railway companies won immediate and massive support—from profit-seeking merchants and civic-minded students and laborers. In Canton, within a period of several weeks in 1906, one governor-general was forced out of office, while six million taels were raised from literally tens of thousands of subscribers.

But these companies, which began with so much promise, failed in the long run. As the campaigns gained force and power, provincial gentry and local officials manipulated the issues to further their own cause in the continuing struggle between regional and central authorities for political and economic domination. Hence, after the construction rights had been recovered from the Western powers, debates and factional fighting continued and spilled over into new issues such as shareholders' rights and officers' duties in the new companies. The result was confusion and leaderless management, followed by renewed state intervention and a decline in public support, both moral and financial.

Thus, on this issue of state and merchant participations in modern enterprise, the Chinese record again contrasts sharply with Japan's. In Meiji Japan, the political leaders had financed a number of key factories from tax revenues and assigned bureaucrats to run them. But by the early 1880s, they sold them out cheaply to entrepreneurs and relinquished control.[12] In late Ch'ing China, the state or individual officials continued to assert claims of direction and ownership.

One can never be certain whether, in the long run, modern enterprise owned and run by Chinese official-entrepreneurs and gentry-merchants could have led to successful economic growth, for the Ch'ing dynastic order collapsed, and the political instability that followed created an inhospitable environment for industrial development. What is certain is the influence these late Ch'ing efforts have had on subsequent Chinese enterprise.[13] State control as well as the contest between center and region remained crucial issues throughout the warlord and Kuomintang periods as each new group of political leaders turned these earlier experiments into precedents and models for their own industrial efforts. Today, under different ideological rules and values, bureaucratic capital has given way to state capital, while provincial domination is being replaced by partnership with Peking. As China pushes ahead to become a fully industrialized state, she and others pursuing the same goal can still profit from the broad experiences gained almost a hundred years ago.

PART ONE

THE MERCHANT CLASS: CHANGING PERSPECTIVES

Chapter Two

MERCHANTS, COMMERCE, AND THE STATE

The earliest Chinese classics are free of the proverbial discrimination against merchants. From the Shang dynasty (c. 1766–1122 B.C.) to the end of the Ch'un-ch'iu period (722–481 B.C.), the size of the merchant community remained small for lack of sufficient demand for merchant services. During this period, the market was already controlled by the state. The classic *Chou-li* (Rituals of Chou) reports that the state established marketplaces at the rear of the palace, and appointed officials to supervise their activities.[1] There was general acceptance that markets were needed for the exchange of goods. One ancient commentator on the *I-ching* (Book of Changes) observed:

> When the sun stood at midday, the Divine Husbandman held a market. He caused the people of the world to come together and assembled the riches of all under Heaven. There they exchanged with one another and then returned home, each thing having found its appropriate place.[2]

Another early classic, the *Shu-ching* (Book of Documents), lists *shih* (food) and *huo* (goods, money) as the first two among eight objects of government (*pa-cheng*).[3]

During the Chan-kuo period (403–221 B.C.), for the first time a small number of wealthy merchants reached social prominence through the purchase of land and offices. Lü Pu-wei, the most successful of these, became the chancellor of the Ch'in state in 249 B.C. Since social mobility affected social class structure, the same period also saw the first serious discussions about the merchants and their place in society.[4]

Early Views of the Merchant's Place in Society

These early discussions generally agreed that merchants should be disesteemed because they were non-productive and parasitic.

The Confucianists were ambivalent, however; both Mencius (372–289 B.C.?) and Hsun-tzu (fl. 298–238 B.C.) readily acknowledged that merchants facilitated the exchange of basic material needs among people. Mencius considered this desirable, observing that people would behave morally only if they were assured of a comfortable subsistence economy.[5] His concern, expressed in the terse exhortation "Let producers be many and consumers few" was to keep the merchants from growing too big and overstepping their role.

While the Confucianists saw both sides of the question, they were hopelessly vague about how to keep merchants within bounds. Should the state permit *laissez-faire* or should it exercise some control? And if control, how much? Those Confucian literati who challenged the Han bureaucrats to a debate in 81 B.C. on the question of state monopoly and control obviously chose *laissez-faire.* They argued unconvincingly that, if left to themselves, the merchants would remain small in number and lowly in social status.[6] Other Confucian scholars, especially those who served as administrative officers of the state, realized how impractical *laissez-faire* would be and adopted control and monopolies of varying stiffness throughout China's long imperial era. In these activities, they borrowed their ideas freely from the Legalist School.[7]

The Legalists had the most emphatic anti-mercantile biases. Neither Lord Shang (d. 330 B.C.) nor Han Fei-tzu (d. 233 B.C.) had anything good to say about merchants. Since the enrichment and power aggrandizement of the state were their paramount concerns, they saw merchants not only as competitors for wealth, but also as promoters of undesirable waste and luxuries among the people. For the Legalists, this meant the impoverishment of the state. The author of the *Kuan-tzu* (Book of Kuan-tzu), a contemporary of Lord Shang, echoed these views when he pointed out one other way commerce could ruin the state. He claimed that the fall of the legendary Hsia dynasty was partly due to the Shang dynasty's deliberate policy of ruining the Hsia economy. To do this, the Shang rulers encouraged the sale of their fancy cloth to the courtesans of the Hsia in exchange for the Hsia's farm produce.[8] It does not matter whether this story was historically accurate. What is significant is this influential author's belief that the Shang's alleged policy was still a valid lesson for his own time.

This analysis, however, did not lead the author of the *Kuan-tzu* or the Legalists to cultivate merchants as useful supporters, or to expand commerce and industry as a means of increasing the state's wealth. Both he and the Legalists believed that agriculture formed the basis of the economy. The *Kuan-tzu* story only re-emphasized the need for the state to monopolize or control all essential commercial and industrial activities. Its author also offered the first formal exposition of the hierarchy of the four classes—scholar-official (*shih*), farmer (*nung*), artisan (*kung*), and merchant (*shang*)—even though some comparable form of social stratification had been customary since the end of the Shang dynasty.

Traditional China, however, was not the only society with strong biases against the merchant class. Joseph Jiang has laboriously examined the records of Egypt and Babylon, Rome, Greece, Medieval Europe and China, seventeenth century New England, eighteenth century England, and nineteenth century France. He found that all these societies held their merchants in disesteem and restricted their legal and political rights.[9]

First, these civilizations were or had been agrarian societies, and their rulers generally relied upon their rural population for revenue and political stability. Even in those societies that had gone through the early stages of industrialization, the psychological pull of their agrarian past remained powerful. Merchants were suspect because their ways were so different from the farmers'. Because of his mobility, a merchant tended to pick up strange ideas from faraway places. Furthermore, his functions put him in contact with a wide variety of social groups within the community, including high officials and aristocrats, lowly government sub-bureaucrats, and social outcasts. He even communicated with foreigners and strangers. With his varied experience, he was more likely to question the ways in which his own society was run and controlled and to have less respect for the agrarian social elite.

Hence, the merchant by definition was likely to incite disturbances.

Second, he was often a stranger in his area of business operation. Kinship ties would prevent a native son from bargaining too hard with the other members of his own community. As Jiang points out, "A man might bear an ostracized life among foreigners in a strange land, but certainly not at his ancestral home."[10] Moreover, rulers of traditional societies often encouraged foreign merchants because, being strangers, they had less opportunity to disseminate seditious ideas while their movements were more easily controlled.

Thus, not only were merchants despised because of their parasitic nature; they were also distrusted because of their threat to the established political authority and its supporting value system.

Merchant and Mandarin: Myth versus Fact

Ideologically, China shared with other agrarian societies the same predilection for disdain and distrust of the merchant class. On paper at least, these biases were translated into various systems of control and prohibition at various times in traditional China. During the Han dynasty (206 B.C.–A.D. 220), the merchants' rights and social status—in terms of social mobility, life style, and so forth—were severely restricted by law. They paid heavy taxes and could not wear silk or own land. Even their descendants were barred from entering into officialdom. Pan Ku's influential *Han Shu* (History of the former Han dynasty) included a treatise on food and money ("Shih-huo chih"). He painted the merchants in stereotypes—selfish, crafty, and profit-seeking. He contemptuously called their profession *yin-yeh* (licentious by corrupt occupation), and held them responsible for the decline of the Chou dynasty. Pan Ku's economic treatise had a moral: he wanted to show how commerce and industry could bring about social and political degeneration.[11]

Since the official histories of succeeding dynasties included similar laws and ordinances of varying severity, they encouraged the growth of folklore and myths about the merchants' social position and economic activities. The merchant stereotype, in the style of Pan Ku, became a familiar figure. Probably the most often quoted comments through the ages, they are included in the standard history text used in modern high schools.[12] Meanwhile, the social or economic historian must read between the lines to discover a more accurate picture of the merchant and the roles he played in his community.

In another part of the *Han Shu,* Pan Ku recalled the words of an earlier Han official, Ch'ao Ts'o, to support his denunciation of the merchants. Ch'ao had found that, in spite of all anti-merchant laws, wealthy merchants fraternized with officials and exploited the peasants. His graphic description of the social realities was contained in a memorial addressed to the emperor in 178 B.C.:

> [The peasants] must sell [to the merchants] what they have at half price in order to pay [the levies], and those who have nothing must take money offered at one hundred percent interest. Thus they are forced to sell their fields and houses, vend their children and grand-children to pay their debts... [The merchants] have none of the hardships of the farmer, yet their gain is ten to a hundredfold. With their wealth they may consort with nobles, and their power exceeds the authority of government officials. They use their profits to overthrow others. Over a thousand miles they wander at ease, their caps and cart covers filling the roads. They ride in fine carriage and drive fat horses, tread in silken shoes, and trail white silk behind them. Thus it is that merchants encroach upon the farmers, and the farmers are driven from their houses and become vagrants. At present, although the laws degrade the merchants, the merchants have become wealthy and honored, and, although they honor the farmers, the farmers have grown poor and lowly.[13]

Y. S. Yü, after examining the economic policy of the Han period, has concluded that its anti-merchant policy, by means of laws, regulations, and state monopolies, "was much more apparent than real. Not only were the general economic conditions conducive to the growth of trade, but the law itself was no sooner established than it was relaxed. Evidence tends to show that, in spite of such a policy, trade, both domestic and foreign, never ceased to grow throughout the period."[14]

The gaps between theory and practice persisted into modern times. Concrete examples of such gaps during the Ming and Ch'ing are better known and are particularly relevant to an understanding of the actual conditions of merchants in the late Ch'ing. Conditions, however, varied widely between the urban centers and the remote hinterland. The following discussion can only illustrate; it cannot sum up the whole scene.

Through a succession of dynasties the legal restrictions against merchants were gradually relaxed until there were hardly any real ones left by Ming and Ch'ing times. The Ming statute of 1394 banned dukes, marquises, earls, and officials of the fourth rank and above, as well as their families and servants, from conducting business. This implies that noblemen and officials below those ranks were permitted to own businesses or invest in trade.[15] Moreover, lands, offices, and conspicuous consumption were no longer prohibited to the merchant family. During the Ch'ing, some merchant groups even received special social privileges. The salt monopoly merchants, for example, were given extra quotas for the enrollment of their sons at government schools, and a disproportionately large number of their sons consequently gained the coveted *chin-shih* degree.[16] Probably from as far back as the T'ang dynasty (618–907), merchants also paid comparatively lighter taxes than peasants. T'ao Hsi-sheng has argued that commercial taxes were further reduced after the introduction of the land-based single-whip tax in the late sixteenth century.[17] Thus, in a period of rapid commercial growth, merchants in effect contributed an even lighter share of the tax burden. But it is difficult to know if this was actually the case; for in the same period, merchants had more and more often to pay irregular contributions (*pao-hsiao*) to the government and individual officials. Then, from the mid-nineteenth century on, the likin taxes were imposed on domestic trade.

Legal liberalizations represented a gradual redefinition of administrative compromises between social reality and ideological ideal; they also made both the reality and the ideal subject to change over time. Around A.D. 1000 Chinese society experienced a massive upsurge of the domestic market and inter-regional trade. This, in turn, accelerated change in the system of state control over the market and the movement of traders. It also affected the relationship between merchants and officials.

Although collaboration between merchants and officials had been commonly acknowledged and widely practiced for a long time, the Sung dynasty provided the first abundant set of records showing officials in business. Many used assumed names or hired managers to run both regular and contraband trades.[18] The Sung records have also revealed the development of occupational diversification within many families. Under such an arrangement, many merchants' sons who showed good aptitude for learning were encouraged and financially supported by their families to study and to take the state examinations. Similarly, others with a comparable aptitude for business stayed in business. The nineteenth-century scholar Shen Yao was the first to point out the social implications of this trend. He contended that it meant that, first, as merchants rose in status, the four-class social divisions broke down; and, second, that scholarly pursuits and official appointments required an economic base of support that the merchants were able to provide.[19]

A variation on the same theme was the development, probably during the Ming dynasty, of the "gentry-merchant clans." Their origins are uncertain; but, throughout the Ch'ing, there were a number of established gentry clans who had had a tradition of dividing gentry and mercantile functions among their members over many generations.[20] Chang Chung-li has documented the geneology of forty-two such clans during the Ch'ing period. One of the geneologies justified such a division by citing the actions of two of Confucius's immediate disciples:

Among Confucius' disciples, those like Yüan-hsien were

> dressed in patched clothing and were extremely poor, while Tzu-kung was engaged in mercantile activities. Critics did not say that Yüan-hsien was more virtuous than Tzu-kung, for Tzu-kung was following his natural ability. The accumulation and hoarding of money by Chi-tzu and the chewing of insect-bitten plums by Ch'en Chung-tzu, however, were both despised by the sages. It is because they feigned [in their acts] against their natural feelings.[21]

In other words, if a gentry member possessed a natural talent for business, he should go into business.

These patterns of family or clan diversification also meant that successful merchant families and clans did not simply disappear by turning themselves into gentry. Some members of each social unit usually stayed on as merchants. This suggests a different scenario from the one generally projected by modern sociologists—that successful merchant families would try to use "the merchant role as a method of lifting the [families] to a gentry role and thence forward getting as far away from the merchant roles as possible." It is thought that, by this means, their talents were drained from commerce.[22]

A third variation was the more common practice where officials and gentry owned business enterprises themselves. They could assume the two socially incongruous roles at the same time because they usually left the actual operation and entrepreneurial decisions to their hired managers and became passive owners themselves, even avoiding public acknowledgment of their ownership. The nineteenth century novelist and social critic Wu Chien-jen included many graphic episodes of this sort in his novel *Erh-shih-nien mu-tu kuai-hsien-chuang* (Strange happenings eyewitnessed during the last twenty years). Wu revealed how officials went into business in secrecy, what motivated them, and what hazards they might face. In one story, a sub-prefect (*t'ung-p'an*) entrusted his pawnshop to an acquaintance who served as his manager and front man. When the pawnshop failed two years later, the front man asked for more capital to keep it going. The sub-prefect refused him. Thereupon, the front man declared ominously: "If you allow the pawnshop to fail, there will be lawsuits, during which it is likely that your ownership will become known. Since you are holding a substantial post in the local area, you will be punished for running a business." This was sheer blackmail, for, having agreed to act as front man, he had also promised to conceal the identity of the actual owner. Now, by threatening to break his trust, the unscrupulous agent "borrowed" 3,000 taels to cover what he called "litigation fees."[23]

Such hazards, however, were probably not frequent. The narrator in the same novel, who used the symbolic pseudonym "Chiu-sheng i-ssu" (Nine Lives), served as the front man for his close friend, County Magistrate Wu Chi-chih. Wu explained why he went into business: "I want to set up a small establishment to serve as 'something to fall back on' (*t'ui-pu*)." As his business prospered, branches were set up. Wu made Nine Lives a partner and offered one more reason to his faithful front man: "I came from a merchant family. How can I ever forget my family's past? Since I am a local official here, I may not manage any business openly. So I use 'such-and-such house' (*mou-chi*) for all transactions, and never my name. Publicly, I claim that the business belongs to you. When you meet with the employees, please don't say differently. [In our Nanking office], only Mr. Kuan Teh-chuan knows the truth. The rest are unaware [of the real ownership]."[24]

Besides such socially revealing novels, another source of information about the traditional merchant came from a specialized genre of merchant literature, the earliest dating back to the Wan-li period (1573–1620) of the late Ming. These are commercial manuals written by merchants largely for itinerant merchants. They contain various information on the local economy, produce, taxes, and regional differences in weights, measurements, and coinage. One important section is devoted to marketing routes over land and water, while another supplies sample letters for different occasions as well as other useful information on proper etiquette and local customs.[25]

Since the traditional merchant was more inclined to burn his account books than to write his autobiography, these manuals become a highly useful source for finding out about his values, attitudes, social origins, and economic activities. They also reveal to some extent the size and influence of the merchant community. For example, in the preface dated 1792 to his manual *Shang-chia pien-lan* (A convenient guide for resident and itinerant merchants), the merchant-author Wu Chung-fu recalled that his ancestors had been scholars. His father continued the family tradition until poor health during his teens caused him to interrupt his studies. Meanwhile, he turned to mercantile pursuits and could not return to his books later on because he needed money to support the family. Wu Chung-fu then added, unconvincingly, that he too had followed his father and elder brother into business because of poor health during his own youth.

One can draw two sociological insights from this account. First, merchants were still looked down upon; hence Wu's repeated excuse of ill health for the family's transition from scholarly to mercantile pursuits. Second, many unsuccessful or impoverished scholars were switching to commerce because the social disesteem meted out to them, while painful, was not unbearably onerous.

The merchant's social worth during the late traditional period was, therefore, a mixture. On the one hand, the wealthy merchant was a successful and influential member in his community. He collaborated freely with officials, and there was some movement between gentry, official, and merchant ranks. On the other hand, officials in their daily routine, and the state in its public statements, continued to promulgate social biases against merchants. Down to the end of the nineteenth century, the great majority of officials, many of whom had undeclared business interests, still talked about the merchant's *mo-yeh* (non-essential occupation), and contrasted it to the exploited farmer's exalted *pen-yeh* (basic or essential occupation).

Joseph Jiang, by studying other agrarian societies, and Ch'ü T'ung-tsu, by examining the Chinese record, have offered a reason for the continuing gaps between what the law allowed and how the social elite actually behaved toward merchants. Both decided that merchants were discriminated against because of their very success.

Gentry and officials resented the fact that many merchants, by their wealth, succeeded in wielding great influence over the ruling elite. As merchants often flouted the legal and social restrictions, so the envious elite used snobbery and social discrimination as defense mechanisms to guard their status and privileges against the merchants' intrusion.[26]

The Late Ch'ing Reappraisal

Although the preceding four or five centuries saw an accelerating rate of growth in the size and complexity of mercantile activities, the gap between theory and practice with respect to the merchant's social position grew even wider. For legal liberalization did not keep pace with the faster rate of social change. But, until the late nineteenth century, the political and intellectual elite did not bother to re-examine their ideology with respect to merchants.

The first changes came from reform-minded officials and scholars who were wrestling with the problem of the Westerners' power and material superiority.[27] They soon realized that the West's secret formula for wealth and power lay in its superior skills in trade and industrial technology. Voices of reform began urging the government to pursue technological development and to sponsor the export trade. Concretely, the reform was a series of steps. The government's initial response in the 1860s was in the limited area of military technology. From the early 1870s on, this was extended into a whole range of industrial efforts in textiles, mining, iron and steel, shipping, and railways. Finally, from about 1900, the central government set up new administrative organizations to push for a national policy of commerce and industry. It also attempted to close the social gap between merchants and officials by issuing a new definition of merchant status.

On April 22, 1903, while endorsing a proposal to establish the Ministry of Commerce (Shang pu), the throne released an imperial edict on the state's new concern for the merchants:

> Since antiquity it has always been an important part of the administration of the state to promote commerce and industry.

> Because by social convention, however, industry and commerce are thought of as matters of the last importance, the national economy and the people's livelihood have progressively grown weak . . . We must now abandon all official habit [of feeling superior toward merchants]; we must unite and not allow any barrier (*k'e-ai*) [between merchants and officials]. . . in order to enrich the people's wealth and to strengthen the state's foundations.[28]

About half a year later, the newly organized Shang pu announced a system of awards of titles and ranks to encourage capital investments in modern enterprise. It observed candidly:

> There has never been any lack of officials making investments in commerce and industry. However, owing to social customs, they have invariably been ashamed of admitting this fact so that they would either use assumed names or ask someone else to manage their businesses. In this way, a barrier (*k'e-ai*) has often grown up between officials and merchants. Now it is the throne's intention to emphasize mercantile policies (*shang-cheng*). We should destroy our past ingrained notions, in order that officials and merchants will make no distinctions between one another, but will work together toward generating a new social climate. Therefore, if any prominent families or large clans organize and raise capital for a company and make it into a successful venture, they will be awarded according to the above listed schedule. Similarly, those who already hold senior official posts or ranks will be given consideration for special awards.[29]

Merchants and Fu-ch'iang. The state's determination to upgrade merchants was based on the new awareness that they could "enrich the people's wealth and strengthen the state's foundations." This assessment was accepted only after many years of debate among the officials themselves. How did it all begin?

One of the areas of major concern throughout nineteenth-century China was the unfavorable foreign trade balance. Concern for the outflow of silver predated the opium war and was an important factor leading to that war.[30] From 1864, when the Maritime Customs began to publish annual import and export statistics, China was almost always in deficit payment. In actual fact, if the trade data were presented differently, and if allowances were made for the trade from Hong Kong, China probably enjoyed an export surplus through 1887.[31] Such economic subtleties must, however, have escaped the Chinese scholar-officials of the time who expressed shock and dismay after examining these trade statistics.[32] In any event, after 1888, China began to suffer a real trade deficit which grew in the 1890s and then galloped to over a hundred million taels a year during the 1900s.[33]

On the question of trade imbalance, Hsueh Fu-ch'eng, an outspoken protégé of Li Hung-chang and China's one-time minister to France and England, simply totaled up China's import and export figures into some 200 million taels a year, then made the exaggerated claim in 1879 that "out of it, the foreign merchants made a profit of about 30 million taels a year. In ten years, this represents 300 million taels of actual drain of our wealth. Little wonder then that, in recent years, the people are becoming poor." Hsueh readily admitted, however, that in spite of those bad effects, China could do nothing to close up the foreign trade. The only alternative left for China, he suggested, was to work on her commercial and industrial enterprises (*shang-wu*).[34]

Ma Chien-chung, another protégé of Li, also made a similar connection between China's poverty and the foreign trade in his *Fu-min shuo* (Discussion on the wealth of the people). He, too, claimed that about 30 million taels were lost each year and offered the maxim that "when exports exceed imports, then it will be profitable [for China]; when exports equal imports, then it will likewise be profitable; but when imports exceed exports, then it will be harmful."[35] Many others were similarly concerned. They prescribed a policy of strict mercantilism—to reverse the foreign trade balance by maximizing exports and minimizing imports.

During the 1870s and 1880s, these proponents were by and large limited to a small number of officials, many of whom like Hsueh Fu-ch'eng and Ma Chien-chung were "barbarian experts."

But they also included a few leading statesmen like Li Hung-chang and Tso Tsung-t'ang. The majority of officials were still vehemently conservative, a representative group being the "Ch'ing-i" (Pure Discussion) Clique which was influential at court and included such a formidable figure as Chang Chih-tung. Although these conservatives were anti-foreign and reacted strongly to the technological borrowing of the 1860s, they were as concerned as the reform-minded officials about some means of strengthening the state. In the end, it was this fundamental goal, expressed in the slogan *fu-ch'iang* (wealth and power),[36] that united them in a common commitment to commerce and industry. Certainly, after 1895 such a commitment could no longer be challenged except by a recalcitrant few. A powerful Japan was cited as living proof of the benefits of overall Western borrowing, while a sense of urgency was injected by the new treaty provisions giving foreigners more trading and manufacturing concessions.

In early 1897, when Ch'u Ch'eng-po, a conservative censor and large landlord from Chekiang known for his association with the reactionary Hsu T'ung, memorialized the throne, he agreed that commerce and industry could no longer be dismissed. Turning to the merchants, he asked the state to abolish the traditional social discriminations, to protect them against foreign competition, and to sponsor adequately-funded industrial projects.[37] Ch'u, who had opposed Li Hung-chang's industrial enterprises during the 1870s, was now reconciled to them because of the need to combat the foreign merchants in China. Another well-known conservative literatus from Hunan, Wang Hsien-ch'ien, went even further by arguing that the merchants' new social status could be justified by traditionalism. Wang separated official platitudes and theories from social realities, then concluded that merchants, proprietors of the handicraft industry, and landlords had occupied the Chinese upper social strata since the Ch'in and Han times. If China was to become a capitalist society, the merchant class would have to take the lead in modern industry.[38]

The conservatives were not unique, however, in having undergone a conversion. Reform-minded officials like Hsueh Fu-ch'eng were different from their predecessors of the 1860s and earlier, even though they shared a common origin that went back to the late eighteenth century intellectual movement. At that time, many scholar-officials began to re-emphasize current problems, administrative efficiency, and pragmatic solutions in reaction to the sterility and scholasticism of the so-called K'ao-cheng p'ai (School of Empirical Research). During that earlier period, from the first "barbarian experts" like Wei Yuan and Lin Tse-hsu to the T'ung-chih restoration leaders like Tseng Kuo-fan and Feng Kuei-fen, reformism was rooted in an orthodox political philosophy that emphasized the primacy of the agrarian subsistence economy. And, even though Fen Kuei-fen had argued for economic innovations, he did not intend them to transform the traditional economy.[39]

The "self-strengthening" movement those restoration leaders proposed during the 1860s was not linked to the "wealth and power" slogan. That link was first made in the 1870s. But it was not until the mid-1880s, with China's defeat in the Sino-French War, that officials and scholars such as T'ang Shou-ch'ien, Ch'en Chih, and Ch'en Ch'iu began to question the utility of the traditional economic and political structure if China was to become strong again. They saw the need to go beyond making better ships and guns and argued for drastic institutional reforms which would begin with a systematic incorporation of Western types of commerce and industry into the Chinese state.[40] Their treatises discussing "commercial and industrial affairs" (*shang-cheng*) reflected this shift of emphasis: Ma Chien-chung's *Fu-min-shuo* (Discussion on the wealth of the people), Ch'en Chih's *Fu-kuo ts'e* (Policies on enriching the state), Wang K'ang-nien's *Lun Chung-kuo ch'iu fu-ch'iang i-ch'ou i-hsing chih fa* (Feasible paths towards China's search for wealth and power), and many others.[41] Indeed they promoted modern enterprise so vigorously that communist historians have come to view them as spokesmen of an emergent capitalist class.[42]

Liang Ch'i-ch'ao's views. Conversions among these reform-minded scholar-officials did not come automatically. Even their most eminent spokesman, Liang Ch'i-ch'ao, showed his psychological biases against the merchant class when he freely expressed contempt for the "subversive, manipulative, and monopolistic" (*ch'ing-chi lung-tuan*) merchants.[43] He wrote this in 1897, just as he had become an avid convert to the importance of commerce and industry. We shall examine in some detail his writings on this subject between 1896 and 1903; not only were they widely read, they also dramatically documented the process of Liang's conversion.

In 1896, when the twenty-three year-old Liang wrote a preface for the periodical of an agricultural society, he heaped scorn on the Chinese "foreign experts" who only emphasized commerce and military training as panaceas for China's troubles. Without trying to discredit the intrinsic value of commerce, he argued that the priorities were wrong because China first needed an increase in her agrarian produce to supply the raw materials for any commerce or industry:

> If industry is not developed, and yet one wishes to discuss commerce; if the agrarian produce is not plentiful, and yet one wishes to expand industry; this is like cutting off one's arms and knees in order to nourish one's fingers and toes. Even if they are miraculous prescriptions, they must fail in the end.[44]

However, in the following year (1897), when Liang published his first thoughtful essay on political economy entitled *Shih-chi huo-chih lieh-chuan chin-i* (The present-day meaning of the "Sketches of the rich" in the *Historical memoirs*), he was much less certain how to deal with the merchants. On the one hand, he expressed his contempt for merchants as noted above; on the other, he explicitly endorsed the paramount importance of commerce and industry for the good of the state. He then rationalized his acceptance by appealing to his own utopian *Weltanschauung:* that in this his own chaotic Darwinian age, far removed from the golden age of the "Great Peace," international competitions in trade and industry were a necessary evil for any state's survival.[45]

Shortly thereafter, while a political exile in Japan, Liang came to know the merchants much better, since the overseas Chinese community there was dominated by merchants who, like him, came from Kwangtung. Liang must have discussed the issue of commerce with them on many occasions. Included in his collected essays for 1899 are three articles dealing with the problems of Chinese merchants' residence in Japan, and the desirability of setting up chambers of commerce (*shang-hui* or *shang-yeh hui-i-so*) all over China and for all Chinese communities overseas.[46]

It is unlikely that Liang completely outgrew his psychological bias against the merchants. But as he knew them better, he began praising them for their industry and frugality.[47] In his book-length treatise entitled *Sheng-chi hsueh hsueh-shuo yen-ke hsiao-shih* (A short history of the development of economics), published in 1902, he pointed out approvingly the Chinese merchants' resourcefulness and their spirit of enterprise. He thought that, if they were only given official protection and encouragement, they could compete favorably with those of any nation in the world.[48]

Liang also discussed a general policy of trade and industry for China. Yen Fu had just published a translation of Adam Smith's *Wealth of Nations*, and it was making an impact on him. Thus, Liang argued that, while Adam Smith's free trade was good for Europe, China with her late start in economic development still needed the protectionism Europe itself had practiced during a similar stage of its own development. Liang's heroes were the two great seventeenth-century protectionists, Jean Baptiste Colbert and Oliver Cromwell, and he lamented that "for several thousand years, China has not produced any man [like them]."[49]

Liang did not, however, advocate strict mercantilism. By that time he had acquired a better understanding of the balance of trade and what it meant in terms of the nation's capital deficit or surplus. In 1896, he had still assumed naively that the amount of goods exported by a nation alone determined whether that nation had a favorable or unfavorable balance of trade.[50] In other words, he read into the foreign trade statistics the same significance as Hsueh Fu-ch'eng had done twenty years before him. In 1902, when Liang devoted a lengthy study to the relationship between a nation's wealth and its balance of trade, he began by asserting that the net outflow or inflow of a nation's capital could not be determined by its foreign trade statistics. Other factors such as foreign travels and living expenses, foreign investments, remittances, shipping freight and insurances, and so forth had to be taken into account. Liang concluded by stating–probably overoptimistically–that, despite a continuous trade deficit, China up to the end of 1909 still enjoyed a net gain of foreign capital.[51]

But Liang did not intend to draw complacency from such a conclusion. He principally emphasized that China must produce more and trade more. He thought that "during the next twenty years, Chinese manufactured goods must compete with foreign products for the China market; after that the competition should be carried on to the world market."[52]

In 1903, Liang suggested explicitly how this might be accomplished. He had just returned from a visit to the United States, where he was evidently much impressed and terrified by the recent development of large business and industrial "trusts." On the one hand, Liang felt that this new economic development which sought greater strength through collective efforts and unity was a step backward for the West, because it meant a retrogression from individual freedom and liberty to the less enlightened "[state] interventionism" (*kan-she chu-i*). It was additional evidence that the age was out of joint, and that there was overproduction and too much competition among nations. Liang commented ruefully that the American anti-trust movement would not succeed, for the trust was a direct result of America's growing imperialism.[53]

On the other hand, Liang was unabashedly attracted to its ideological implications. He had already discussed elsewhere the concept of *ch'ün* (grouping) as a source of national unity and power.[54] Liang's main concern was the Chinese merchants' and industrialists' ability to compete with their foreign counterparts. Unity among these Chinese entrepreneurs was therefore of crucial importance; and unity was the quality Liang thought they lacked most. Indeed, such a concern had led Liang and other scholar-officials to propose chambers of commerce. The trust seemed, therefore, a ready-made institution designed to unify the economic resources of the nation vis-à-vis the outside world. And, in order to assure its success, Liang thought the merchants should manage it under state supervision.[55]

Liang described the trust alternatively as the "Great Spirit" and the "Satan." Although he did not formally propose the adoption of the trust for China, he was clearly in favor of it. He warned his fellow countrymen to take the trust seriously, for its influence would reach China in less than ten years, at which point China would have to respond with her own trusts or be swept under. "In less than one hundred years, the whole world's political order will be reduced to a few large states; in less than fifty years, the whole world's economic order will be reduced to a few scores of large companies."[56]

It is ironic that Liang Ch'i-ch'ao who in 1896 had expressed his contempt for the merchants' love of monopolies should, by 1903, be actively encouraging them to combine their efforts with the Chinese government into the biggest possible monopolies. In this sense, Liang was a casuist. In spite of his professed moral abhorrence of the trust, he nonetheless advocated its use because, as he put it, from the twentieth century on, "what will determine a nation's strength or weakness and, indeed, its very chance of survival, will be its ability to gain a place within the economic developments of the world."[57]

Commerce versus industry. As the scholar-officials accepted the expanded role for commerce and industry, they soon made a distinction between them. At first, all such discussions were lumped together under the term *shang-cheng* (mercantile affairs), for both kinds of economic activities were carried out by *shang-jen* (merchants). When Li Hung-chang launched his shipping company in 1872, he turned to the merchant community for funds and management. The Chinese name for the China Merchants' Steam Navigation Company was Lun-ch'uan chao-shang chü (lit. "The Bureau to Invite *Shang* [*-jen* to Invest in] Steamships"). The first textile project, which later became the Shanghai Cotton Cloth Mill, was proposed by a *shang-jen,* P'eng Ju-tsung, to Li Hung-chang in 1878.[58] Indeed, the institutional framework of these early industrial efforts assumed that they would be "*shang-jen* management under official supervision" (*kuan-tu shang-pan*).

Since the merchant was carrying out both commercial and industrial functions, discussions about him before the 1890s tended not to differentiate his social role and status on the basis of which function he was performing. By the late 1890s, however, a growing distinction was made between *shang-yeh* as commercial enterprise and *shih-yeh* as industrial enterprise. When the progressive monthly *Tung-fang tsa-chih* published its first issue in February 1904, there were separate sections devoted to *Shih-yeh* and *Shang-wu.* The term *shih-yeh* had just come into current usage, having been borrowed from Japan to emphasize the modern aspects of industrial enterprise. The old term *kung-yeh* retained its traditional meaning and referred to the artisan's profession or the handicraft industry.[59]

This development reflected the growth of social distinctions between the two groups of merchants. Yet, to elevate one and degrade the other seemed to be the work of officials who could not get rid of their old prejudices against the commercial entrepreneurs. Officials had already been warned by imperial decrees to close the social gaps between themselves and merchants. In the 1900s, it was much easier for these officials to accept as their social equals promoters of modern industry. Many of them had an official or gentry background. Others such as the compradors who did not have such a background had new specialized skills instead. In any case, they too possessed official status through the purchase of ranks and titles.

Besides emphasizing the industrial entrepreneurs as a new breed of *shang-jen* very different from the traditional trading merchants, these officials also argued on the comparable values of commerce and industry. Both Chang Chien and Chang Chih-tung contended that it would be superficial to think that the Western states were built on commerce, for their wealth and strength came from their industry. K'ang Yu-wei pointed out that the West had already entered into the industrial age, and, if China was to obtain wealth and power, she needed to industrialize and learn the physical and engineering sciences upon which industrial technology was based.[60]

The only kind of commerce that mattered was international trade. But it was assigned a supporting role. Even less acknowledged was the view of one student publication pointing out that the West had to improve its domestic market first before it competed well in the world market.[61] The consensus was that, without a strong industrial base, no amount of commercial effort could stop the flow of imported goods that flooded the domestic market. Besides, only by improving industrial products through scientific training and by imitating foreign models could China hope to replace imported items and compete with foreign products overseas.

One other conclusion can be drawn from the commerce versus industry debates. They logically followed the other debates on the wider subject of formulating a new "commercial and industrial policy" (*shang-cheng*) that would increase the "wealth and power" (*fu-ch'iang*) of the state. All of the pro-merchant converts, Liang Ch'i-ch'ao, Hsueh Fu-ch'eng, Chang Chih-tung, Chang Chien, and others, had little or no organic grasp of modern economics. Totally absent was any understanding of the trader's role in creating new demands and facilitating the flow of commodities at home and across national boundaries. Consequently their arguments were propped up by half-understood economic theories and reflected how "backward" the scholar-official's ethos still was. Few Chinese intellectuals at the time were thrilled by the Western concept of an ever-expanding economy, or by the prospect of more and better material comforts. The Chinese discussed commerce and industry in terms of what they could do for China vis-à-vis the rest of the world.

Officials in business: legal liberalization and restrictions. Another consequence of these late Ch'ing reappraisals of modern enterprise was the further liberalization of the legal code for officials and gentry to participate in either the new or traditional types of business. Yet, in spite of state encouragement, most officials continued to be wary of openly admitting even passive ownership for themselves and for their immediate families. In the social novel *Strange Happenings Eyewitnessed During the Last Twenty Years* already mentioned, County Magistrate Wu Chi-chih certainly believed that he could not use his name or that of a family member for trade. Wu's fears were expressed at a time when legal restrictions were gradually being lifted. Around 1855, for example, the law forbidding gentry members to apply for brokerage (*ya-hang*) licenses was apparently repealed. Governor Hu Lin-i had informed the court that the prohibition was not only unenforceable, but was also defeating its original intentions, which were to enforce control and guard against any private monopoly. Hu added that a number of gentry members had become brokers under assumed names, while many brokers had acquired official titles through purchases.[62]

From the 1870s on, as officials openly canvassed their colleagues for investments in modern industry, all the major legal restrictions were simply ignored. It is not certain if official permission was ever formally given. But one imperial edict, dated March 20, 1897, officially "allowed all officials of senior and junior ranks, in the provinces and at the capital" to invest capital in the nation's textile factories and other industrial developments.[63] Although this imperial approval was given in response to a plea to counteract the impact of foreign factories in China, liberalization had probably already been extended to include both commercial and industrial enterprises. Certainly, by 1903, when the Ministry of Commerce published regulations to award investors, it was clear that these were applicable to officials who had made capital investments in either commerce or industry.

There were various ways in which officials and gentry concealed ownership. Magistrate Wu's employment of his confidant to act as front man was probably the most common. A second method was the use of various *t'ang* (hall) names to represent individual families, associations of partners, or groups of related families. This is a practice that has continued into the present.

A third method was the adoption of assumed names.[64] This

worked well both for officials who wanted to engage in business and for the many merchants who wanted to acquire gentry status, since different names gave them social and even legal separation for their different and socially incongruous roles. Thus, the prominent hong merchant Howqua IV (1810–1863) was known as Wu Shao-yung by his business associates, but as Wu Ch'ung-yao, a *chü-jen* scholar and gentry leader, in the local Gazetteer. Indeed his biography in the gentry-oriented Gazetteer did not even discuss his business enterprise.[65] As for gentry and officials in business, Governor Hu Lin-i's report to the throne discussed above already suggested that it was a common practice.

The government hoped these legal liberalizations would encourage officials who had flouted the old prohibitions to make their investments openly and be held legally accountable for any abuse or bankruptcy. But this failed to happen. The first set of legal definitions of a merchant published in 1903 by the Ministry of Commerce conceded that "any merchant, for purposes of operating his enterprise, may use his own name or any other name, company name (*tien, hao,* or *chi*), or hall name (*t'ang*) as he sees fit."[66] In 1905, when the Company Registration Law was promulgated, the government required all shareholders and partners of any company that sought registration to give their real names, geographical origins, current addresses, and amounts of capital invested. Besides keeping check on the officials, the government was also concerned about foreigners, especially Japanese, who were using Chinese as front men to set up companies outside the treaty port areas.[67] Such government efforts in themselves represented a compromise solution, for those companies which would register with the government formed only a very small fraction of all the private companies in China. They were mostly new type industrial joint-stock companies of limited liability. Moreover, it appears that even that compromise was not usually enforced, since many shareholders still used only their *t'ang* names so as to cover up their true identities.[68] The reason is simple. Even those officials who openly invested in government sponsored or approved industrial projects did not wish to divulge *the full extent* of their investments, lest the state discover how much personal wealth they had accumulated individually.

In 1909 the court suddenly reversed itself. Apparently many senior officials were taking advantage of the legal liberalization to increase both the scope and the volume of their entrepreneurial activities without, however, disclosing their ownership. The prince regent early in 1909 claimed that he feared that conflicts of interest were involved, that the interests of the state had been compromised in many instances, and that these officials abused their power and authority by engaging in unfair competition with the people for profit.[69] This was followed by the prince's order to the Bureau of Legal Code asking it to devise a new law which would, in essence, make it illegal for officials to be in business. The bureau was instructed to follow legal practices similar to the West's. The prince then added that it was his understanding that the West generally forbade officials in office to run businesses just as it did not allow active merchants to take up official appointments.[70] It is uncertain if this new set of guidelines was made into law. But, for all intents and purposes, the legal liberalization which vaguely allowed officials to engage in business was officially dead by early 1909. And concealment continued onto the end of the dynasty and beyond.

Chapter Three

CHANGES IN THE MERCHANT'S ROLES, CLASS COMPOSITION, AND STATUS

During the second half of the nineteenth century, Chinese merchants enjoyed a real rise in social status. But such a rise was not brought about by imperial exhortations or ministerial directives affirming the need to do away with the social barriers between officials and merchants. The haughty attitudes of the great majority of Chinese officials towards the merchant class reflected a cherished set of cultural values that could not be swept away by imperial or administrative fiats. As Benjamin Schwartz has observed, "The prejudice against any revaluation of the merchant and his presumed ethos was still bone-deep and grounded solidly on both the class interest and the deepest convictions of the literati."[1]

How then did the merchants improve their own position? First, foreign trade brought with it new types of enterprises, new socio-economic values, and a new environment for work in the treaty ports. These Western ideas and practices gave the Chinese merchants in the treaty ports a sense of importance about their place in society. The treaty ports and modern enterprise, by creating new merchants such as the compradors and the industrial entrepreneurs, contributed to a general rise in the social status of the whole merchant community.[2] Second, there was an influx of men from official and gentry backgrounds into the merchant class. From the merchants' side, there were also many who made use of their wealth to purchase official ranks and titles. These persons were called upon by government officials to give expert advice on public finance and to help manage industry. By the late nineteenth century, such an interchange of social and economic roles meant in effect that mercantile activities had become an acceptable alternative to an official career.

Some Merchants' Views

The merchants themselves failed to advance intellectually stimulating arguments that would lend support to those literati who advocated their cause. Instead, they were surprisingly unoriginal–resorting to the classics and repeating the usual caveat about further national humiliation and weakness if the state continued to ignore commerce and industry. Like the "pro-commerce" literati, they emphasized that China needed commerce as a means of combating the West and of regaining her former power and prestige. They neglected to explore the nature of the entrepreneur or his potential for making broad social contributions.[3]

Not even Cheng Kuan-ying (1842–c. 1923), perhaps the only outspoken intellectual who was also a practicing merchant, was an exception. He was among the first Chinese to see and discuss the connection between national self-strengthening and commerce. His first published volume, entitled *Chiu-shih chieh-yao* (Important suggestions for the salvation of the time), was dated 1862. Then barely twenty years old, he had already served more than three years as the comprador of the large English firm Dent & Co. in Shanghai. Cheng was concerned about China's weakness vis-à-vis the West as well as by the official lack of interest in commerce. In a later expanded work he suggested that "if China hoped to control the Westerners by a program of self-strengthening, then she could do no better than to promote her commercial affairs." Asked Cheng rhetorically, "How then can 'commercial affairs' be equated with 'non-essential affairs?'"[4] Although Cheng's flash of insight appeared very early, he had few new ideas to add when the great debate on this issue took place in the 1890s.

Cheng's argument was that changing times had invalidated such old adages as "Let agricultural profits be the basis [of the wealth of a State], and let commercial profits be its non-essentials." This "changing times" concept did not, however, lead him to reject the classical tradition. Instead, Cheng delved into the classics, especially such early works as the *Chou-li,* and tried to show that anti-commercial thoughts came later and were, therefore, deviations from the honorable place commerce had enjoyed in classical times.

He listed a number of statesmen who had once been merchants. They were mostly ancient Chinese personalities but included, interestingly enough, Peter the Great of Russia.[5] By making such an appeal to history, Cheng hoped to lend respectability to his arguments and to win converts among traditionalists.

Cheng felt that the state should lead in the promotion of commerce and industry, for its past neglect had been responsible for the merchants' weakness in China. Among other things, he argued that the state should: 1) establish a Ministry of Commerce (Shang pu) to take charge of commercial and industrial affairs; 2) appoint men of integrity to run it; 3) commission merchant directors in the provinces to report directly to the central government without intervention by the local authorities; 4) set up technical schools, a research center for silk, and new commercial bureaus (Shang-wu chü) to examine the state's resources and their use; 5) organize trade and industrial exhibitions; and 6) give achievement awards.[6]

One other publication of this period which provides a view that is close to that of another merchant was *Hsin-cheng chen-ch'üan* (The true meaning of new government) by Ho Ch'i (Ho Kai) and Hu Li-yuan.[7] Neither Ho nor Hu were, strictly speaking, merchants. Ho was a prominent Chinese leader in Hong Kong who, as a British-trained surgeon and barrister, shared many committee seats with the local merchants and was concerned with many of their problems.[8] Hu possessed other talents. His Chinese classical education was complemented by a Western education, as well as "modern" experiences in publishing a newspaper, advising the sultan of a small state, and running a trading post for a British merchant in Southeast Asia. Although he came from a Hong Kong merchant family, Hu appears to have engaged in business partially and then only briefly.[9]

Ho, Hu, and Cheng shared many qualities. They discussed commerce and industry in much the same way. They pleaded for governmental concern, pointing out the relevance of commerce and industry to the nation's survival.[10] All three men came from the same Hong Kong-Canton area. As products of the treaty ports, their views were probably not representative of those of most Chinese merchants. But the fact that they, and only they, articulated their thoughts for public consumption is in itself significant and reflects the crucial role the treaty port played in changing society's attitudes toward the merchant class.

The Changing World of Commerce

While the official advocates of modern enterprise ignored the domestic scene, the nature of domestic commerce was changing rapidly during the second half of the nineteenth century. Many of these changes were caused by foreign trade.

During the eighteenth century and down to about the 1850s, two monopolistic groups of merchants were among the most prominent commercial groups in China. These were the salt and the Cohong merchants. P'ing-ti Ho's study on the eighteenth century Yang-chou salt merchants has given us a vivid picture of their fantastic wealth, their high-flown style of life, and their great social privileges.[11] Liang Chia-pin, William Hunter, and others have also described the affluence and the economic importance of the Cohong merchants in Canton.[12] No doubt other major groups of merchants existed to service the thriving inter-provincial trade in silk, tea, medicine, and other regionally based produce. The growth of *hui-kuan* (Landsmannschaften or geographically based guild halls) in the various commercial cities of this period attested to the size and prominence of the merchant community. However, one knows very little about them. The great merchants during the Ming dynasty, such as those from Hui-chou (or Hsin-an) of Anhwei and those from T'ung-ting Lake in Kiangsu, had become much less prominent, while itinerant merchants from other areas such as Kwangtung, Chekiang, and Szechwan with their widespread network of *hui-kuan* had grown in size and importance.[13]

During the civil strife of the 1850s, the various merchant communities, especially those involved with inter-regional trade, suffered great losses. Peng Tse-i, in his study of the urban handicraft and commercial organizations of this period, noted that many guild halls were destroyed or had otherwise fallen into disuse.[14] Similarly, the salt merchants, having suffered years of gradual decline, were hit the hardest in the profitable Liang-huai area by the Taipings, and many went into bankruptcy.[15] As for the Cohong merchants, the Opium War and the establishment of the treaty system spelt their end.[16] Although individual Cohong merchants and their companies continued to exist as tea and silk merchants, they lasted only until 1856. Then a fire set by a Canton mob enraged over the Arrow Incident burned out the commercial district and much of its remaining influence.[17] Although Liang Chia-pin lists many scholarly descendants from among the Cohong merchants, he could find no prominent merchant successors.[18] The Cohong sites were apparently taken over by small merchants with their small shops. In 1901, one merchant by the name of Lu Chieh challenged the local government's claim to an empty plot of land in the area. Probably a direct descendant of the first Mowqua (Lu Kuan-heng), Lu claimed that Mowqua's Kuang-li (Kwong Lee) Company once stood there, that it properly belonged to his family, and that the government had appropriated it over the years.[19]

In their places were new kinds of merchants with new entrepreneurial functions. A major type were the compradors in the treaty ports. The compradors began early under the Cohong system as licensed clerks and purveyors. After the end of the British East India Company's monopoly in 1834, they began to be hired by independent foreign merchants as their resident stewards, treasurers, and guarantors of their Chinese staff. Then, with the demise of the Cohong system, the compradors rose to prominence. Previously they had to be guaranteed by the hong merchants. Now they themselves became the guarantors for any business transactions between their foreign employers and other Chinese merchants. Even as purveyors and treasurers, the early compradors were already known to conduct some trading on their own accounts. These activities did not, however, amount to much until after the 1840s when they became the compradors' dominant concerns. In time, the comprador's status vis-à-vis the foreign merchant changed successively from steward to business assistant and finally to business associate and independent merchant.[20] The comprador, with his close observance of the Western merchant's commercial practices and social outlook, helped bring about innovating economic and social values to the Chinese merchant class.

The impact of the foreign merchant, however, was not limited to those who could claim direct contact with him. Even merchants of the traditional sort, dealing in general commodity trading and financial services, were often affected by the foreigner's presence. One example was Meng Lo-ch'uan (c. 1850–1939) who, between 1893 and 1917, transformed his old but rather unimpressive family business in native cotton cloth into a business empire of some twenty-four branches in Peking, Tientsin, Shanghai, and the major towns in Shantung. At its height it employed about 1,000 men and involved many lines of business: cotton goods, medicine, tea, handicraft weaving, pawnshops, and imported goods such as foreign-made cloths. Meng belonged to a Shantung merchant clan that dated back at least to the early seventeenth century. His own family began different lines of business in the late eighteenth century. But by Meng Lo-ch'uan's time, only his own branch of the family, operating under the name of Jui-fu-hsiang, remained successful. Until 1893, his business changed very little and was still known in Tsinan as a prominent local establishment dealing in native cloth. Then in 1893, through the enterprise of Meng Chin-hou, his manager, Meng the owner opened a shop in Peking and began branching out into "silk, Cantonese goods, and foreign piece goods." Meng had been won over by his manager's argument that native cloth alone was too restricting. The change apparently worked well for the company, which began to register very rapid growth.[21]

Meng Lo-ch'uan remained a model of the traditional merchant throughout his long life. He was hard-working, conservative, frugal, and lived in a simple, traditional home. His pastime was to read and reread his company's books and records, which alone filled the shelves of his bedroom and study. He ran his many branches by a system of checks and balances among his chief assistants, some of whom were selected on the basis of their talent, others on the basis of their personal loyalty to him. These two types of men were often kept in pairs and assigned to the same posts. In addition, he had a network of trusted informers.[22] His business, too, remained traditional. Although he was ready to diversify from native cloth to pawnshops and handicraft weaving, he balked when asked to modernize his hand-operated wooden looms into a full-fledged machine-operated weaving factory. He pleaded that he would be a complete non-expert (*wai-hang*) to the factory system and could not understand—and one might add, control—the technicians and their work.[23]

The traditional distinction between the "professional of a trade" (*nei-hang*) and the "non-expert" was not a barrier preventing the Chinese entrepreneur from branching out into other traditional lines of trade, finance, or even handicraft manufacturing, for all the big merchants in traditional China invested in and managed a wide range of businesses. The distinction, however, was a real barrier keeping many who might otherwise have the capital and the spirit of enterprise from moving from the traditional into the modern types of industry. Meng Lo-ch'uan apparently thought so, even though he was fully aware that foreign trade and foreign type industry played a vital role in his own phenomenal growth after 1893.

The post-1850s also saw the development of new banking institutions. Although the first *p'iao-hao* (remittance bank) of the Shansi merchant-bankers, the Jih-sheng-ch'ang, was founded in or about 1831 to handle remittances between Tientsin, Hankow, and Chungking, it was from the 1860s that such banks grew rapidly into a "national" network of branches.[24] The same period also saw the phenomenal growth of the *ch'ien-chuang* (local bank) in the lower Yangtze area, so that an 1876 survey reported that there were 105 in Shanghai alone. In the area of finance there is little doubt that development of both the *p'iao-hao* and the *ch'ien-chuang* were influenced by foreign trade. The impact on the *p'iao-hao* is less obvious, for they often served as the agents and depositors of official funds. Yet their large deposits and busy movement of funds for their private and official clients must have been affected by the general increase in trade volumes brought about by foreign trade. The close connection between the *ch'ien-chuang's* growth and the growth of the foreign banking facilities during the same period is better known. Just as Chinese merchants in Shanghai depended on the *ch'ien-chuang* for their credit facilities, so did the *ch'ien-chuang* depend on the foreign banks for making them loans and honoring their bank orders which matured in periods ranging from three to thirty days.[25] The extent of this form of dependence was clearly demonstrated when the foreign bankers' threats to halt these credit facilities led to a serious financial crisis in Shanghai in 1910.[26]

The Contrast Between Two Traditional Merchants

The foreign merchant and foreign trade, however, were not alone responsible for the changes taking place in the Chinese world of commerce. Nor was that world reshaped entirely by individual entrepreneurs and private enterprises as exemplified by the compradors, the traditional Shensi and Chekiang bankers, traditional merchants such as Meng Lo-ch'uan, and their wide-ranging private interests. Indeed, internal developments such as the phenomenal rise in population and the increased government spending during and after the Taiping Rebellion led to the need for new public fiscal policies and a new group of men with the proper financial expertise to manage them. Hu Kuang-yung (c. 1825–1885), an entrepreneur and traditional merchant-banker, but in many ways the antithesis of Meng Lo-ch'uan, owed his rise to prominence to these internal developments.[27]

Hu belonged to the first group of merchant advisors to officials who needed not only the usual expert advice their private secretaries (*mu-yu*) could provide, but also management and improvisations that would help solve the increasing complexities of public finance because of the wars against the Taipings, the Niens, and other rebellions.[28] Often by means of a *pro forma* purchase of titles, these merchant-advisors acquired semi-official status. They became insiders to the bureaucratic world and continued to carry on their private or semi-official enterprises. Hu Kuang-yung thus became an expectant taotai by purchase, and beginning probably from the mid-1850s, became a part-time advisor to Wang Yu-ling, at that time the Provincial Treasurer of Kiangsu. When Wang was promoted to the governorship of Chekiang, Hu, a native of Chekiang, followed him to his yamen in Hangchow and soon opened up a remittance bank, the Fu-k'ang Bank, there. The next governor, Tso Tsung-t'ang, turned to Hu for help in public finance and appointed him his purchasing agent during his 1870s campaign in the northwest.[29]

Hu rose rapidly meanwhile as a merchant-banker. Within a dozen years, he emerged from obsurity to become perhaps the wealthiest man in the lower Yangtze area. Such a phenomenal rise could not have been achieved by personal enterprise and good fortune alone. It was made possible by the new political situation Hu was able to exploit because of his official and secret society connections. While other entrepreneurs in the past had enjoyed similar entrée into and collaborations with the official world, Hu had the added advantage that his official world had newly acquired the freedom to discard old, rigid revenue quotas and to improvise new, non-statutory sources of revenue. Hu benefited from these public funds since he was able to channel a good deal of money through his banks. This included taxes collected from foreign trade and assigned to his many customs banks for deposits or remittances. Then, while the capital was temporarily in his care, he used it in the commodity markets.

Existing official records, which touch upon Hu's official dealings, treat only partially Hu's complex system of private financial and trading management. Hu did not leave his own private accounts to posterity, but one of his contemporaries, using the Japanese pseudonym Ohashi Shikyu, wrote a factionalized account of him in Chinese entitled *Hu Hsueh-yen wai-chuan* (An unofficial biography of Hu Kuang-yung [Hsueh-yen being his courtesty name or *tzu*]). Although the novelist overemphasized Hu's alleged personal depravity, what little he had to say about the social background, Hu's rise to fortune, his economic relations with the government, and his eventual bankruptcy appears to be historically accurate.[30] It is from this kind of literary source that one can get a better understanding of how public funds and political connections augmented personal wealth among this group of merchants who straddled the two worlds of commerce and officialdom.

Hu Kuang-yung and Meng Lo-ch'uan represented two types of traditional merchants, both successful during this period. While Hu readily invested money in both Chinese- and foreign-owned cotton mills, Meng refused even to introduce power looms to his handicraft weaving industry by pleading *wai-hang*.[31]

Hu made use of his banks and official deposits to support his own large-scale trading and speculation. Meng, on the other hand, depended on his family wealth to trade conservatively and used his extra capital to invest in two pawnshops, which never became his main business. Hu the entrepreneur was greatly benefited by Hu the semi-official. Meng on the other hand was slow in seeking official support. In the early period, he cultivated friendship with officialdom only in order to minimize official squeeze. When he first opened his branch in Peking, he had no connections with the local officials. As a result, the headman (*ti-pao*) of his precinct took him to court when he committed the petty irregularity of paving the front of his shop with stone.

It is interesting to note that, by the 1900s, Meng began to seek out positive support from the officials. He bought himself the rank of an expectant taotai. In 1909, six months after Tsinan had set up its first general chamber of commerce. Meng was appointed its vice-president. Sometime after 1910, Meng became president of the Association of Chambers of Commerce of Shantung, while his manager, Meng Chin-hou, became a special director and was reported to be the man with the real power behind the Peking Chamber of Commerce. Apparently, Meng Lo-ch'uan had become a friend of Yuan Shih-k'ai when the latter spent his early official career in Shantung. After 1912, the year Yuan appointed him an advisor, Meng committed himself to supporting Yuan and the warlords who succeeded him. His own children were married into the families of such prominent Peking warlord leaders as Hsu Shih-ch'ang and Ts'ao K'un. In 1885 Hu abruptly found himself bankrupt because he had speculated recklessly during the Sino-French war. Meng's fortune lasted longer. His gradual decline began in 1926 when the warlords who supported him were themselves losing power.[32]

The Influx of New Elements into the Merchant Ranks

Hu Kuang-yung and others like him were not the only kind of merchant-advisors required by the officials. Beginning in the 1870s, as officials began to sponsor profit-making industrial enterprises, they recruited merchants with money and presumed expertise in modern industry. As a result, the new recruits were largely drawn from the compradors. Although their direct contacts with foreign merchants did not make them experts in industrial management, yet their exposure to things foreign somehow made them more ready to go into these new enterprises. The first recruits were the compradors Tong King-sing (T'ang T'ing-shu) and Hsu Jun, who in 1873 resigned from their foreign firms and accepted Governor-general Li Hung-chang's invitation to manage the Chinese Merchants' Steam Navigation Company begun earlier that year.[33] They and other compradors thereby added a new dimension to their entrepreneurial roles. And as they moved from shipping to textiles and mining, they were no longer merely private, "non-productive" traders; they had become semi-official manufacturing industrialists. Another change was thus brought into the Chinese world of commerce.

As these merchants assumed some measure of official status, others with official backgrounds began to infiltrate the merchant ranks. In one sense, this was nothing new. Most officials who had commercial investments kept them secret, for there had been no ideological justification to support them. In contrast, during the late nineteenth century, a number of the regular officials and their sons who showed aptitude for the management of finance began to express openly their interest in private and government-sponsored entrepreneurial activities. This was particularly true from the 1870s when the switch to industrial management became possible. Some retained their official appointments but devoted most of their energy to the supervision of government-sponsored and private enterprises. Others made a formal exit from the official world to devote full time to enterprises. The following personalities will give some idea of the kinds of men involved and of the nature of relationships they still retained with the government.

Sheng Hsuan-huai (1844–1916), the best known of this group of officials, requires only a brief introduction.[34] He probably acquired his own entrepreneurial interests at a very early age from his father who had had a long career in the management of public finance. During the Taiping Rebellion, the senior Sheng worked for many years in the Hupei provincial tax and likin bureau. After the rebellion, he was appointed salt administration taotai in Wuchang, Hupei. Sheng himself does not tell us how much he learned from or was influenced by his father, but after he had failed to achieve any degree higher than the *sheng-yuan* degree, he joined the official staff (*mu-fu*) of Li Hung-chang where he was soon assigned to a supervisory post in the China Merchants' Steam Navigation Company.

From this first footing Sheng gradually moved into telegraph, railways, mining, iron and steel mills, textiles, and modern banking. In 1879, some six years after his steamship company assignment, he received his first regular administrative appointment as acting military administrative taotai of the Tientsin-Hochien circuit. Sheng stayed on in his official career, and ultimately made use of his own promotions and the patronage of such senior statesmen as Li Hung-chang and Chang Chih-tung to protect and further his control over his various private and *kuan-tu shang-pan* enterprises. However, Sheng never succeeded in acquiring a provincial power base. His later official positions were with the central administration, from the director-generalship of the Imperial Railway Administration to various ministerial assignments, and finally the presidency of the powerful Ministry of Posts and Communications. In the course of this career, he ran into several conflicts of interest with provincial power holders such as Governor-general Yuan Shih-k'ai. Since the central government usually came out second best in any competition for power with the provinces, these clashes contributed to

Sheng's loss of control over a number of his major enterprises during the 1900s.[35] This is not the place to discuss the theme of the unequal contest between provincial and central authorities; that will come later. The point here is that Sheng was able to control and expand his industrial complexes while serving in substantive official positions.

Yen Hsin-hou (c. 1838–1907), also known as Yen Hsiao-fang, probably began his career as a merchant in Shanghai in the 1850s. His first connection with the official world was through Tso Tsung-t'ang, who asked him to arrange food supplies for his army. Then, sometime in the early 1860s, Hu Kuang-yung recommended him to Li Hung-chang. Hu had become impressed by Yen's literary accomplishment and refinement which he found "unusual in a 'mercenary broker' (*shih-kuei*)." Thus, although he was credited with having a *kung-sheng* degree when he joined Li's *mu-fu,* it was probably a purchased title. It was also probable that he came from a merchant family, for his biographers did not mention any official forebears. Besides his native home, Tz'u-ch'i, near Ningpo, was famous for its many prominent merchants. Under Li, he was assigned to manage salt transport in Honan.

Yen's early career in some ways paralleled that of both Sheng Hsuan-huai and Hu Kuang-yung. With Sheng he shared a similar *mu-fu* career and management in financial affairs. Like Hu, he entered into semi-official status through similar routes. It is probable that Yen's relationship with Tso was like Hu's early relationship with Provincial Treasurer Wang Yu-ling. However, Yen later developed into an entrepreneur very different from either Sheng or Hu.

Sometime in the 1870s, having acquired considerable wealth from his official functions in public finance, Yen resigned from Li's service and moved on to private industry and finance. He involved himself first in textiles, then flour mills, oil presses, railways, river transport, traditional banks, and finally, from 1896 on, as Sheng's partner in China's first modern bank, the Imperial Bank of China. Although Yen never resumed his official career, he bought the rank of an expectant taotai and continued to retain his official links. Between 1890 and 1903, hardly a year went by without his appointment to some government-sponsored commission to raise funds for relief, national debts, or military provisions. Between 1901 and 1903, he cooperated with Sheng in preparing for a merchant association in Shanghai which later became China's first chamber of commerce. When the chamber was opened in Shanghai in 1904, Yen became its first president. Yen was also very active in the Ningpo guild and a number of charitable halls in Shanghai. Unlike Sheng, who was known as an official involved with entrepreneurial activities, Yen was known by his fellow merchants in Shanghai as an entrepreneur with official and gentry status. He was a good example of the so-called "gentry merchant" (*shen-shang*).[36]

Chang Chien's (1853–1926) family had for many generations been small farmers. His father was the first to become literate, and he did it through sheer strength of will, for the grandfather would have preferred that he devote full time to helping him in the fields. Chang Chien's father did not learn enough to qualify him for the imperial examinations. A capable and resourceful man, the senior Chang managed to find the money to repay the family's debts, then went on to become a man of moderate means and a respected mediator in the village. It seems that he owned a small commercial shop to supplement his income from the farm. At first he sent Chang Chien and an older son, Chang Ch'a, to school together; only later did financial difficulties force him to withdraw Chang Ch'a so that he could help with work at home and in the family business.[37]

The family had a previous connection with a porcelain artisan and trader surnamed Wu. Chang Chien's grandfather had married the comparatively wealthy Wu's only daughter and had agreed to let one of their children be adopted into his wife's family. It is not clear which of the sons was so adopted, because some of them died afterwards. Probably, Chang Chien's father and then Chang Chien himself were designated for adoption. Thus the father was sent on frequent and lengthy stays with his artisan-trader maternal grandfather while Chang Chien himself was given the surname Wu until ten years of age, by which time his father had become very much impressed with his intellectual promise.[38]

It is not known what sort of residual impact these commercial and artisan antecedents had on Chang Chien when he later decided to turn to industry. It is, however, worth noting that Chang Chien did not come from a strictly peasant background as is often supposed.[39]

Chang Chien passed his first set of imperial examinations in 1868 when he was only fifteen years old. From then on, he was plagued by examination misfortune. He did not become a *chü-jen* until his sixth attempt in 1885. This was followed by four more failures to gain the *chih-shih* degree. When he finally succeeded in 1894, he was awarded the much coveted first place among his fellow *chih-shih* graduates for that year. By then he was already forty-one years old.

Meanwhile, in between sitting for his examinations, Chang had a long and successful career as a respected *mu-yu* and scholar. Then from the mid-1880s on, he was home in Nan-t'ung (near Shanghai) as a gentry leader working on such local affairs as tax reforms, militia, flood relief, and the promotion of sericulture.

In 1894, with his examination triumphs, Chang was appointed a senior compiler in the Hanlin Academy. But before the year was out, he was home again to observe a two-year home leave because of his father's death. The enforced rest gave Chang a chance to reconsider his official career. Although he had long been a *mu-yu* type of "unofficial" official (he had refused official recommendations to gain a regular post because he stubbornly wanted to acquire the *chih-shih* degree and become an official by the regular route), and had only become a regular official for less than a year, there was already much that displeased him: the rigidity of the bureaucracy, the slow promotions, and the merely advisory and academic nature of a post in the Hanlin Academy. Later on, he claimed that one of the reasons he went into industry was his strong urge to prove that a scholar like himself was not just a bookworm. Another reason was the servility of court officials, which disgusted him. One incident in Peking Chang personally witnessed in 1894 is said to have helped him quit his official career. Chang was shocked to see court officials, old and young, high and low, all drop to their knees as required by court etiquette on the muddy road after a heavy downpour in order to greet the empress dowager on her return to the capital. Yet, as Chang sadly observed, the old lady did not even turn her head to acknowledge this public display of feudal homage.[40]

Another factor that influenced him was the shock of China's defeat in 1894 and the new treaty provision allowing foreigners to set up factories in China. It appears, however, that, when he finally made the decision to devote full time to industry, he came upon it by a devious route. Chang was convinced that thorough reform was needed and that the foundation of such a reform lay in the introduction of a modern system of education. When he realized that the new education needed funds, he decided to turn first to industrial enterprise as a means of raising money for his educational program.[41]

Between 1896 and 1898, Chang Chien worked hard to set up his first industrial enterprise, the Dah Sun Cotton Mill, to be discussed hereafter. Suffice it here to say that his final success in the mill was owing to the support he received from Governor-general Liu K'un-i.[42] From cotton spinning Chang applied his entrepreneurial talents to other industries, then to land reclamation, river conservancy, and fisheries. In these activities, Chang was helped by his older brother Chang Ch'a, who had become a county magistrate through Chang Chien's connections. Chang Ch'a relinquished his official career and apparently turned himself into a very able industrial administrator. Their long-term association also assured a stable managerial leadership, rare in China at the time. Undoubtedly it contributed to the profit-making capacity of many of Chang's ventures. It is also symptomatic that Chang Ch'a, despite his conservatism, also left officialdom in order to become an industrial manager.

Change Chien returned to officialdom only briefly during the early Republican period to serve as Minister of Industry and Agriculture. During the 1900s, he was made a counselor of the Ministry of Commerce, was sought after by such senior provincial officials as Liu K'un-i, and remained politically active in a series of modernization efforts in the fields of education and local and constitutional government.

Nieh Ch'i-kuei (c. 1850–1911), although he came from a family in Hunan which for many generations had produced scholar-officials, failed when he tried to acquire the *chü-jen* degree. However, through the well-placed connections of his wife, Nieh Tseng Chi-fen, a daughter of Tseng Kuo-fan, he was given a minor official post by Governor-general Li Han-chang in 1882. Soon afterward, having come to the attention of another governor-general, Tso Tsung-t'ang, by similar means, he was first made an assistant director and then, in 1884, Director of the Kiangnan Arsenal in Shanghai. In 1890, he became the customs taotai of Shanghai. Again, he owed this promotion to his wife's uncle, Governor-general Tseng Kuo-ch'üan. According to the wife, Tseng submitted a special memorial on his behalf and then appointed him to the post for which he by-passed nine other candidates.[43] Nieh rose rapidly through the provincial hierarchy, then received successive appointments as Governor of Kiangsu (1900), Anhwei (1901), and Chekiang (1903). In 1905, his official career was abruptly terminated after he was attacked by a censor for abuse and misappropriation of official funds.[44]

With the Shanghai customs taotai office came a great opportunity to acquire wealth and influence. Until then, while serving at the Kiangnan Arsenal, Nieh did not have access to sizeable official funds. Since the family estate was moderate, one may presume that Nieh had not made any substantial business investment even if his long residence in Shanghai had so encouraged him. In 1890, with his new appointment and improved financial position, Nieh and another taotai joined a number of merchants in founding the New Hua-hsin Cotton Mill in Shanghai. In 1893, he invested in another mill, the Hua-sheng Cotton Mill, headed by Sheng Hsuan-huai. Then sometime around 1904, Nieh, while serving as governor of Chekiang, gained control over the failing Hua-hsin and put in his oldest son, Nieh Ch'i-chieh, as manager. The new management turned the mill into a moneymaking venture, yielding a net profit of over 100,000 taels in its first year. In 1908, Nieh bought the mill outright for 320,000 taels.[45]

Nieh Ch'i-chieh and a younger brother, both still in their twenties, now took charge of the mill, which was renamed Heng-feng. Ch'i-chieh had learned English from Mrs. John Fryer in his childhood because, as his mother put it, "I realized the importance of Western language and science."[46] The two brothers were also given an engineering training, the family having apparently decided that modern education and skill offered a respectable profession. Both stayed on in the cotton industry and became major industrialists in Shanghai during the 1920s. Between 1920 and 1922, Nieh Ch'i-chieh was elected President of the Shanghai General Chamber of Commerce.

While one could sketch the career of many other "new" entrepreneurs, the purpose here is to take a few examples to show how officials in their various ways began to take up entrepreneurial roles. Some, like Sheng Hsuan-huai, continued to act and think of themselves as officials first and entrepreneurs second. Sheng, for example, ran his industrial enterprises in a most bureaucratic manner. Right down to 1912, Sheng as director-general allowed the nominally merchant-operated (since 1907) Hanyehping Coal and Iron Company Ltd. to greet him as a bureaucrat-potentate whenever he showed up at the company on an inspection. Before his arrival, the offices would be cleansed and decorated. Then all the officers would line up by the gate, in formal dress, to welcome him and his party. An elaborate banquet at company expense would follow. Other unbusinesslike practices included large family expense accounts, including contingents of bodyguards, for all senior officials. There were also cases of embezzlement of company funds, many of them by sinecure holders related to Sheng by kinship and personal loyalty.[47]

These bureaucratic practices inspired the novelist Wu Chien-jen to write many satirical pieces about the official managers. In one episode, Sheng, as director-general of the China Merchants' Steam Navigation Company, was thinly disguised as the director-general of a large steamship company. What followed was high comedy. The director-general had become infatuated with a "low class" girl he had met only briefly in Hankow while on his inspection tour. The local manager, pandering to the director-general's desires, devised an elaborate scheme in order to present the girl to him. Everything worked according to plan until the jealous wife got wind of it from her brother, who, predictably, held a sinecure in the company. The wife then requisitioned one of the company's large cargo ships and ordered its captain to take her non-stop from Shanghai to Hankow. At the end of the story, the wife dismissed the girl, took her husband back to Shanghai, and put the Hankow manager on probation.[48]

Others, like Chang Chien and Yen Hsin-hou, not only relinquished their official posts, but also behaved primarily as entrepreneurs. But they did not thereby lose their official and gentry status. They received considerable support from their official connections. Indeed it was support of this kind that made them as successful as they became. Chang's son and biographer, Chang Hsiao-jo, put it in this way: "In Chinese society, you cannot accomplish anything without having close ties with the officials. They can help you or break you. When a private person takes over something, if he can get official support, then naturally he will achieve success at double measure for only half efforts."[49]

Nieh Ch'i-kuei and his son Nieh Ch'i-chieh represent another kind of official or, more precisely, official family who made an entrance into merchant ranks. For them, the transformation took place over three generations. Nieh Ch'i-kuei's ancestors had been regular officials, while his father-in-law, Tseng Kuo-fen, was the foremost T'ung-chih restorationist leader. They were as far away from being "merchants" as one could imagine. Nieh himself, however, began his official career without the minimal *chü-jen* degree, and he entered it by an irregular route through his wife's family connections. Many of his contemporaries who later became prominent officials, including Yuan Shih-k'ai, began their careers in similar ways. Nieh had all the "right" mandarin background; he prepared himself for an official career, became a successful official, and throughout his life acted and thought like an official. Thus, although he readily combined his official duties with industrial investments and management, it is not certain how openly he admitted his involvement with those activities at the time. His wife's autobiographical chronology, written in 1932, though very candid about his official appointments through personal connections, is devious about his business ventures. She brushed aside Nieh's early involvements. Nieh had rejected such offers because he "felt that, as an official, he should not manage any business." As for Nieh's taking over control of the cotton mill in about 1904, she argued that Nieh had reluctantly agreed to it only after the manager's repeated pleadings, "followed by prolonged beggings on his knees." Finally, as for Nieh's outright purchase in 1908, she credited it to her two sons' requests. It is likely that in her old age and in her desire to paint her late husband as a model of rectitude, she tried to shield him more than he had actually shielded himself.[50]

When these men are considered along with those who came originally from a merchant background, and who by various means had attained official or semi-official status while continuing to be merchants–men as diverse as Hu Kuang-yung, Men Lo-ch'uan, Hsu Jun, and Tong King-sing–then it can be readily admitted that new elements had crept into the merchant ranks. One might even suggest a typology of merchants. The only difficulty with any such model is that there could be no clear demarcation lines between the various types. The blurring effect was underlined by the term *shen-shang* (gentry-merchant) which had come into popular use during the late nineteenth and early twentieth centuries. It connotes a close but ambiguous relation between merchants and gentry, and it suggests a group of men who assumed interchangeable mercantile, gentry, and official roles. Moreover, the term *shen-shang,* though broad, was not broad enough. It excluded, on the one hand, those who went on to become senior officials and, on the other, the numerous merchants whose only claim to gentry status was the money they spent on some petty official titles.[51]

Other causes of the influx. Besides the growing conviction among scholar-officials that industry and commerce were crucial to the state's wealth and power, other factors also contributed to the swelling number of officials and gentry in business during the late Ch'ing.

It is generally known that officials and gentry have consistently put their excess income into land investments; farm lands were not only stable, but, as Fei Hsiao-t'ung and many others have pointed out, they could also be leased out "at high rentals, for 2,000 years close to 50 percent of the crop raised."[52] Even when the 50 percent crop yields could be collected *in toto,* however, they did not assure a high profit because the prices of both land and rice were variable. According to Chang Chung-li, throughout the nineteenth century, the slower rise in rice prices relative to land prices led to a progressive decline in profit for land investors. In the late eighteenth century, the annual rate of returns on land investments stood at 10 percent before taxes. By the 1820s, with an almost fivefold increase in land prices and a mere twofold increase in the cost of rice, profits dropped to 4 percent. Then, in the 1880s, because land prices had again risen three times, profits slid further to below 2 percent after taxes. In the 1920s, a field survey conducted by J. L. Buck showed that the rate of return remained low, at about 2.5 percent.[53]

Such a diminishing level of profits should have made land investments unattractive. However, even after due allowances are made for the more rapid rise in population relative to acreage of arable land, the soaring land prices (about 1500 percent in one century) could only mean that demands for land were keener than ever before. How can one explain this seeming economic paradox?

First, land was still regarded as a worthwhile, long-term investment because, unlike commercial enterprises, it was stable and without risk. Second, and more important, it had a value other than its purely economic value. While degree-holding gentry and officials did not require land possessions to maintain their social distinction, wealthy urban merchants with or without purchased titles presumably did, if only to establish and consolidate their "gentry" status back in their ancestral villages. Moreover, they were the ones who could best afford to pay the spiraling price increases. Indeed, the unattractive profit returns could be written off as a small cost to pay for the social status and long-term stability to be gained.

On the other hand, the combination of soaring land prices and dwindling profits from rents were good reasons for the gentry and officials to sell or limit the size of their holdings. Moreover, conditions for individual investments in both the traditional and the modern forms of commerce and industry were excellent in the second half of the nineteenth century. Although accurate statistics are unavailable, it seems that, as the nineteenth century progressed, more and more urban merchants became landowners, while more and more of the regular gentry and officials sold their land or diverted their bureaucratic income from more purchase of land into industrial and commercial capital.[54]

Such a tentative theory is supported by at least two pieces of circumstantial evidence. First, it is known that the post-Taiping decades saw an increase in absentee landownership in the commercially most active lower Yangtze Valley. This had been shown by Muramatsu Yuji's study on the "landlord bursaries" (*tsu-chan*). By means of these bursaries, many urban merchants were able to enlist the services of the rural elite to collect rents for a percentage commission on their behalf.[55] Coupled with the Chinese urban merchants' uniquely strong ties to and close identification with their ancestral rural homes, these landlord bursaries successfully served as an institutional link between the merchants and the rural elite. Second, there is evidence that, in spite of tax exemptions and other benefits that only gentry landowners received from the state, the gentry as a whole were not large landowners. Chang Chung-li, who estimated that the large landowners among the gentry and officials owned some 25 percent of cultivated lands, found evidence suggesting that large numbers of gentry, including retired officials, were landless.[56]

Another factor influencing the large number of officials and gentry in business was the social tension within the gentry class during the nineteenth and the early twentieth centuries. As the population rose, the quota of degree holders and official posts failed to keep pace. As a result, there was keener competition among the literary elite for degrees and offices.[57] On the other hand, the cheapening of official titles and ranks through commercialization and the general demoralization of the bureaucracy must have contributed to a growing number of dissatisfied literati who altered their professional pursuits from officialdom to the world of the entrepreneur. Chang Chien was a case in point. Only by stubborn persistence did he succeed in the traditional civil service examinations. Almost immediately thereafter, he chose to discard his hard-won official career in order to take up a career in industry.

Since more officials and gentry went into commerce and industry one may assume that a greater amount of their wealth was put into these enterprises during the late Ch'ing period. How much of it went into the traditional types of commercial enterprises—pawnshops, general trading, local banks, and the like—may never be known, since, like Magistrate Wu, their investments both in terms of their size and extent were largely secret. Presumably a greater portion of their capital went into the traditional types because these were better understood (that is, they were more *nei-hang*). Besides, their concealed ownership notwithstanding, these enterprises were often protected from the excessive official demands which so often plagued usual business operations.[58]

The part of their capital that went into modern industry is, however, somewhat better known. The number of industrial enterprises of this period was relatively small and, after 1905, most of them were registered with the government, which then tried to record the identity of their investors. According to Yen Chung-p'ing, the social backgrounds of the major founders of some twenty-six textile mills established in China between 1890 and 1910 were as follows:[59]

Senior Officials	13
Retired Officials and Gentry	7
Compradors	6
	26

A similar study which deals with forty-one industrial companies of all types founded in Shanghai before 1912 gives the following distribution of the main founders:[60]

Officials and Retired Officials	11
Compradors	14
Merchants	6
Overseas Chinese Merchants	2
Apprentices, Workers, Craftsmen	6
Unclassified, priests and monks	2
	41

These occupational and social categories were rough approximations, since many merchants, officials, and gentry played overlapping roles. Yet these two sets of figures show the active participations of official and gentry capital in industry. It was particularly true of the cotton textile industry, where official founders predominated, probably because of the early sponsorship of this industry by both Li Hung-chang and Chang Chih-tung.

One question of great interest to social historians of modern China is whether there was a new social stratum of official and gentry merchants and, if so, whether it had become committed to economic modernization.[61] Why were several prominent gentry-merchants associated with the development of modern industry? Who benefited?

This study has suggested that the emergence of a new social stratum of gentry-merchants from the old scholar-official and merchant classes was real. That stratum had not, however, developed into a distinct social class during the period of the late Ch'ing and early Republican China. In a few large treaty ports, the number of gentry-merchants might have become so considerable that a kind of common lifestyle, values, and social and political orientations had become quite evident. But there remained a lack of broad unity of purpose and a persistence of strong commitment to traditional patterns, such as the old identification with native place and clan ties, extraneous to any bourgeois interest.[62]

The fusion of a large number of merchants and gentry was the result of several drastic and interlocking social changes in nineteenth-century China: the growth of commercial and industrial activities through foreign impact, the oversupply of scholars for available official posts because of population pressures, and the emergence of specialists in public management and technical skills because of internal rebellions and external influences. These developments converted scholar-officials ideologically to the idea that the nation's survival depended on their ability to sponsor modern enterprises. Yet, since the gentry-merchants were the only ones with the proper management skills to run the new enterprises, they were also provided with an opportunity for personal gain. For both public interests and private benefits, therefore, they established for themselves a rationale for economic modernization and became its ardent advocates.

PART TWO

THE PROVINCIAL GOVERNMENT: INITIATIVE AND DOMINATION

Chapter Four

FROM MERCHANT TO BUREAUCRATIC MANAGEMENT

The early Legalists were the first to make "wealth and power" the primary concern of the state. Though acutely aware of the connection between political power and economic power, both Lord Shang and Han Fei-tzu rejected commerce and industry in favor of a "physiocratic" theory which argued that agriculture alone provided the source of real wealth. When later Legalists, including Emperor Wu-ti of the Han dynasty, finally pushed the connection to its logical conclusion and emphasized the importance of trade and industry, they argued that all major commercial and industrial activities should be controlled or monopolized by the state. Although such a view was challenged from time to time by Confucian literati who believed in the more passive and morally self-regulating economic policies (*wu-wei*), Emperor Wu-ti's basic assumptions for the activitistic and interventionalistic economic policies (*yu-wei*) were accepted by succeeding dynasties. Thus, in spite of the continuing ambivalence in Confucian ideology, recurrent debates on the state's economic policy after the Han dynasty often dealt with the extent and the nature of state intervention and seldom with the question of whether state intervention was necessary.[1]

During the late nineteenth century, as officials and literati became convinced that commerce and industry had assumed a crucial importance to the state, all of them—from the conservative senior statesman Chang Chih-tung to the liberal intellectual and political exile Liang Ch'i-ch'ao—could think only of encouraging and expanding the nation's commerce and industry within the framework of state supervision. Even the merchant-intellectual Cheng Kuan-ying believed that Chinese merchants could not run any modern enterprise without government support and protection.

Two basic premises inherent in these views—that the state had the right to run, or at least intervene in, the affairs of any major business enterprise, and that the state had prior prerogatives over its profits—were in sharp contrast to those prevalent in the West. In the classic expression of the eighteenth and nineteenth century liberalism, state intervention was inevitably harmful. All productive, creative, and profitable business enterprises were assumed to be the activities of individuals by themselves or in "voluntary" association, acting freely and without state coercion. A government might, however, extend encouragement to private investors and offer a favorable environment such as light taxes and a minimum of rules required for the smooth and orderly functioning of their entrepreneurial activities.[2] Government-run enterprises were also objectionable, for as the authors of *The American Business Creed* have pointed out,

> they do not obey the rules. They do not operate at a profit. By their ability to run at a loss they drive out private competition and thus become monopolies, with all the evils of monopoly. Moreover, they do not obey the rules in terms of accounting, taxation, and the like, so that their costs are never honestly known. The objections on incentive grounds are even stronger and more fundamental. Governments are run by bureaucrats and bureaucrats are always irresponsible. They are motivated by political and not by business-like aims; they are not judged by the consequences of their actions; therefore they can never function as effectively as can the executives of business operating under the stimulus of the profit motive.[3]

Even more reprehensible were the Chinese state's presumed claims over the profits of commerce and industry. For not only did they challenge the operation of free enterprise, they also called into question the whole system of capitalism. In the West, the profit motive of the capitalist has always been seen as an indispensable incentive for undertaking the risks of owning productive capital equipment and making commercial transactions. The profits so acquired are then added to his stock of capital which an owner can use in whatever way he sees fit. This does not, however, lead to antisocial, personal greed because, in the long run, the individual's profit will benefit the rest of society. For example, profits help create savings, and savings lead to reinvestments for more plants, more equipment, and larger volumes of business. These in turn produce new jobs and more goods.[4] If the state laid prior claims to the profits, then few individuals would be motivated to make any investments, and fewer still would be left with any substantial accumulation of capital from their trading or industrial enterprises.

Although the Chinese state made different theoretical claims, it did not always put them into practice; and, even when it did, it concentrated its efforts in selective fields. After all, the entrepreneur in imperial China could accumulate private capital, and, when left to himself, also believed ideally in the legitimacy of the profit motive, the general good that it could bring to his community, and the importance of reinvesting his profits. From the 1870s a new set of problems confronted him, however, when the state invited him to become a partner in a modern type of industry requiring more capital than he could raise from among his relatives and friends. For, unlike his Western counterparts, he had very hazy notions of his overall legal status, much less of his rights vis-à-vis the government-appointed official managers.

Merchant Management in Kuan-tu Shang-pan *Operations*

Since the Chinese officials, literati, and merchants all agreed on the need for the government's involvement in developing the nation's commerce and industry, it is small wonder that China's first wave of profit-oriented industrial enterprises, begun in the 1870s, was sponsored and supervised by government officials. It should also be noted at the outset that, down to the end of the dynasty, these government sponsors were by and large provincial governors-general and their assistants.

Beginning in the 1860s the government had set up a number of government funded and managed (*kuan-pan*) modern industries which, as arsenals and shipyards, were directly involved with national defense. On the other hand, the new enterprises of the 1870s were business ventures. Some, such as textiles and shipping, were in areas traditionally reserved for the private entrepreneur. Others, such as mining, had a strong tradition of government control or monopoly.

In 1872, when Governor-general Li Hung-chang proposed setting up the first non-military modern industry, the China Merchants' Steam Navigation Company (Lun-ch'uan chao-shang chü), he did not envision government ownership. In any case, he realized that the government was without sufficient funds of its own to undertake all such ventures. Instead, Li recycled a bureaucratic term *kuan-tu shang-pan* (government supervision and merchant management) from the salt monopoly to suggest that the organizational structure for these new industries should incorporate features from both the salt administration and the Western model of joint-stock companies. The former was useful because it had already established a precedent of co-opting wealthy merchants who then provided capital and managerial skills. The latter was necessary because modern enterprise was borrowed from the West and because it opened up the possibilities of attracting investment from large numbers of merchants. Private investors, under official sponsorship and supervision, would then assume all the risks of profits and losses. Beyond these general principles, however, neither Li nor any other official promoters at this time had any precise institutional format for the *kuan-tu shang-pan* organization.[5]

It is sometimes thought that, from the very beginning, Li Hung-chang did not intend to leave the running and management of the *kuan-tu shang-pan* enterprises to the merchant investors, even though the second half of the term, *shang-pan* clearly suggested, in direct translation, "merchant management."[6] Certainly, Li did not intend that the merchant investors in the joint-stock companies would hold shareholders' meetings and form boards of directors, which in turn would appoint their own management personnel. But, even if Li had agreed to such a close copy of the Western corporation model, it could not have succeeded. In the 1870s, the concept of management's responsibilities to a board of directors and ultimately to the corporate body of shareholders was little understood among Chinese investors. Some thirty years later, when a number of private joint-stock companies gave their directors and shareholders such rights and responsibilities, many factional and petty squabbles erupted.

For an alternative meaning of merchant management as understood by Li and those merchant investors who responded to his call, one must look to more traditional models of cooperation between groups with comparably different functions. To begin with, Li and the merchants were familiar with the salt administration's policy of co-optation in which the state appointed wealthy merchants to be *tsung-shang* (chief merchants). These merchant-managers were given official status and ran their operations with broad administrative power and influence not only over the smaller merchant salt shippers but also within the network of official supervisors.[7]

Another model was the traditional company. Although such companies were smaller, each usually dependent upon the resources of one extended family or a few partners, many were run by hired managers. In such a company the owners gave the manager almost absolute control, and did not intervene on a daily or monthly basis. Usually once a year the manager would review the business with his passive owners and present a statement of the company's accounts. If his work was found unsatisfactory, he would be dismissed and a new manager with similar power would be hired.[8]

In spite of many obvious differences between such a traditional company and the three major *kuan-tu shang-pan* companies Li sponsored during the 1870s—the China Merchants' Steam Navigation Company of 1872, the Kaiping Mining Company (K'ai-p'ing k'uang-wu chü) of 1877, and the Shanghai Cotton Cloth Mill (Shang-hai chi-ch'i chih-pu chü) of 1878—their management structures shared several similar elements.

First, they were all headed by merchant-managers. The China Merchants' was first led by the junk-owner Chu Ch'i-ang (1872–73). When Chu's knowledge of running wind-driven junks (*sha-ch'uan*) proved inadequate to manage a fleet of steam-powered ships, he was replaced by two ex-compradors, Tong King-sing (T'ang T'ing-shu) and Hsu Jun (1873–84). It was also Tong and Hsu who started the Kaiping mines in 1878. Until 1892, when he died, Tong was in charge of the mines as chief manager (*tsung-pan*). For the Shanghai Cotton Cloth Mill, Li assigned another ex-comprador, Cheng Kuan-ying, to work with another merchant, P'eng Ju-tsung, who made the original proposal for the mill. In 1880, after P'eng had left because of disputes with the other merchant investors, Li retained Cheng and appointed five other merchants to run the reorganized mill. Only Kung Shou-t'u, an expectant taotai put in charge of the mill's official affairs, was primarily an official with business experience.[9]

Indeed, all of them were gentry merchants (*shen-shang*). They purchased official titles (usually of the rank of an expectant taotai) because these had become a *sine qua non* for merchants who wanted to gain admission into any official yamen to conduct business and to seek official support or sanction. Most of them were also former compradors. This in itself is significant, since the comprador-merchant's managerial functions in a foreign firm were in some ways comparable to those of the hired manager in a traditional company.

Second, while retaining his hold as sponsor and patron, Governor-general Li allowed these merchant-managers much freedom of action in carrying out their roles as entrepreneurs. To take the case of the faction-ridden Shanghai Cotton Cloth Mill, Li did not step in to order a drastic reorganization until it became clear that Cheng Kuan-ying's departure in 1884 had taken away many investors' support and the management's know-how for organizing a mill. As for the two other enterprises, as long as they were under Tong King-sing and Hsu Jun, Li used his supervisory authority only sparingly. The Kaiping mines greatly expanded its capital from merchant resources, while the China Merchants' competed successfully with its foreign competitors, and increased its tonnage enormously by taking over the fleet of the American-owned Shanghai Steam Navigation Company. Thus, although Tong, Hsu, Cheng, Kung, and the other *shen-shang* managers served at Li Hung-chang's pleasure, Li, much like the owner of the traditional company, did not as a rule interfere with their business activities. His protection against excessive official squeezes as well as his many timely and egregious loans of official funds benefited the companies far more than the increased opportunities for personal gain and patronage he received in return benefited him.

Third, like the traditional company's lesser partners, most shareholders in these early years did not question their powerlessness under management. The relative ease with which individual merchant-managers like Tong were able to raise merchant capital suggests that these shareholders made their investments out of loyalty to and trust in the managers. Whether the trust was warranted is a different matter. In 1884, Tong and Hsu were forced to relinquish their control over the China Merchants' to the official-entrepreneur Sheng Hsuan-huai because they and others had diverted some company funds into their own private business. Similarly, Cheng Kuan-ying had apparently made private use of the cotton cloth mill's capital he had raised. It, too, led to his resignation in 1884 as well as the mill's eventual reorganization and transfer of control to Sheng Hsuan-huai.[10]

Such managerial malpractices, however, were not a direct result of the *kuan-tu shang-pan* organization. On the contrary, they are further evidence of the persistent influence of the traditional company's practices, which called for no independent auditor to check a manager's accounts. Financial irregularities of this sort were a constant feature of the traditional enterprise, and were tolerated as part of the risk in any business investment for as long as both the company and the manager's private use of the company funds were doing well. After all, an analogous case can be made in the Chinese official's use or misuse of revenues on a personal basis. He, too, was tolerated so long as he did not lose money on these transactions. In 1884, a financial crisis in Shanghai over the impending Sino-French conflict led to many business failures, including those in which Tong, Hsu, and Cheng were involved.[11] When they could not repay the company funds and when court censors began attacking Li Hung-chang for covering up their malpractices, they were forced out of the shipping company.

Such managerial malpractices were so deep-rooted, however, that they continued to engage in them. Cheng Kuan-ying reported that in 1891, while serving as the Kaiping mines' manager in Canton, he had bought a piece of land for the company with money from both company and private funds: 10,000 taels from the company funds of the mines, another 10,000 taels from Tong, 5,000 taels from a Mr. Li, and 5,000 taels from himself. Cheng also reported that he and Tong had acquired interest in a land and agricultural development company after he had intermingled company and private funds to buy it in the name of the company. Apparently, these individual capital participations in company ventures were not legitimate because Tong's successor, Chang Yen-mou, later refused to credit their private shares. They could do it and reap its benefit only as long as they were in charge of the company.[12]

Growing Bureaucratization of the Kuan-tu Shang-pan *Enterprises*

Sometime around 1885, management control over two of these three *kuan-tu shang-pan* operations was transferred to Sheng Hsuan-huai who, as an official-entrepreneur, believed in keeping a close watch over the business decisions of these companies. Li Hung-chang remained the unobtrusive patron. Sheng's active direction over the two companies, however, brought a new element into the *kuan-tu shang-pan* organization. Although the merchant-managers practiced nepotism and misuse of company funds, the companies were relatively uncluttered by bureaucratic practices. Under Sheng, however, the China Merchants' turned bureaucratic. Little tonnage was added, and the company was barely able to maintain its profits and position by "pooling agreements" with its foreign competitors.[13] Sheng also took over the Shanghai Cotton Cloth Mill in 1887, and quickly tripled its capital—from about 300,000 to over one million taels—by means of government loans and the transfer of some China Merchants' funds he controlled. In 1894, after a fire had almost completely ruined the original mill, Sheng converted it into another *kuan-tu* company, funded almost exclusively by himself and a small group of his friends. His efforts in trying to attract a wider number of merchants to subscribe shares ended in dismal failure. In 1901, Sheng took it over completely under an assumed name and made it entirely private.[14]

At the Kaiping mines, ex-comprador Tong's death in 1892

marked the beginning of gross corruption and creeping bureaucratization. The new manager was Chang Yen-Mou, a Chinese bannerman and bureaucrat who owed his rise to his patron, Prince Ch'un. Ellsworth C. Carlson has noted that, during Tong's period, expansion of the plant and facilities was funded by new merchant capital; Chang, being unable to find any merchant support, had to depend on foreign loans, thus opening the way for foreign control of the mines later on.[15]

These were changes within the *kuan-tu shang-pan* format that could hardly have escaped the notice of the merchants. To take one tangible index of change, that of office titles, Tong King-sing's title in both the China Merchants' and the Kaiping mines, though indicating official or quasi-official status, was chief manager (*tsung-pan*). When Sheng succeeded him at the China Merchants' in 1884 as a substantive taotai, he was given the decidedly official title of director-general (*tu-pan*). The post of chief manager was apparently dropped, for Sheng's main assistants were associate managers (*hui-pan*) and merchant directors (*shang-tung*). Similarly at the Kaiping mines, Chang Yen-Mou, the bannerman bureaucrat, first succeeded Tong as chief manager. But in 1898, he, too, was elevated to director-general.[16] From the merchants' point of view, Tong on the one hand and Sheng and Chang on the other represented very different types of managers. When seen from Li Hung-chang's perspective, however, they performed nearly identical roles of official supervision.

Merchant disenchantment with the *kuan-tu shang-pan* type of enterprise stemmed from the replacement of merchant-managers by men of bureaucratic background. The merchant investors had not been deterred by their lack of voice in company policies (in fact, one suspects that all of the large shareholders or their friends became directors and managers). But they began to shy away from further investment when they became convinced, rightly or wrongly, that government bureaucrats were in control and making use of their capital for bureaucratic and personal ends.

When the *kuan-tu shang-pan* operations first began, their merchant-managers had relatively little difficulty in raising sufficient merchant capital. Although Chu Ch'i-ang, a junk owner and China Merchants' first manager, had trouble attracting merchant capital, Tong and Hsu, who took over the company in mid-1873, had none, and, by the end of the year, they had raised a paid-up capital of 476,000 taels.[17] Chu's failure probably had nothing to do with his secondary role as an expectant taotai in charge of the sea transport for Chekiang province. He failed apparently because his contacts were with the wrong kind of merchants—traditionalists like Yü Hsi-sheng (most likely another large junk owner) who hesitated to enter into modern ventures. On the other hand, Tong and Hsu, with their comprador contacts, succeeded not only with the China Merchants', but also with the Kaiping mines, for which they raised another one million taels between 1878 and 1882 alone.[18] Similarly, another ex-comprador, Cheng Kuan-ying, raised most of the 352,800 taels for the cotton cloth mill in Shanghai around 1880.[19]

In this sense, these early operations fulfilled Li Hung-chang's intention to use merchant capital at the merchant's own risk. From the 1880s, however, as these operations passed into the hands of official-managers and their merchant assistants, and as new ones were founded without responsible merchant-managers, merchant capital too, was conspicuously absent.

The Mo-ho Gold Mine (Mo-ho chin-k'uang chü). One example is the Mo-ho Gold Mine, which began in 1887 along the Sino-Russian frontier under the joint sponsorship of Li Hung-chang and the Tarter General of Heilungkiang. They dispatched Li Chin-yung, "an expectant prefect versed in mining and frontier affairs," to take charge.

Li was probably one of the typical "official-entrepreneurs" whose type recurred in practically all of the late nineteenth century's officially sponsored industries. Though less successful than Sheng Hsuan-huai, they combined official mentality and values with a keen sense of business. As unsuccessful candidates for the higher civil service examinations, these official-entrepreneurs were nonetheless gentry members whose minor degrees and purchased ranks entitled them to enter the *mu-fu* service of official luminaries like Li Hung-chang and Tso Tsung-t'ang (himself a mere *chü-jen*). From such an official base, as irregular officials assigned on specific commissions, they cultivated friendships with merchants and gradually acquired a reputation for commercial or industrial expertise and good relations with the merchant community.

Li Chin-yung was a native of commercially active Wusih in Kiangsu. In 1861, while still a young man with a minor degree and the purchased rank of an expectant sub-prefect, he joined Li Hung-chang's military staff. He was involved in some of Li's campaigns against the Taipings and, for a time, supplied Tso Tsung-t'ang's army with food and arms. During the 1870s and 1880s, while still on Li's staff, he worked on many land reclamation assignments and helped settle frontier disputes in Manchuria. Li Chin-yung took numerous leaves to organize famine relief in his own province, then all over north China and Manchuria. He was also a founder of many charitable organizations, including two major ones in Tientsin and Shanghai. In appointing him to take charge of the Mo-ho Gold Mine, Li Hung-chang was no doubt influenced by Li Chin-yung's knowledge of the Sino-Russian frontier and his wide and amiable connections with the merchant communities of Shanghai and Tientsin. Li Chin-yung went to Mo-ho in the summer of 1887 and opened the mines early in 1889.[20]

Between 1887 and 1889, Li Chin-yung made repeated attempts to raise 200,000 taels from the merchants as the mine's initial capital, but they yielded only 60,000–70,000 taels. The Heilungkiang provincial treasury finally granted him a loan of 30,000 taels, while one Tientsin merchant supplied the other 100,000 taels as a loan after Li Hung-chang agreed to guarantee its repayment.[21]

Sheng's management of other kuan-tu *enterprises.* The Mo-ho Gold Mine was just one of several *kuan-tu shang-pan* operations that languished for lack of private financial support. More significantly, there were several others that continued to find adequate funding and to operate profitably in spite of the merchants' disengagement. This was accomplished through an increasing reliance on government funds by well-connected official sponsors. As a result, the nature of *kuan-tu shang-pan* operations was altered while the bureaucratic practices already going on were justified and consolidated.

Sheng Hsuan-huai was the most successful official-entrepreneur in developing such an alternative means of funding modern enterprises, and this explains why, during the 1880s and 1890s, he came to control a number of other major *kuan-tu shang-pan* operations. The first of these was the Imperial Telegraph Administration which he acquired in 1882 when Li appointed him its director-general. In funding it, Sheng depended heavily on provincial treasuries' funds and the loan of existing lines that were only later repaid. Some merchant capital was available to Sheng for the commercially profitable lines running through the lower Yangtze and the southeast coastal areas.

In 1882, the change to bureaucratic control was less obvious. Supporting Sheng was a small côterie of business associates who continued to provide him with private capital for his other enterprises.[22] Their contributions constituted almost all of the private capital of the Hua-sheng Spinning and Weaving Mill (Hua-sheng fang-chih tsung-ch'ang) in 1894, the Hanyang Ironworks (Han-yang t'ieh-ch'ang), and the Imperial Bank of China (Chung-kuo t'ung-shang yin-hang), in 1896. This capital, however, formed only a small part of the total operational capital. In the case of the Imperial Bank of China, Sheng had hoped that, out of the 2,500,000 taels initial capital, 1,000,000 taels would be taken up by his business associates and himself and another 500,000 taels by public subscription. His associates supplied him with the allotted amounts, but the public subscription ended in failure. At first, the merchants responded enthusiastically toward this first attempt at the formation of a modern bank. Many applied for shares, which were put on sale at the various China Merchants' offices. But reports of the Tsungli Yamen's objections to some of the bank's proposed regulations quickly turned into ugly rumors of impending official squeeze. No more merchants came forward, and most of those who had already applied demanded refunds.[23]

As for the Hanyang Ironworks, when Sheng took it over from Chang Chih-tung in 1896, he did not promise to raise from the merchants an amount even close to the staggering 5,600,000 taels of official funds already spent. Chang had reluctantly agreed to let Sheng change it from official management to *kuan-tu shang-pan* because success continued to elude him even after he had spent so much of the official funds. Meanwhile, the central government was unwilling to commit any more funds. Since 1894, he had been ordered by the court "to invite merchants to take over its management." Chang stalled for about a year by pleading that he still needed more experiments to prove that the right kind of coal to make steel had been found; for, without it, he claimed that no merchants would step forward. On October 16, 1895, he informed the throne that the search for the right coal had been successful and that a high price had been offered for the finished product. He was now ready to invite merchants to take over, he stated, but, in order for them to have time to look over the plant and mine sites properly, he needed a further appropriation to keep the ironworks running until the end of the year.[24]

By late 1895, Chang was so pressed by the court that he would accept Sheng's help on almost any terms. In one of Chang's private letters to a senior official at court (probably Li Hung-tsao, then President of the Board of Rites), he admitted that he had to "bribe" Sheng into taking over the ironworks. First, Chang promised to protect Sheng who in 1895 was under indictment by the censors. When the attack quieted down, and the "wily and crafty" Sheng, or so Chang described him, again slackened his interest, Chang had to entice him with other offerings: the supervision of the Peking-Hankow Railway and a guarantee that the rails of this railway line would use the steel of the ironworks.[25]

After Sheng reorganized the ironworks into a *kuan-tu shang-pan* enterprise without an influx of new merchant capital, he set up a plan to repay the government by means of a levy of one tael per ton of pig-iron produced. Sheng tried to raise a limited amount of capital from the merchants to improve on existing facilities, but he ended in failure. He complained that the merchants were hesitant because the success of the coal mines and iron smelting was in doubt. As part of the bargain he had arranged with Chang Chih-tung, however, he was able to draw upon the prepayment of 1,900,000 taels of government funds, which came from the Peking-Hankow Railway for the purchase of steel. By 1904, some 2,000,000 taels were raised from two sources: the larger portion from a transfer of funds from the China Merchants', the remainder from himself and the same merchant associates who were contributing to his other *kuan-tu* ventures in banking, shipping, telegraph, and textiles.[26]

The transfer of one company's funds to another was a technique he frequently employed. Sometime between 1890 and 1891, on his own authority and over his associate manager Cheng Kuan-ying's protest that the merchant investors had not been consulted, Sheng transferred some 300,000 taels from the China Merchants' to the Shanghai Cotton Cloth Mill. In 1896, Sheng ordered another massive transfer of funds to his new venture, the Imperial Bank of China–800,000 taels from the China Merchants' and 200,000 taels from the Telegraph. These transfers amounted to 30 or 40 percent of each company's total capital at the time.[27]

The Merchants' Disenchantment

The reasons for the merchants' growing reluctance to invest in *kuan-tu* enterprises are obvious. While some of the major enterprises already cited, such as the Kaiping mines, the China Merchants', and the Imperial Telegraph, turned out to be eminent moneymaking ventures–Albert Feuerwerker has estimated that, between 1873 and 1914, an investor of the China Merchants' could have made a fivefold gain on his capital and a 15 percent annual return in dividends[28]–many smaller ones were failures. And when they failed, the provincial government usually stepped in to make prior claims on official loans, deposits, and capital, leaving very little for the merchant shareholders. In 1893, after having been in operation for more than ten years, the Silk Bureau in Chefoo went out of business. After it had fully met the government's claims, its official-managers offered the investors ten taels for every share for which they had paid two hundred taels as first installment, or twenty taels if the additional two hundred taels second installment had been paid up.

The refunds thus stood at 5 percent of the original capital investment. Apparently this was done without consultation with the investors who, according to Hsu Jun, complained bitterly about such unfair proceedings. Hsu, who was no friend of Sheng Hsuan-huai, laid the blame on him, claiming that Sheng later took over the bureau and turned it into a profitable business. Hsu then commented: "[Official-managers] have strong authority but lack righteousness. How could they obtain the respect of others? There is nothing one can do. For [to have us merchants] fight them would be like striking rocks with eggs. Truly we can do nothing."[29]

Such sentiments of merchant frustration over official control must have become common knowledge by this time. One can cite much evidence from the various official writings that officials themselves were well aware of the merchants' dissatisfaction. Governor-general Liu K'un-i, when asked to express his opinion on applying the *kuan-tu* format to building the railways, memorialized the throne in 1895 as follows:

> If we restrict ourselves to the *kuan-tu shang-pan* formula, then nothing is achieved except by the officials. When officials hold all authority and merchants are given none, this will not lead to success. When capital is collected from the merchants, and profit is scattered by the officials, then indeed the government has yet to acquire trust from those to whom investment invitations are extended. Moreover, even though enterprises such as the China Merchants' Steam Navigation Company and the [Hua-sheng] Cotton Spinning Mill have achieved commendable results, yet their management remains with the officials. Moreover, their profits have not been much. Merchants still feel they are set apart.[30]

Sheng was well aware of similar complaints from the merchants themselves. Later in the same year in which Hsu accused him of having unfairly treated the Chefoo Silk Bureau's investors, Sheng tried to work out a more equitable compensation for the shareholders of the Shanghai Cotton Cloth Mill after it had been burned down in October 1893. With Li in agreement, Sheng held back government claims on its 265,390 taels of official loan. He then offered to pay the merchants from the mill's remaining assets in cash and in the form of shares of the successor company. For the Hua-sheng Spinning and Weaving Mill was being formed in its place.[31] As a result, the merchant shareholders received a cash refund at 20 percent of their initial investment, and the rest in Hua-sheng's shares. If Sheng had secretly hoped that such a demonstration of generosity and good will to the merchant investors would bring them back with new capital for Hua-sheng, he was to be disappointed. The merchants remained skeptical, and, since his small côterie of overworked business associates had access to only a limited source of capital, Hua-sheng remained undercapitalized. After a promising start, it ran consistently at a loss throughout its short existence to 1901. In that year, Sheng turned it into a private company after he had received the court's permission to declare worthless all the company shares, including those issued in exchange for the shares of the old cotton cloth mill.[32]

However, merchant sentiments toward the *kuan-tu shang-pan* were not totally negative, and this explained why this type of enterprise continued right through to the end of the dynasty and beyond. If there was considerable disenchantment, there was also general awareness that something like the *kuan-tu shang-pan* was needed to serve as a mechanism of merchant-official collaboration. Such a feeling of ambivalence was best exemplified by Cheng Kuan-ying, himself a merchant-manager in at least two of these enterprises. On the one hand, Cheng conceded that the merchants needed official protection because there was no commercial law or constitutional guarantee to safeguard their rights and properties. He suggested, therefore, that the *kuan-tu* formula was justifiable. On the other hand, Cheng felt that any long-term solution must lie in the setting up of a fair and enforceable law for the merchants.

Cheng contended that the bureaucracy, corruption, and administrative inefficiency had greatly reduced the profits of some enterprises and caused the failure of others. Referring to three profit-making *kuan-tu shang-pan* enterprises, the Imperial Telegraph, the China Merchants', and the Kaiping mines, he exclaimed that if only they were to be run by the merchants, "their profits will know no bounds!"[33] Cheng also observed that *kuan-tu* operations were too dependent on the whims of provincial official patrons. "Even if one accepts the fact that Li Hung-chang is very enlightened and will not overtax merchant enterprises, the fact remains that Li cannot be the superintendent of trade for the northern ports forever."[34]

Later on, writing in the early years of the Republican era, Cheng became much more caustic toward the Ch'ing government's involvement in various industries. He accused the officials of "inflicting losses on the merchants and promoting benefits for themselves," while they pretended to help the merchants. He recalled how the *kuan-tu shang-pan* Telegraph Administration was nationalized during the late 1900s without proper compensation for its shareholders. He contrasted it to the Japanese government's policy, where new and infant industries were given financial and disinterested management aid to tide them over their initial years of experimentation. Cheng then related one specific Japanese case he had learned about from a Japanese friend. The latter, a copper merchant, told him that his company was suffering from such heavy losses during the first few years that he was about to declare bankruptcy. The government, however, stepped in to investigate and, after having dealt severely with those officers who were corrupt, helped the company with funds, management advice, and general supervision. When the company began to make a profit after a few years, the government relinquished all its authority over the company and returned it to the merchant directors. Cheng implied that the Chinese government should have adopted such a model for its own *kuan-tu shang-pan* enterprises.[35]

Here, then, were widely disparate perspectives on what the *kuan-tu shang-pan* operations ought to be. The merchants welcomed official encouragement and sponsorship. They would even accept, for the initial period at least, state control in the form of official capital loans and managerial direction. In contrast, Sheng Hsuan-huai and the other official-entrepreneurs had very different concepts of official-merchant relations in such a partnership. Because the state had little excess capital for these economic developments, the merchants' resources had to be tapped and their capital co-opted to work toward national goals. But the modern enterprise was too important a business to be left solely in the hand of the merchants. Therefore they, the official-entrepreneurs, needed to retain control.

Given the state's traditional role in the Chinese economy, it would be hard to fault the officials' self-righteous perspective about state control. But in the process of maintaining such control, they went beyond Li Hung-chang's original vision of general supervision and promotion of modern industry. They went directly into management and capital campaigns for these enterprises. As official managers and investors, they had a natural tendency to confuse state and bureaucratic control, and to lapse from working for the national goal to looking after their own personal interest. Then, when more officials became involved with the growing number of modern enterprises, these problems increased until they came to shape the style and nature of industrial developments in China.

Chapter Five

THE ILLUSIONS OF MERCHANT PARTNERSHIP

From the late 1880s onward, as it became clear that fewer and fewer merchants would risk their investments in bureaucratically controlled *kuan-tu shang-pan* operations, provincial officials began to offer alternative formulae for inviting merchant participations. Avoiding the term *kuan-tu shang-pan,* they came up with new ones. These may all be subsumed under the most widely used phrase, *kuan-shang ho-pan* (officials' and merchants' joint management), first used by Ma Chien-chung in the winter of 1879–1880 in an article entitled "T'ieh-lu lun" (On railways). Ma, a senior advisor of Li Hung-chang, did not elaborate on the details of such a partnership. For example, he did not consider defining the rights and responsibilities of each party. He was ambivalent about the merchants' ability to raise sufficient capital even if they were willing. At one point, he observed that the merchants had the money if only they and the officials could be united. At another, he argued the need for foreign loans, which he claimed were not harmful if put to productive use. In general, Ma was advocating a more responsible and independent partnership for the merchant investors when he put forward his ideas on *ho-pan* and *i-kuan tso-shang* (putting the officials to help the merchants).[1]

Ma's essay made an impact on his official patron, Li Hung-chang, and on other officials looking for merchant support. The dilemma, however, persisted because officials could not reconcile the needs of state control with those of private capital. In the end, the *kuan-shang ho-pan* slogan, with its apparent promise of more or less equal partnerships between state and private interests, became a convenient cover for several enterprises which, in spite of their varying patterns, were no different from the *kuan-tu shang-pan* companies. Then as their number grew, the nature of state control was further modified. The following examples will illustrate this trend.

Two Early Kuan-shang Ho-pan *Enterprises*

The Kweichow Mining and Ironworks (Kuei-chou chi-ch'i k'uang-wu tsung-chü), established at Ch'ing-ch'i hsien by Governor P'an Wei in 1886, is often thought to be the first *kuan-shang ho-pan* operation.[2] This is inaccurate, but the confusion had arisen because provincial official sponsors like Governor P'an liberally used this and other similar terms to describe such projects. Whether or not they were sincere about offering more equitable partnerships, these officials were anxious to have some evidence of merchant support. The central government seemed more ready to sanction their projects if they could promise to draw upon private financial resources. Vague claims of merchant participation, therefore, were useful to the many provincial official sponsors who were planning on purely official management, for they knew that, once the project was officially approved, some amount of official funds from local sources could always be found.

Governor P'an Wei's first proposal of this mining and ironworks to the throne on February 25, 1886 fell into this pattern. He called it "a merchant enterprise, with official supervision and [guarantee] of sale" (*shang-pan, kuan-wei tu-hsiao*). He did not mention if official funds would be required either as loans or capital, but stated that merchant capital would be solicited locally and in Shanghai and Hankow. In the follow-up memorial dated April 22, 1886, P'an laid out in greater detail how he hoped to make the company's shares more attractive to merchants. He had asked a number of provinces to agree on a set amount of iron which they would individually buy from the company. This would allow him to guarantee sales, and his new memorial was to seek the court's support. He then added that he had already assigned a 20,000-tael loan from the province's likin revenue for the initial operating cost, and a number of officials to conduct surveys and to set up branch offices at appropriate locations.[3]

It is unlikely that P'an found much cooperation from the other provinces. Tseng Kuo-ch'üan, Governor-general of Liang-kiang and patron of the Kiangnan Arsenal, would have been in a position to buy considerable amounts of iron. But he did not appear enthusiastic. He informed P'an that the ore sample sent him was of B-grade, that he usually bought his iron close by, but that he would buy some from Kweichow if only to help out the company's difficult initial period.[4]

In any case, from P'an's two memorials, it is certain that he intended to run the ironworks as another *kuan-tu shang-pan* operation. His promise of a guaranteed market to the prospective merchant investors was similar to Li Hung-chang's initial promise to the China Merchants' Steam Navigation Company's investors of a guaranteed quota of tribute rice to be transported by the company's ships. And, in both cases, there was an official loan to start the operation. Its similarity to the early *kuan-tu* model, however, ended there. While Li appealed to merchant managers to run the company, P'an followed the later and more bureaucratic type of *kuan-tu* operation by allowing trusted officials to dominate the company. Heading the list of these official-managers was his younger brother, P'an Lu, an expectant taotai with some technical skill in mining, for he was at the time employed by the Kiangnan Arsenal.[5]

These bureaucratic maneuvers did not encourage the merchants. In the first year, merchants were still enthusiastic enough to put up 50,000 taels for the ironworks. Although this was far short of the 300,000 taels projected for the initial stage, it was large compared with the results of the next four years. From 1887 to 1890, when the first iron was finally produced, the company received approximately another 30,000 taels of public subscriptions. As for the total expenses, they stood at the much higher figure of 276,000 taels. Almost 200,000 taels, therefore, had come from borrowed provincial funds.

On July 20, 1890, P'an memorialized again. The ironworks had finally begun production, but, since merchant capital was still not forthcoming, he now petitioned the throne for permission to contract a foreign loan of 300,000 taels, to repay all the official debts, and to keep the remainder as working capital.[6] Just as P'an received the court's approval, however, his brother and chief manager, P'an Lu, died on August 31. Since he alone had the technical skill and knew where everything was, the other official managers in the head office decided that they could not go on. Negotiation for the foreign loan was therefore halted. But Governor P'an was not ready to give up. He recalled another official manager, Tseng Yen-ch'üan, from the field office in Hankow and asked him to carry on with a further 20,000 taels official loan. Tseng, an expectant prefect who had personally raised more than half the merchant shares, was probably another official-entrepreneur sharing a common background with Li Chin-Yung of the Mo-ho Gold Mine. He accepted P'an's offer and took over the ironworks on January 7, 1891.[7] From available records, it does not appear that Tseng was able to attract any more merchant capital. Renewed attempts were then made to secure a foreign loan. But, by this time, a change had occurred in the governorship (P'an was called to Peking shortly after Tseng took over), and the company, having lost its official patron, was refused permission by the new governor to negotiate for any foreign loan.

In 1893, without further support from either the merchants or the new provincial governor, the ironworks was finally closed down. In 1898, it was leased out to one expectant taotai named Ch'en Ming-yuan on a five-year trial basis. Ch'en promised to repay its official debts by means of a drawn-out levy of one tael for every ton of iron produced. He was evidently following the example set by the Hanyang Ironworks in 1896 to repay its past debts. Ch'en, however, never reopened the works, and, when his license ran out in 1903, the debts the company owed to the province had only been reduced by his first payment of 30,000 taels, which was the only payment Ch'en had to make when he took over the company.[8]

This brief recounting of the Kweichow Mining and Ironworks has revealed nothing that might distinguish it from a regular *kuan-tu shang-pan* operation at the time. There was nothing the two P'an brothers did or attempted to do that would suggest that they were trying out an alternative way of merchant and official collaboration. Instead, it was a typical example of the many medium-sized bureaucratically controlled *kuan-tu* operations, most of which failed in the end as official loans were depleted and their provincially based patrons reassigned.

The New Hua-hsin Spinning and Weaving Mill (Hua-hsin fang-chih hsin chü) was another early company advertised as a *kuan-shang ho-pan* operation.[9] It was organized on the basis of an existing cotton-ginning factory by the same name. In around 1888, its merchant owner, T'ang Tzu-chuang, agreed to accept partners and expand its eight gins into a modern cotton mill. The primary promoter was the incumbent Shanghai taotai, Kung Chao-yuan, who apparently petitioned Li Hung-chang for approval. Kung was joined by three other entrepreneurs of official background, Taotai T'ang Sung-yen, Yen Hsin-hou, and Chou Chin-chen. In early 1890, when Nieh Ch'i-kuei succeeded Kung as the Shanghai taotai, Nieh too received shares of the mill. One other recorded shareholder, Su Pao-sheng, was a merchant dealing in traditional medicine.[10]

The total amount of paid-up capital, probably 225,000 taels, or one half of its authorized capital of 450,000 taels in 4,500 shares, was quite modest for a textile mill. There were 12,000 spindles, 80 looms, and the original 8 gins when the mill opened in 1890 or 1891 (versus 35,000 spindles and 530 looms for the Shanghai Cotton Cloth Mill).[11] Much of the officials' capital was probably taken from the Shanghai Customs revenue. Yen Hsin-hou, who ran Hua-hsin in these early years, was also in charge of the Hui-t'ung Customs Bank, which was supervised by the Shanghai taotai who used the bank as his treasury. Such a transfer of public funds into private accounts would explain how Nieh acquired 450 shares, which represented 22,500 taels in paid-up capital, when he became taotai of Shanghai.[12] Mrs. Nieh's less-than-candid record of her husband's involvement with Hua-hsin revealed as much when she tried to explain it away by stating that her family owned these shares a few years later. It appears that, when Nieh left his taotai office in 1894, his official accounts were short some 600,000 taels in addition to another 200,000 he had inherited from his predecessor, Kung Chao-yuan. According to his wife, Nieh's treasurer, Hsu Tzu-ching, had embezzled the funds, portions of which had gone into paying for the Hua-hsin's shares which the family then reclaimed. Mrs. Nieh's version of the transaction was meant to explain two things: first, how Nieh Ch'i-kuei, an official holding local office, came to possess these company shares when he reportedly believed strongly that it would be improper for officials to do so; second, how Nieh found the money to buy these shares when the wife's autobiography was full of references of tight family budgets, at least up to this time. What Mrs. Nieh does not explain is why, if the shares had been bought by official funds, they remained with the family, or how the treasurer, presumably a trusted subordinate, could embezzle so much without Nieh's acquiescence.[13]

Apart from the support of official shareholders with public funds, Hua-hsin shows other evidences of close official connections. It will be recalled that, since its reorganization in 1887 under Sheng Hsuan-huai, the Shanghai Cotton Cloth Mill had been trying to raise additional capital from the merchants, but without much success. By 1891, Sheng had to transfer some 300,000 taels from the surplus funds of the China Merchants' to the mill. Probably the difficulty he experienced in raising any merchant capital prompted some associates of the Shanghai Cotton Cloth Mill to organize the new mill under a different set of rules. In any case, there was an overlap of personnel between these two mills. Nieh had earlier been appointed by Li Hung-chang to share responsibility with Sheng in taking charge of the reorganization of the Shanghai Cotton Cloth Mill. Moreover, the establishment of the Hua-hsin could not have been permitted in Shanghai if Li Hung-chang and Sheng Hsuan-huai had not given their consent, for the Shanghai Cotton Cloth Mill, through Li Hung-chang's memorial, had a ten-year monopoly on cotton textile production granted by the court.[14]

All these factors point to a connection between the Hua-hsin Mill and Li Hung-chang. But Li failed to mention it in any of his memorials seeking a court sanction for the project.[15] This in itself is significant, suggesting that Li had deliberately stayed out of the preparation and organization of the new spinning mill so that merchants and medium-ranking officials could negotiate more or less equally as between private investors.

In this sense, it was a radical departure from the normal *kuan-tu* format, where no attempt was made to distinguish between private investors of official and of merchant backgrounds. Both, in theory, were accepted and treated equally, while the state, not individual officials, was to have the authority of supervision. In the case of the Hua-hsin Mill, the *kuan* in its *kuan-shang* came to denote not the state or the corporate body of officialdom as when it was used in the phrase *kuan-tu shang-pan.* The Hua-hsin type of *kuan-shang* meant collaboration between "officials" and "merchants" on a private, individual level. The Hua-hsin Mill was in fact a private enterprise from the start, invested in and managed by private individuals, a number of whom were officials.

There was, strictly speaking, no state control except by those officials who were also major shareholders. Since the government did not come in, there could be no official patron for a senior official like Li. Hence there was no need for Li to petition the throne for its approval. Presumably Hua-hsin hoped to attract merchants by the absence of formal official ties, while its official shareholders assured the enterprise of official protection. On the other hand, if the officials' half of the partnership had involved the state, then Li Hung-chang would, at some point, have memorialized the throne on its behalf.

The first few years of Hua-hsin saw some expansion. Some 3,000 more spindles and 150 more looms were added in 1893. But the new organizational setup had apparently created no stir among the merchants. In 1894, as the burned down Shanghai Cotton Cloth Mill was being transformed into the Hua-shang Spinning and Weaving Mill, Hua-hsin became its subsidiary, and the *kuan-shang ho-pan* structure was apparently discarded.[16]

Hua-hsin did not become an industrial success, and Hua-sheng's takeover only led to bad bureaucratic management and financial losses. In 1904, T'ang Kuei-sheng, a shareholder and Nieh Ch'i-kuei's confidant, got Nieh's tacit approval to form a new company called Fu-t'ai, to lease out Hua-hsin, and run it as a private enterprise. By this time, its shares were quite worthless because it had not paid any dividend for many years.

The Fu-t'ai Company, with Nieh's son Nieh Ch'i-chieh as manager, made a tremendous comeback in its first year by registering some 100,000 taels in profit. When T'ang died suddenly in 1905, Nieh, by then governor of Chekiang, bought over the entire stock of Fu-t'ai and sent in a second son as assistant manager. In

1908, as Fu-t'ai's lease ran out, Nieh forced through a resolution to auction off the plant and its equipment by claiming that "the old shareholders were unable to pay off the company's old debts." He then bought the entire mill's interest for his family for 325,000 taels and changed its name to Heng-feng.[17]

The Hua-hsin Mill, therefore, was never a "public" company subject to state control. Its official promoters sponsored the company in their individual capacities. They were low-keyed, of medium rank, and probably never submitted the company to a public subscription of the company's shares. Only the merchant and official friends of the original promoters were invited to subscribe. In around 1890 the belief was prevalent that a spinning mill, properly managed, could be very profitable. In addition, it seems that the major official shareholders, by reason of their control over the Shanghai customs receipts, were able to divert sufficient government funds to finance such a medium-sized enterprise. Public subscription could thus be ruled out. Undoubtedly, some of the official shareholders used their savings from public office for their investments. The fact remains that much of their invested "capital" came from a transfer of public money into private accounts. Hua-hsin was not an isolated case in this respect, and one must assume that this form of financing a modern enterprise contributed immeasurably to the size of bureaucratic capital during this period.

One other aspect of the Hua-hsin Mill which reflected the trend of official entrepreneurship was its several reorganizations by which finally its largest and politically most powerful shareholder made himself sole proprietor. One is reminded of Sheng Hsuan-huai's own adroit maneuver in 1901, when he ended the *kuan-tu shang-pan* status of the larger Hua-sheng Mill by selling it to a new private corporation owned largely by himself and his family.[18]

Chang Chih-tung and His Ho-pan *Type Enterprises*

Both the Kweichow Ironworks and the Hua-hsin Mill were *kuan-shang ho-pan* companies in different but equally misleading ways. While Governor P'an subscribed to the *ho-pan* formula without any intention from the very beginning of fitting his mining operations into that formula, the Hua-hsin managers conformed to the ideal of a joint undertaking between individual merchants and officials until much later, when the official owners took it over. Surreptitiously, Governor P'an brought government funds in so that he, as the state's representative, could dominate the enterprise. Also surreptitiously, Hua-hsin's official investors transferred government revenue in, but kept state control out.

These distinctions are important because their contrasting modes of dealing with the issue of state control and its related problem of capitalization contributed ideas and set patterns for subsequent industrial developments. From the 1890s, Governor-general Chang Chih-tung's several *ho-pan* type enterprises featured variations on the same themes as those first practiced by the Kweichow Ironworks. In the 1900s, official-entrepreneurs such as Chou Hsueh-hsi and Chang Chien improved upon Hua-hsin's techniques and succeeded in gaining even greater government protection without state control

Following the Sino-Japanese War of 1894–1895, as Li Hung-chang declined in power and influence, Governor-general Chang Chih-tung's own developing industrial complex in the mid-Yangtze basin began to assume the pre-eminence long enjoyed by Li's industrial empire along the coast. The same years saw Sheng Hsuan-huai, who until then had depended on Li Hung-chang's patronage, seeking out Chang Chih-tung for protection against his critics and for new patronage from Chang's growing industrial and railway complex.

While Sheng's entrance into Chang's Hanyang Ironworks and railways has been noted, there were other portions of Chang's industrial promotion over which Sheng did not have control. These were Chang's various ventures into the textile and related industries. The arrangements he attempted to make with the prospective investors of these industrial projects show that he was looking for an alternative to the *kuan-tu shang-pan* formula.

Unlike Li Hung-chang, Chang was generally very distrustful of the merchants' conservative outlook and therefore of their willingness to invest in modern industry. Since state capital was in short supply, however, he was forced to look to the merchants for a number of industrial projects which demanded much less capital than his programs in the heavy industries–iron and the railways.

The Hupei Cotton Cloth Mill (Hu-pei chih-pu kuan-chü). This cotton cloth mill, introduced to the throne in a memorial dated August 31, 1889, was one of Chang Chih-tung's earliest ventures into modern industry. Arguing that foreign textile imports were flooding the domestic market and driving Chinese handicraft producers out of business, Chang observed that China needed quickly to establish her own mechanized weaving and spinning factories to stem the foreign tide. He then proposed to open the cotton cloth mill in Canton, where he was governor-general, and asked for the court's approval.[19]

Although he had already found a way to raise the capital, Chang did not explain this to the throne, except by vaguely stating his intention to set up the operation where "officials would promote [the industry] on behalf of the merchants" (*kuan wei shang-ch'ang*). Chang and his advisors had been studying the weaving industry for at least a year. In November of 1888, he had sent Li Hung-chang a telegram confiding to him his interest and asking for his assurance that the ten-year monopoly Li had obtained for the Shanghai Cotton Cloth Mill did not extend to places as far away from Shanghai as Canton. After consulting with Kung Shou-t'u, Li's official manager of the Shanghai mill until 1887, Li telegraphed back, affirming that, since the opening of the Shanghai mill was still being delayed indefinitely, and since Canton was indeed far away, a second mill in Canton "would appear to be all right" with him.[20]

Thus reassured, Chang and his advisors proceeded to look for the required capital. Sometime in 1889, they found an answer when they successfully committed the local *wei-hsing* lottery merchants to an enforced contribution of 400,000 taels for 1889 and another 560,000 taels for 1890. The *wei-hsing* merchants were licensed to run lotteries in which winning depended on accurately predicting the surnames of the successful candidates of the imperial civil examinations.[21] Since the year 1889 was one in which both the provincial and metropolitan examinations were held, these merchants were more vulnerable to official pressure. They succumbed to the governor-general's "intensive lecturing and guidance" (*to-fang k'ai-tao*) and offered to contribute these egregious amounts on top of the three million taels of regular levy each year.

Chang did not bother to wait for an imperial sanction. Soon after he had made the proposal to the court, he began to order the needed machinery. Because the first installment of the *wei-hsing* merchants' contribution was not immediately available, orders for the machines were placed with advances drawn on the provincial treasury. Chang's precipitous action won him a strongly-worded reprimand from the throne.[22] But on January 16, 1890, the central government simply accepted his *fait accompli.* Chang continued to keep the throne ignorant of the details of the arrangement he had made with the merchants, until his reassignment as Governor-general of Hu-kuang forced him to petition the throne for permission to move the funds from Canton to Wuchang. On March 24, 1890, he finally informed the throne of the arrangements he had made with the *wei-hsing* merchants.[23]

Perhaps Chang was not certain how the court would react to them. His own formula, "official promotion on behalf of the merchants," did not fit into any of the categories such as *kuan-tu shang-pan* or *kuan-pan.* In 1890, he tried to soften his formula by claiming that the arrangement with the *wei-hsing* merchants was the only available means he could find. Chang told the court that regular merchant shares were slow in coming, and that he hoped to find greater interest among the merchants when the enterprise had passed its initial tests.[24]

In fact, by making use of this particular means of drawing upon merchant wealth, Chang accomplished two things. He was able, first, to by-pass the depleted government treasury and, second, to establish a weaving factory that was essentially *kuan-pan* under him. There was no question that Chang meant the extra levy to be confiscatory. Chang was also concerned with the problem of keeping the mill under his personal control. He informed the throne that he had negotiated with his successor, Li Han-chang, who had agreed to let the 1889 contribution of 400,000 taels leave Kwangtung for Hupei, where his new appointment took him. Li, however, insisted that, owing to Kwangtung's own heavy expenditure, only 160,000 taels out of the 560,000 taels for 1890 would go to Chang and the Hupei mill. Chang then added that he had accepted the new arrangement with Li, but that the smaller receipt together with some expansion of the facilities on his original plan had led him, in 1890, to contract loans from various sources at high interest rates.[25]

In 1893, when Chang again sought additional government loans, he released figures on what they were up to that time: 1) 200,000 taels which the Reorganization Bureau of Shansi had deposited in Kwangtung at interest (with Li Han-chang's consent, this interprovincial loan was transferred from Kwangtung to Hupei in 1890); 2) 100,000 taels from Hupei's own official reserves earmarked for relief, and which ordinarily was deposited in the local pawnshops at interest; 3) 100,000 taels from the Hongkong and Shanghai Bank in anticipation of the 160,000 taels' contribution, which could not be released before the end of 1890 or early 1891; and 4) some unspecified amounts from local merchants.[26]

This apparently was the mill's indebtedness as it stood on July 16, 1893. It was to borrow a good deal more by the time it was completely reorganized in 1902. Apart from a total of 560,000 taels received from the *wei-hsing* merchants during 1889 and 1890, its other sources of income came from at least the following loans:[27]

Hupei's Reorganization Bureau's transfer	300,000 taels
Hupei's Arsenal's transfer	78,375
Hupei's Government Bank's loans	49,000
Hupei's Government Bank's advances	60,000
Shansi's Reorganization Bureau's transfer	196,000
Total	683,375 taels

The Hupei Cotton Cloth Mill went into production in 1892, and, in spite of its many high interest loans (by 1896, it had paid out some 138,000 taels in interest alone), it was an immediate success. In 1894, Chang tried to raise merchant shares by public subscription of up to 500,000 taels or one-third of its assessed assets. Chang offered some very attractive terms for sharing profits, including the rather unusual concession that, in case of insufficient profit, the "guaranteed dividends" (*kuan-li*) of 15 percent would be paid on the merchants' shares first. No promise was made, however, on sharing management responsibilities. On the evidence of the continuing resort to government loans, Chang's efforts to attract private capital must have been ineffective.[28]

The merchants' hesitancy was not unwarranted. The mill's profits and even some of its capital were used to support Chang's other industrial projects. Chang himself was quite open about this. In 1894, while proposing a cotton spinning mill, he suggested that some of the government's share of the new company would come from the profits of the Hupei Cotton Cloth Mill. Moreover, the money so earmarked could then be loaned to the ironworks temporarily until its use was needed to pay for the machinery. Chang admitted that he had always thought of the mill and the ironworks as one, and that the mill had helped the ironworks with its problem of finance.[29] On an earlier occasion, he expressed the hope that the three major industries in Hupei—the Hanyang Ironworks, the Hupei Arsenal, and the Hupei Cotton Cloth Mill—would support each other as one so that they would succeed together and need no recourse to government funds.[30]

Since the ironworks was in constant financial crisis, the support had been one-sided. When the ironworks was reorganized in 1896 into a *kuan-tu shang-pan* operation under Sheng Hsuan-huai, Chang presumably terminated the interchange of funds. But by then, the Hanyang Ironworks had already drawn on the mill a total of 340,000 taels. In return, it had paid out only some 60,000 taels of freight and insurance charges on behalf of the mill.[31]

After 1896, it appears that a complex and untidy system of accounting between the mill and Chang's other industries proceeded as before. Moreover, it continued to be plagued by the high interest loans and bureaucratic waste. In the summer of 1900, the cotton cloth mill ran out of working capital and ceased to operate.[32] Then, two years later, it was leased out to a private company, together with a number of Chang's other unsuccessful industrial projects.

The Hupei Cotton Spinning Mill (Hu-pei fang-sha kuan-chü). One can hardly take Chang Chih-tung or his official-manager, Sheng Ch'un-i, to task for running the Hupei Cotton Cloth Mill as another *kuan-pan* enterprise even though it was euphemistically called "an enterprise promoted by the officials on behalf of the merchants." The *wei-hsing* merchant contributors had little or no interest in a modern textile mill. As for Chang's other promise that private merchants could eventually be invited to invest in it after it had achieved stability and profitability, he apparently kept that promise in 1894. Thanks to the unorthodox arrangement he made with the *wei-hsing* merchants, Chang was able to avoid using terms like *kuan-tu shang-pan* and *kuan-pan.* Given the options, Chang's new phrase was an imaginative cosmetic device that did little harm to his credibility.

However, when Chang proposed to the throne in 1894 to set up a cotton spinning mill as his second textile mill, he included elements in his proposal which suggested that merchant capital would be sought. And in spite of its official sounding name *kuan-chü* (official agency), Chang stated that merchant investors would be brought in as more or less equal partners. Once more, he avoided the term *kuan-tu shang-pan* but called it *kuan-shang ho-pan,* or interchangeably, *chao-shang chu-kuan* (an operation in which merchants are invited to assist the officials).[33]

Chang outlined his plan of collaboration to the throne. His shares of the mill might be one-half, one-third, or two-thirds of the total capital outlay. He had no plans to use regular provincial funds, but intended to transfer excess profits from the Hupei Cotton Cloth Mill, and to borrow the remainder from local bankers. If the merchants provided all the capital (and he would only allow it if he had difficulty raising capital from the above two sources), the company would be turned over to the merchants who would manage it entirely. Chang's own cotton cloth mill would then serve as the new mill's parent company, collect a set levy based on its production, and check its books.

There was no question that Chang planned to commit official capital to the new cotton spinning mill. The same memorial requested the throne's approval for his two appointees to serve as chief managers (*tsung-pan*) of the two projected branches, north and south. The north branch, outside the northern city wall of Wuchang and close to his cotton cloth mill, was to be headed by Sheng Ch'un-i, an expectant prefect of official background serving concurrently as the *tsung-pan* of the cotton cloth mill. The south branch's appointee was another official-manager of the cloth mill, Chao Pin-yen, with the rank of a provincial taotai.[34]

Chang Chih-tung's sincerity in offering partnership (*ho-pan*) to the merchant investors under such a plan is questionable, for its original outline looks very similar to the *kuan-tu shang-pan* formula. At the time when it was presented to the throne, there were no clearly spelled out guidelines on the extent of the merchants' authority and rights in the management of the company. For, if such guidelines existed, they would undoubtedly have appeared in his memorial. It seems, however, that sometime in the next two years such an agreement was drawn up. In 1896, when Chang proposed to the throne to extend the *kuan-shang ho-pan* formula to the Soochow-Shanghai Railway, he submitted details about the partnership presumably based on an earlier model.[35] Nonetheless, in actual practice, Chang was not ready to give up his controlling voice on major issues. The "partnership," as he saw it, was between merchants and the government, not between merchants and individual officials investing in their private capacity as in the case of the Hua-hsin Spinning and Weaving Mill in Shanghai. Shortly after the court's approval, Chang had already appointed the acting provincial judicial commissioner to be director-general (*tu-pan*). Then, as the north branch, with a total of 50,064 spindles, was finally ready for production early in 1897, Chang appointed an expectant taotai of official background, Wang Ch'ang-ch'uan, to be his resident representative to supervise all the affairs in the plant.[36]

Chang had been quite successful in raising capital from the

merchants, who by 1897 had contributed 300,000 taels, representing a 50 percent interest in the company. There was also evidence that an agreement giving the merchants managerial responsibilities was in force while the company was engaged in its preparatory stage. For, despite the formal appointments of two new official supervisors, the merchant shareholders were in actual control of the company accounts, equipment, and management of the plant. For example, when the mill was later returned to official management, Chang instructed the *tsung-pan,* Sheng Ch'un-i, to go over the books and machines with the merchant-managers. But there were also growing signs of official interference. Wang's appointment as the official-in-residence virtually turned the merchants' growing uneasiness into open revolt.

Sometime in the spring of 1897, they approached Wang to express their dismay. Wang argued that, since the government's capital investment also stood at 50 percent, it was only fair for the government to have an equal share in the management. He offered to draw up more precisely the different areas of control to be divided between them. The merchants demurred, then lodged a formal complaint. Pleading that any official interference would eventually lead to total official control, they asked for a reaffirmation by the government that it would only extend protection, leaving public management to the merchants. Chang rejected it firmly, rebutting:

> If the merchants do not wish to share the rights of control with the government, then they should be held responsible for everything. The government does not feel warranted to increase its capital. It will not ask about profits or losses but will collect interest on its 300,000 taels already assigned to the mill.[37]

The private investors declined to take complete charge, insisting that they needed a further official loan of 200,000 taels. When Chang rejected it, they reportedly asked the officials to buy back their shares and to manage it themselves. On July 14, 1897, Chang instructed his official-manager, Sheng Ch'un-i, to accept their withdrawal. As for the reimbursement of their capital, Sheng was to return 150,000 taels (one-half) outright. The other 150,000 taels, however, were to be paid in bonds at 8 percent interest and to be matured in a year.[38]

One does not have the merchants' version of this first major contest between themselves and the officials under the *kuan-shang ho-pan* framework. Presumably Chang's letter of instruction to his manager cited above, which constitutes the only available source of information, does not tell everything. Chang's version would have one believe that the merchants, in effect, rejected his very generous offer to give them full control in return for changing the government's 300,000 taels capital into a loan at a predetermined rate of interest, which had to be paid regardless of profits or losses. If there were no other conditions, it seems most unlikely that these private entrepreneurs would have turned it down. It would have represented a major breakthrough for them when contrasted with the position they held under the usual *kuan-tu shang-pan* format. Indeed they would have exchanged their roles with the officials. Under the *kuan-tu* operations, the officials made use of merchant capital and were ultimately in charge of the management, irrespective of how actively they performed their supervision. Under the new plan, as reported by Chang, the merchants would have been the ones to make use of the official capital and have control over the management. As for the guaranteed interest on the official loans, this was very similar to the "guaranteed dividend" (usually referred to as *kuan-li*) which all private and official capital was promised whether it was invested in the *kuan-tu* or any other type of enterprise.

In late nineteenth-century China, a *kuan-li* of 7 to 10 percent annually was expected as a matter of course by all investors using private and government capital. It was paid out even in those enterprises operating at a loss. No company could claim to have made any profit until the *kuan-li* was paid and there were still some "net profit" left to distribute as regular dividends and bonuses. This system made the Chinese investment capital almost indistinguishable from loans, and was a problem with which industrial managers and promoters had to contend.[39] Yen Chung-p'ing, also relying solely on Chang's July 14 letter, has suggested that the merchants of the Hupei Spinning Mill had rejected Chang's offer because it would have meant that they had to "contract loans in order to run the industry."[40] This was most likely not the reason, since all industrial managers knew they would have to pay interest on loans, or *kuan-li* in the case of investment capital. Chang's "loans," being official, could not be charged the exorbitant interest rates the same merchants might have to pay if they had to contract private loans.

It is not clear what the actual concessions were that Chang Chih-tung tried to give the merchants. What is certain is that, in the end, they rejected them, and the spinning mill was changed into a *kuan-pan* operation with only half of the private capital returned. This apparently created much ill will: Chang Chien, who during 1897 and 1898 was working hard to raise private capital for his first textile project, the Dah Sun Cotton Mill, reported that Chang Chih-tung's action led many private investors to withdraw their pledges of support to his project.[41]

The Hupei Cotton Spinning Mill, after it had relinquished its merchant partners, did not go on to make a profit. In 1902, it followed the way of the cotton cloth mill and was leased out to a private concern.[42]

Carpeting and other "reformed" ho-pan *enterprises.* The cotton spinning and weaving mills were the two major ventures Chang Chih-tung had launched in his efforts to attract merchant participations in modern industry without loss of bureaucratic control. With their failures in 1902, Chang realized that he could continue to sponsor new *ho-pan* companies only if he promised conciliatory changes in the partnerships between merchants and officials. This was what he conceded he would do when, in 1905, he outlined his plan to open a series of new factories in Hunan and Hupei to manufacture carpets, woolens, cement, paper, leather, prints, needles, nails, and glass.

Chang began by affirming that merchant management of the

modern joint-stock type was indeed superior to official management because the former, by the wide participation of the small investors, was more likely to benefit the common people. He conceded that "in the past, the government has intervened in the affairs of these [private] joint-stock companies. This has led to much abuse. Many failed to last very long, thus causing wealthy and upright families to avoid them."[43]

Chang proposed to form joint-stock corporations whose management would be responsible to the shareholders. The link with the government, however, would be maintained by means of the *kuan-shang ho-pan* format. Chang still believed that such a combination would attract merchant capital. He also offered an attractive addition, by promising the merchants investors guaranteed profits and monopoly rights over their products. Thus, by official subsidy if needed, the government would assure them a minimum of 5 percent net profit on their capital outlay for the first five years. As for the production monopolies, they were to last for fifteen years. In return, the company's books would be inspected regularly by government auditors. Chang expected that the company would be making a substantial profit by the end of the fifth year. From the sixth year onward, the government would get together with the company to decide on a reasonable rate of levy.[44]

The merchants, however, remained distrustful, and Chang's offer was not well received. The largest of this new series of manufactures, the carpet factory, was established below its projected capital of 800,000 taels. In 1906, it was opened with 300,000 taels of official funds and only 100,000 taels from private sources.[45] By 1908, owing to a chronic shortage of working capital, it was closed down, and a Hunanese merchant was given a twenty-years' lease to run it. In return, he paid a 6,000-tael annual rent for use of the plant facilities and a one-time payment of 30,000 taels as dividends and bonus on the official share of the capital.[46]

Some of the other enterprises never emerged from the planning committees. The rest, including the paper mill, the glass, cement, needle, nail, and leather factories, failed after a very short existence.

The general cause, according to one report, was inexperienced and wasteful bureaucratic management. For example, the needle and nail factory finally opened in 1908 after having been equipped with the most modern machinery from Europe; its chief manager, Huang Hou-ch'eng, an expectant taotai and from all accounts a likeable person, had no experience in running a factory. He had once served as a Confucian tutor in Chang Chih-tung's household, and apparently owed his position to this connection. In 1910, after he had declared bankruptcy for the company, he was accused, convicted, and imprisoned for embezzling at least 50,000 taels of company funds.[47]

This particular episode is instructive, because it shows that, in spite of Chang's open assertion that official management was a mistake not to be repeated, his new ventures turned out to be no better. Probably, given the merchants' lukewarm response, Chang Chih-tung had few alternatives. The fact remains that a personal friend and a scholar-official who had no entrepreneurial talent or managerial experience was asked to run it.

The Pei-yang Tobacco Company. This company, founded in Tientsin in 1905 under Governor-general Yuan Shih-k'ai's sponsorship, demonstrates that other *ho-pan* enterprises of this period promoted by other senior provincial officials suffered similar weaknesses attributable to bureaucratic control. Run by an official-entrepreneur, Huang Shen-chih, who had already distinguished himself in setting up the first officially sponsored Bureau of Industry (Kung-i chü) in Peking, the company promised that it would be a "reformed" *kuan-shang ho-pan* enterprise. Old bureaucratic practices would be banned. There could be no ostentatious display or lavish entertainment. The government would not appoint any director-general, but would be represented on the board of directors. Yuan Shih-k'ai thus echoed Chang Chih-tung's sentiment for inviting merchants into a modern joint-stock corporation in partnership with the government. Furthermore he did not call it a *chü* (bureau or agency), a term by which Chang Chih-tung's *kuan-shang ho-pan* projects were known. It was called a *kung-ssu* (company). The government's role was to offer protection, not interference.

Finally, Yuan generously offered 20,000 taels as the government's share, and expressed the hope that, as the company proved its profitability, merchants would give it sufficient capital through public subscription.[48]

Yuan's encouragement seems to have been unnecessary. The capital involved was relatively small, and tobacco had a demonstrably profitable market. Shares amounting to 33,000 taels were quickly pledged by private individuals, who included both merchants and officials. But, in spite of Yuan's expressions of good intention, it seems that, from the beginning, the company was staffed by bureaucrats who engaged in factional feuds among themselves. When Huang Shen-chih apparently lost out, he set up a competing cigarette factory within the Bureau of Industry in Peking. Meanwhile, he continued to intervene actively in the affairs of the Peiyang Tobacco Company. This led to more acrimonious disputes. In 1908, as the different factions brought management to a standstill, the company was forced to declare bankruptcy. Yuan sent his representative to assess the company accounts, then proceeded to lay claim to the government's share of the capital.

The Peiyang Tobacco Company had by this time committed a total capital outlay and loans of about 100,000 taels, divided in this way: 20,000 taels of government shares, 33,000 taels of private investments, 10,000 taels of mortgage, and 36,000 taels in loans from private sources. When Yuan's assessor discovered that only some 27,000 taels of assets were left, Yuan ordered that 10,000 taels be sent to the bank to pay for the mortgage in full, since, without it, the bank would refuse to release the collateral for the mortgage. Of the remaining 17,000 taels, he apportioned 16,000 taels to repay the government shares, leaving a mere 1,000 taels to reimburse the far larger private investments and loans. Understandably upset, the merchants voiced their complaint. In the end, Yuan relented somewhat, and returned another 6,000 taels to reimburse the shareholders. The government's refund thus represented half its original investment, while the private individuals received just slightly more than one-fifth. As for the private loans, Yuan refused to honor them since they had been contracted without first consulting the shareholders.[49]

Official sponsors of modern enterprise desired merchant participation for a number of reasons. The state revenues that could be diverted to industrial projects were insufficient. Where revenue surplus was available, the provincial officials' enthusiasm to use it was tempered by the central authorities' reluctance to have local revenue become excessively diverted to industry. Most likely Peking also realized that such a transfer of local revenue would increase regional power. Thus, when seeking court approval, the provincial government resorted to vague claims of merchant investments or to the need for official funds to serve as seed capital.

Merchant partnerships were sought also because of their management or technical skills, especially from among the compradors. But just as state capital from provincial coffers raised the problem of political power between central and regional authorities, so the sharing of rights and responsibilities between merchants and officials raised the issue of state and bureaucratic control. Chang Chih-tung, a senior official patron and major promoter of modern enterprise, was so obsessed by control that he refused to trust his own appointed official supervisors, much less the merchant-managers. He thus opened his iron smelting factory right next to his yamen, even though it was close to neither the coal nor the iron mine. As he later told Shang Hsuan-huai, he did it deliberately in order to keep a close watch, for he feared that even his own men might use it for their private gain. Chang then continued: "This is the Chinese way; it is not the Western way. In China this sort of evil practice and abuse have traditionally been present, and one must guard oneself against them. This is why I do it the Chinese way."[50]

Chang's "Chinese way" of control had even less success than Li Hung-chang's. Li, having been far abler at delegating authority, attracted many good managers and administrators from both merchant and official ranks. On the other hand, Chang Chih-tung had no assistants with the caliber of a Sheng Hsuan-huai or a Tong King-sing. Private investors, who had already shied away from the *kuan-tu shang-pan* type of enterprise, now concluded that the more equitable partnerships promised by the *ho-pan* slogans were similarly hollow. The search for a viable framework to develop modern enterprise in China continued.

Chapter Six

STATE CONTROL AND THE OFFICIAL-ENTREPRENEUR

The failure of both the *kuan-tu shang-pan* and *kuan-shang ho-pan* experiments to attract merchant investments in modern enterprise was the failure of official promoters like Chang Chih-tung and Li Hung-chang to convince merchant investors that their interests would not be sacrificed by official-managers representing the government or the official sponsors. By the 1900s, the merchants' message was clear: leave us out unless we are respected as full partners. On the other hand, their financially unspectacular and uncoordinated attempts at setting up genuine privately-owned enterprises at that time demonstrate that merchants by themselves were still too weak and disunited to lead the nation to industrialization. In the end, with the official promoters unwilling and unable to relinquish control, a partial way out of the impasse was found in new arrangements that totally eschewed or rendered *pro forma* formal government sponsorship.

The key was the transformation of the official-entrepreneurs. Late Ch'ing reappraisals of the role of commerce and industry had already made it ideologically respectable for official and gentry members to engage in modern enterprise. At first these officials did little more than general supervision. But, as time went on, they began to invest some of their own money, took on managerial power, and ended up making entrepreneurial decisions. Such a metamorphosis from officials to official-entrepreneurs was not completed by all, especially among the early group. Nieh Ch'i-kuei supervised and invested, but left the second half of the transformation process to his sons. Sheng Hsuan-huai, perhaps the most successful official-entrepreneur, completed the entire process. Still others, such as Chang Chien and Chou Hsueh-hsi, who began their entrepreneurial careers around 1900, not only went through the metamorphosis quickly, but also adopted new values and ideas compatible with their new roles.

Thus, if Sheng Hsuan-huai sought to amass a large fortune from his management of several enterprises, he still considered that goal subsidiary to his dominant concern for success in the world of officialdom. He was acutely aware of the connection between economic and political power. In order to further his own political goal, he made good use of the large amounts of public and private funds and the sizeable patronage provided by his economic empire. As an official-entrepreneur, Sheng favored bureaucratic manipulations at the expense of sound business judgments. He was successful in those enterprises where he clearly enjoyed a monopoly or massive official subsidies; he often failed in others where there was competition.[1]

On the other hand, Chang Chien and Chou Hsueh-hsi, as later starters, did not view their industrial activities as a means to achieve greater political success. Probably one reason for their different orientation was the political upheaval after 1900 and the problem of political legitimacy that followed the 1911 Revolution. As political chaos intensified, the world of officialdom became less attractive. Political power had lost its Confucian idealism as the means of fashioning out an orderly and ethical society.

The main reason for preferring sound business practices to bureaucratic manipulations, however, was the different kind of capital involved. While the first group of official-entrepreneurs like Sheng risked some of their own money as investments, they did not do it so massively as to hold a controlling share. In any case, they were more interested in attracting merchant capital and transforming government funds into industrial loans and capital under their supervision.

From the 1900s, a second group of official-entrepreneurs began to raise most or all of the required capital from among themselves or their friends. And they accomplished it in their private individual capacities, without formal government sponsorship. As a result, profit and loss affected them personally, and it became easier to separate their bureaucratic functions from their entrepreneurial roles. There was greater incentive to run a more efficient business organization. Undoubtedly they were concerned with maintaining their political influence and backing. But this was thought of almost as a means to ensure continued control over their enterprises. They had, therefore, reversed the priority, in terms of value and function, of economic power and political success as personal life goals.

As managers and owners who were also directly in charge of, or in a position to influence their colleagues in charge of, government policy towards modern enterprise, this second group of official-entrepreneurs no longer required formal official sponsorship in order to make their enterprises safe from official exploitations. This had already been the case when medium-ranking officials, with Li Hung-chang's unofficial blessing, invested privately in the New Hua-hsin Spinning and Weaving Mill in Shanghai during the 1890s. In the following decade, with the backing of Governor-general Yuan Shih-k'ai, Chou Hsueh-hsi, another medium-ranking official, built up a successful industrial complex without or with only *pro forma* state control. A second approach that achieved similar results was practiced by Chang Chien, who left government service entirely but relied on his old official background and connections to build up his own industrial successes. These later official-entrepreneurs, by combining their roles as investors, managers, and official sponsors, were able to provide modern enterprise with state protection without its stultifying control.

Chou Hsueh-hsi and His Official Partners

Chou Hsueh-hsi (1866–1947) came from a wealthy official family with extensive land holdings. His father, Chou Fu, rose to be Governor-general of Liang-Kiang (1904) and then of Liang-Kuang (1906). Through his family's connection, Chou began his association with Yuan Shih-k'ai around 1900. As governor of Shantung, Yuan commissioned him to set up a modern school in the province. In 1901, Yuan was promoted to be Governor-general of Chihli. Since Yuan's successor was Chou Fu, the son took the excuse that no father and son should work as officials in the same province and followed Yuan to Chihli. Once in Tientsin, Chou rose rapidly from expectant to substantive taotai, then to salt commissioner, and finally, by 1907, to provincial judicial commissioner.[2]

From the very beginning, Yuan was impressed by Chou's

efficiency and administrative skill in economic affairs. While on his way to take up his new post in Tientsin, Yuan ordered Chou to set up a Bureau of the Mint (Chien-yuan chü). Chou completed his assignment so well and so expeditiously that Yuan sent him to Japan on an inspection tour of her industrial program. On his return in 1903, Chou offered Yuan a plan for industrial development within the province. With Yuan's support, he quickly set up the provincial Bureau of Industry (Kung-i chü) which, with its many subsidiary offices added later, became Yuan's chief vehicle for industrial development. Since Chou remained to take charge of the profit-making Bureau of the Mint, and since Yuan allowed him to use the mint's profit for his industrial programs, Chou was able to get adequate funding and successful results.[3] Then, with the reputation and experience gained from these ventures, Chou moved into industry as a private investor. This took place around 1906 when he became involved with two major industrial projects, one in mining, the other in cement manufacturing.

The Lanchou Official Mining Company Ltd. (Pei-yang Lanchou kuan-k'uang yu-hsien king-ssu). Chou Hsueh-hsi's interest in mining went back to the pre-1900 era when, for a while, he was an officer of the Kaiping mines. They had, however, fallen under British control during the Boxer Uprising, and litigation all the way to London to try to recover them had not been successful.[4] Sometime during 1905–1906, Yuan, in whose jurisdiction the mines were located, asked Chou to look into the matter and to see if a new mine could not be opened under strictly Chinese control.

Chou's report stressed the importance of coal for China's industrialization and the inadequacy of the Kaiping mines' output to satisfy China's needs.[5] He favored a new mine next to the old mine sites which, because of official mining regulations, were conveniently restrained from spreading out beyond a 30-square-li area.

The result was the formation of the Lanchou Official Mining Company Ltd. in 1908. In 1906, Yuan had commissioned the Tientsin Official Bank (T'ien-chin kuan-yin-hao) to set up a committee to organize the company. Chou, already an officer of this official bank, was placed in charge.

The first set of regulations, submitted to Yuan in 1906, suggested that its organizers intended the mining company to be a private venture. It made no mention of official supervision or connection beyond the usual promises of official protection. On the other hand, many articles were devoted to enumerating the rights of the shareholders and the company's accountability to them. It is clear that it would subscribe to the recently established company laws, especially those rules regarding limited liabilities.[6]

However, even though its organizers wanted to run it as a private enterprise, it is doubtful if this could be accomplished. The existing law was extremely harsh on private owners of mines, for traditionally mining was thought to be a government monopoly. Even the reformed legal statutes on mining sponsored by Chang Chih-tung and enacted into law in 1907 did not entirely favor the private operator. Article 18, for example, gave him only 50 percent of the profit, the rest to be divided equally between the landowner and the government.[7] Given these legal liabilities, it is understandable why, in the final draft approved by Governor-general Yang Shih-hsiang on May 7, 1908, Article 4 specifically stated that the company was to be a *kuan-tu shang-pan* enterprise. Furthermore, the provincial government was to invest 500,000 taels in it. The other portions of the regulations remained substantially unaltered. Thus, the role of the private shareholder still predominated. He would elect a board of fifteen directors as well as the chief manager (*tsung-li*) and the associate manager (*hsieh-li*).[8] The flexible *kuan-tu shang-pan* format had once again been liberally interpreted to fit current needs.

In the preceding decades, several experiments using various *kuan-shang ho-pan* slogans had already demonstrated that what mattered was content, not name. Chou Hsueh-hsi profited from such a lesson when he changed the *kuan-tu shang-pan* formula into a *pro forma* acknowledgment of official sponsorship. As a personally-managed corporation with the name "Official Mining Company" in its title, the *kuan-tu* nomenclature had only assets and no liabilities. For example, as an official company, it could waive the 30-square-li area limitation imposed on private mining companies.[9] On the other hand, the investors' usual distrust of official domination would not apply in this case, since the great majority of the company shares were held by a relatively small number of men who were themselves officials. Many of them served in the management of the company. One tangible result of such an arrangement was the abolition of the bureaucratic supervisor under the name of director-general (*tu-pan*). This office, a direct appointee of the senior official patron, had always been present at the head of any *kuan-tu shang-pan* organizational chart. In the case of the Lanchou Mines, this would have made little practical difference, since Chou, who would have been the *tu-pan,* was made *tsung-li* first by Yuan Shih-k'ai and later by his successor, Yang Shih-hsiang. Chou enhanced his legitimacy, however, not only because *tsung-li* sounded more entrepreneurial to the investors, but also because his assumption of the office prior to the shareholders' approval was necessary and in any case recognized by company regulations. For it was not until June 12, 1909, that the shareholders finally met in session for the first time. At that meeting, Chou's office was duly confirmed in spite of his ritualistic request to be excused. Also confirmed at that meeting was the associate manager, Sun To-shen.[10]

In order to assure that control of the company would remain with a small group of men, the company regulations were heavily weighted in favor of the major investors. First, Chou made certain that there would be close identification between these major investors and the administrators. The two senior managers were to be elected from among the directors. Each was required to hold at least 2,000 shares, which, at 100 tael each, amounted to the sizeable investment of 200,000 taels. As for the directors and the two auditors, each was to own at least 1,000 shares. All shareholders who held 200 shares or more were entitled to recommend one person to be employed by the company on the basis of ability and qualifications. More significantly, shareholders' privileges were tightly confined to the larger investors. Thus, only those holding five full shares were entitled to introduce proposals; ten, to vote in elections; and fifty, to propose policy resolutions. Moreover, to further increase the influence of these shareholders, each was allowed to have up to twenty-five votes for every fifty shares under his name.[11]

If one assumes that the fifteen directors and two auditors elected at the first shareholders' meeting followed these rules, then, between them, they held a minimum of 19,000 shares (Chou and his associate manager were both managers and directors, and owned at least 2,000 shares each). This represents just under 40 percent of the total number of shares, even when 1909's additional capital-raising efforts of 3,000,000 taels are combined with the initial 2,000,000. Then if the government's 10 percent (or 5,000 shares) is added, the directors and the government held essentially a majority. Besides, there were those unrepresented shares owned by smaller investors with less than five shares.

Until the 1909 subscription, there were probably only a small number of shareholders. There was no effort to attract wide public participation. The company reported that the 2,000,000 taels were quickly taken up, all within a year. In the 1909 campaign, however, there was some initial uncertainty, since potential investors held back because the British controlled Kaiping mines had brought a suit against the Lanchou Company. Probably this was a factor forcing the company to welcome fractional shares as an appeal to small investors, even though an earlier regulation had rejected these lower investments.[12]

As to the identity of the seventeen original directors and officers, there is only partial evidence. Most likely they were Chou's friends, most or all of whom were officials working under Yuan Shih-k'ai and shared common geographical origins like Anhwei (Chou's native province) or Honan (Yuan Shih-k'ai's). They included Sun To-shen, Yuan K'o-ting, Kung Hsin-chan, Li Shih-wei, Ch'en I-fu, Li Sung-ch'en, Li Shih-chien, and Wang Shao-lien.[13] Yuan K'o-ting was Yuan's eldest son and later heir to his imperial dream. Sun To-shen, the associate manager, shared some of Chou's characteristics: both came from Anhwei; both had very distinguished fathers, for Sun's father was Grand Secretary Sun Chia-nai (1827–1909). Since 1898, supported by his family's wealth, Sun had become a major entrepreneur in his own right by opening China's first modern flour mill (The Fu-feng Flour Mill) in Shanghai. Kung, the two Lis, and Ch'en were minor officials at this time but later rose to prominence both as officials and official-entrepreneurs.

For example, Kung, another native of Anhwei, was Finance Minister during the Peking government, and later became Board Chairman of the China Industrial Bank, the Yao-hua Glass Factory, and the Chee-Hsin Cement Company.[14] Kung was not alone. At least Li Shih-wei, Li Sung-ch'en, and Ch'en I-fu also found their way onto the board of directors of the same cement company, which at this time was Chou's other major industrial project.[15]

Chee Hsin Cement Company Ltd. (Ch'i-hsin yang-hui yu-hsien kung-ssu). In name, this was structurally different from the Lanchou Official Mining Company since it was organized as a private corporation of limited liability and did not become a *kuan-tu shang-pan* enterprise. In practice, it was managed and financed in much the same way. First, there was considerable government support; and second, there was a similar close identification between the management and its major official investors. One may assume that the *kuan-tu shang-pan* formula was dropped because the special restrictions private mining companies were subjected to no longer applied, while the power and influence of its individual investors-cum-managers were sufficient to ensure its protection and support from the government.[16]

Chou Hsueh-hsi's initial interest in the cement industry dated back to 1900 when he, as associate manager of the Kaiping mines, learned about Tong King-sing's unsuccessful attempts at cement production. Tong ran a cement factory between 1889 and 1893 with some 100,000 taels invested jointly by the provincial government, the Kaiping mines, and himself. Chou sought the advice of German engineers and was planning to reactivate Tong's old plant when political events intervened and the cement plant, like its parent company, the Kaiping mines, fell under British control. In 1906, while working under Yuan Shih-k'ai in Chihli, Chou fought for its return as a separate entity from the mines. After Chou's repeated challenge, the British managers finally agreed to return it in the summer of 1906.[17]

Meanwhile, he had secured Yuan's backing in settling the old company's indebtedness at no expense to the new organizers, for the old shareholders and other creditors were paid off *pro rata* from its remaining assets. In addition, he was assured a monopoly of the cement market and production over the entire province. Then, even before the British had given up their claims, Chou, with Yuan's approval, had been promised a loan of 400,000 taels from the Tientsin Official Bank to help him reactivate the company. The loan, carrying a low interest rate of 5 percent per annum, was to be repaid in seven installments from the fourth to the tenth year. On December 4, 1906, Chou and the Tientsin Official Bank concluded the loan agreement and, by the following month, government money began to pour in to support this private company. According to the unsympathetic view of the editors compiling the company's archival materials, Chou wanted to make sure the company would be profitable before committing his own and his friends' funds.[18]

If Chou had any such doubts, they were quickly put to rest. The company was an immediate success, and his friends seemed more than ready to accede to his request for an initial capital of 1,000,000 taels. It was fully subscribed in less than six months.[19] By September 1907, the company repaid in full both the principle and interest of the 400,000 taels government loan.[20]

Chee Hsin continued to enjoy adequate funding. Its report for 1910 was self-congratulatory over its past performance and confident of its future. In 1907, the first year the company paid out dividends, they amounted to 18 percent. Between 1908 and 1911, the annual dividend (which included the 8 percent guaranteed dividend or *kuan-li*) maintained a fantastic 16 percent return. In 1912, each share was split into two, doubling the company's capital value.[21] Chee Hsin then planned for an additional 1,500,000 taels capital investment for development and expansion. Half the new stock offerings were reserved for existing shareholders, while the other half were offered, not to the general public, but to the provincial government of Chihli, and the railway companies in the various provinces. Since the company files show no investment by either the government or the railway companies in the later years, it is most probable that the entire 1,500,000 taels were subscribed by the same shareholders and their official and gentry friends. Similarly, when the company raised another 300,000 taels shortly thereafter to set up a northern branch factory, new shares were specifically limited to the old shareholders.[22]

Official support was also expressed in other ways. Governor-general Yang Shih-hsiang continued Yuan's protective policy. He refused to entertain a plea from the Acting Governor-general of Hukuang to stop Chee Hsin from building a southern branch factory in the Anhwei-Kiangsu area in order to extend the company's market to the lower Yangtze Valley. He called Yang's attention to the struggling cement company Chang Chih-tung had sponsored in 1905 at Wuchang, and its need for time to establish its market in the neighboring provinces. Yang replied that Chee Hsin would enjoy no monopoly in the lower Yangtze, that the southern branch had already been approved by Peking, and that, in any case, no branch would be built inside Hupei—a meaningless concession since the cement factory in Wuchang already had a monopoly over its own province.[23]

But even such a forceful assertion of its rights was not enough for the company. During 1908 and 1909, the Ministry of Industry, Agriculture, and Commerce reconfirmed its right to be the sole manufacturer of cement in Chihli. It also had prior claims of suitable sites for branch factories throughout Manchuria and the lower Yangtze Valley.[24] Other benefits the company acquired included special tax reduction and exclusive rights to supply cement to the China Merchants' S.N. Company and the government-run railways in the north. All these enterprises were dominated by men subservient to Yuan Shih-k'ai.[25]

Just as in the case of the Lanchou mines, Chee Hsin was able to enjoy such massive government support because its managers, directors, and other shareholders were officials. Although the list of directors in the early period includes no member of Yuan's immediate family, the family probably had some shares. From the late 1920s on, one of Yuan's sons emerged onto the board of directors.[26]

There is no complete list of the shareholders in this early

period. But from the few listed, and from the more complete lists of later years, one may assume that they were largely the same men who at about the same time were investing in the Lanchou mines.[27] The same small group of investors continued to hold the majority of the company shares in spite of its many capital-raising campaigns. How this came about has already been described: by changing the company's reserves and assets into new capital (as in the 1912 share-splitting), and by restricting portions of each subsequent issue of new shares to the old shareholders. Thus, in the company's revised regulations of 1912, it is reported that new shares "were assigned to the original shareholders according to the size of their holdings, and only when they could not take on any more did the company managers step in to arrange for subscription by some other means." As for these original shareholders, they apparently managed to meet the call for new capital because they plowed back most of their dividends and bonuses.[28]

They differed from those others who had earlier invested in the *kuan-tu shang-pan* enterprises such as the China Merchants' S.N. Company. Albert Feuerwerker's study on the latter has shown how, during the same period, its shipping business went into gradual decline in spite of its great profitability. It seems that there was no plowing back of profits. Instead, its shareholders (in far larger number than Chee Hsin's) and managers continued to draw their dividends like a miner exhausting a vein of coal or copper.[29] However, the difference between the investors of the Chee Hsin and those of the China Merchants' lay not in their different values or entrepreneurial goals, but in what each group knew the government and officials might do to their enterprise. In the case of the cement plant, the managers-cum-investors were the same men who formulated political decisions affecting the company. In the case of the shipping company, there was no such close identification. After the fall of Li Hung-chang, the company was subject to official exactions from various sources.

Chou Hsueh-hsi went on to found other enterprises. In 1909, he organized the first water works company in Peking. During the Republican era, he ventured into banking, glass works, and textiles, while the Lanchou mines were amalgamated with the Kaiping mines. Chee Hsin spread out its market and eventually dominated the entire country's cement output.[30]

Chou retained the consistent support of Yuan Shih-k'ai until 1915, when he failed to endorse the latter's monarchical scheme. By this time, a new political context had emerged in China. The central political authority had finally collapsed, and regionally-based warlords and military cliques had come in. Chou realized that the relationships between merchants and officials, industry and government, were no longer the same. Around 1916, although he appeared to have been unenthusiastic, he joined the Anhwei clique to tender his economic support in return for political protection.[31]

Chang Chien and His Merchant Partners

Chang Chien (1853–1926), whose transformation from scholar-official to entrepreneur has been discussed earlier, was a different type of official-entrepreneur. While Chou Hsuen-hsi turned to his official colleagues for financial and managerial backing, Chang appealed to the merchants. Although he argued that his considerable official status and personal integrity would assure his merchant partners official protection, the merchants would only give him partial support. In the end, Chang owed his success as an official-entrepreneur to his ability to make use of official funds and influence without sacrificing his operation's independence of state control.

Chang's initial interest in industrial promotion went back to 1895, when he was residing in his native home in T'ung-chou on leave from official duties because of his father's death. Since he was the most prestigious gentry member in the area, and since, also, Acting Governor-general Chang Chih-tung had asked him to organize the local militia, he began to assume leadership in local affairs. This led him to become involved in a local campaign petitioning the provincial government to lessen bureaucratic abuses by unifying the sundry taxes imposed on cotton cloth—the region's major handicraft product. Although he failed in that venture, it apparently captured his interest and won him the friendship of the local cotton cloth merchants. When Sheng Hsuan-huai began his cotton mill in Shanghai a few years before, he had bought a lot of cotton from T'ung-chou and even tried to set up a mill there. But Sheng was blocked by the local merchants who wanted to preserve the area's handicraft spinning and weaving industries. By 1895, however, local opposition had faded, since the merchants saw the growing popularity of machine-made cotton yarns and realized the possibility of building their own textile mill.

Meanwhile Chang Chih-tung also had become interested in setting up some cotton mills in Kiangsu other than the ones in Shanghai and Hupei. He was visibly upset by the terms of the Treaty of Shimonoseki of April 1895, by which foreigners obtained the right to build factories in the treaty ports. Chang Chih-tung planned for two additional mills, one in Soochow and the other in T'ung-chou, areas known for their cotton. For the first, he approached Lu Jun-hsiang, a prominent Soochow scholar-official then on home leave from his official post in Peking. Lu responded positively, but relinquished his management shortly afterwards in order to resume his official career.[32]

The Dah Sun Cotton Spinning Mill (Ta-sheng sha-ch'ang). Chang Chih-tung's plan for the second cotton mill went to Chang Chien.[33] Two local cotton goods merchants, Liu Kuei-hsing and Ch'en Wei-yung, introduced him to two wealthy merchants in Shanghai, P'an Hua-mao, a native of Kwangtung, and Kuo Hsun, a native of Fukien. They then decided upon a medium-sized, 600,000-tael, 20,000-spindle spinning mill to be built at T'ung-chou. P'an and Kuo, joined by a third merchant, Fan Fen from Ningpo, would form the Shanghai team of directors and be responsible for raising 400,000 taels. Liu and Ch'en, joined by Chang Chien's trusted friend and neighbor, Shen Hsieh-chün, would form the local team of directors and be responsible for the remaining 200,000 taels. In this earliest format, Chang Chien, who had no substantial capital of his own, was not one of the directors. He was the official promoter and responsible for all dealings with the government. Chang's role reveals starkly how difficult it would be at the time for any group of private individuals without official credentials to start a large modern industry.[34]

When Chang Chien initiated this industrial project with Chang Chih-tung's blessing, he probably had no idea what a private enterprise of this size and nature would mean in practice. As a scholar-official, he could not imagine how it could be managed without official support and direction, or why official supervision would be harmful so long as the official managers were capable and upright men. According to his son-biographer, he asked to extend his official leave late in 1896. This request was presumably granted, for he did not return to Peking until the spring of 1898, when he finally made up his mind to resign from his official post.[35] Moreover, Chang's official cast of mind was expressed in other ways. When his merchant directors discovered that they could not find sufficient investors, Chang's solution was to invite the government in as a partner. When the Shanghai group protested, fearing government interference, Chang promptly declared that "he alone could counter any such moves."[36]

Chang Chien's organizing committee of six directors received Chang Chih-tung's endorsement in early 1896. It ran into problems almost immediately. First, there was a change in the governor-general's office. With Chang Chih-tung's recall to his original post in the Hu-Kuang provinces, Governor-general Liu Kun-i returned to Kiangsu. Although Liu was friendly to Chang Chien, he informed the committee that the tax exemption promised earlier by Chang Chih-tung would be withdrawn. Second, market conditions in Shanghai in 1896 for textiles were disastrous. The end of the Sino-Japanese war had led to a steep rise in the price of raw cotton, at the same time when the level of competition had risen sharply. Four new foreign-owned mills were being opened in the city. As a result, the existing mills were doing so poorly that rumors of bankruptcy were frequent.[37] As Chang Chien observed sadly, whenever a prospective investor was confronted by him or any of the company directors, they "became close-lipped, smiled, or else covered their ears and took off."[38]

The impact was contagious. At their meeting in the summer of 1896, Fan Fen and Ch'en Wei-yung resigned, while P'an Hua-mao and Kuo Hsun, the remaining two Shanghai directors, advised Chang to postpone the subscription campaign for another year since they had failed to raise any capital. Since P'an, Kuo, and Fan were natives of Ningpo, Canton, and Fukien respectively, they were presumably well connected in Shanghai with the major commercial groups from these three places. From the start, they recognized that most of the money would have to come from Shanghai, and even promised to make up the difference for the T'ung-chou directors if the latter were unable to fulfill their shares. Thus, P'an and Kuo had been appointed company treasurers.

Undaunted, Chang Chien quickly found two new directors, Chiang Shu-chen and Kao Li-ch'ing of T'ung-chou, to replace the two who had left. At the same time, Chang seized upon the government's offer to sell some unused spindles and turned it into a counter-offer of partnership with the government. Governor-general Liu Kun-i had inherited 40,800 spindles his predecessor Chang Chih-tung had bought in 1893 for a second mill in Wuchang that was never opened. Instead, the spindles had to have a foreign maintenance team and a rented warehouse to store them. In that same summer of 1896, Liu ordered Taotai Kuei Sung-ch'ing, head of the newly established Bureau of Commercial Affairs in Nanking, to sell them. Kuei approached Kuo Hsun, whom he knew, and the matter was brought before the Dah Sun organizers.[39]

Chang proposed to take in all 40,800 spindles, to increase the mill's capital to 1,000,000 taels, and to accept Liu's spindles as government shares. Since the spindles were finally appraised at 500,000 taels, this would represent a 50 percent interest for the government. The merchant directors would then raise the other 500,000 taels, to be split evenly between the Shanghai and the T'ung-chou groups. Chang's proposal was strongly opposed by P'an and Kuo, who feared future official interference. With the support of the T'ung-chou group (now grown to four directors as against Shanghai's two), however, Chang Chien's motion carried, and he proceeded to sign an agreement with Taotai Kuei on December 6, 1896.[40]

Chang's tactics, based on majority vote and not on the more traditional consensus, appear to have alienated P'an and Kuo once and for all. They continued to voice opposition to Chang, and began to squabble with each other. By the summer of 1897, while the T'ung-chou directors had raised 120,000 taels, the Shanghai directors could produce only 20,000 taels. They now asked to withdraw. The organizers tried for another compromise. The T'ung-chou merchants would assume roughly two-thirds or 340,000 taels, leaving one-third or 160,000 taels for the Shanghai merchants. Thus, the various shares' proportions between the two groups had come full circle. First, Shanghai's shares had been twice T'ung-chou's, then equal in amount, and now, some twenty months later, only half as much. When P'an and Kuo still refused to release any money so long as the government remained a partner, an impasse was reached. The T'ung-chou group offered to resign; so did the Shanghai group. Finally, Governor-general Liu K'un-i intervened.[41]

Liu had apparently been able to secure the help of Shang Hsuan-huai, even though at the time Sheng's Hua-sheng Cotton Mill was suffering losses of several thousand taels each month because of undercapitalization and keener competition.[42] When Chang approached him on Liu's instruction, Sheng agreed to take over half the spindles as well as the cost of running them. This meant that Chang's proposed mill was split in two, each requiring a capital of only 500,000 taels. For Chang and his group, it also meant that they would return to their original size of about 20,000 spindles. As for their fund-raising efforts, they would need only 250,000 taels instead of the 600,000 taels of the original plan or the 500,000 taels for the bigger mill. Sheng and Kuei further promised to give additional capital support if required. The new arrangement was concluded on August 16, 1897, whereupon P'an and Kuo withdrew.[43]

It is probable that Sheng made his promises simply to placate Liu K'un-i, for the promised funds never came. When Chang pressed him repeatedly, Sheng acidly informed Chang that he could have the budget of all of his under-financed mills in Kiangsu if Chang would assume the responsibility of running them as well.[44] Taotai

Kuei's promise was almost equally unreliable. From an original commitment of 60,000 or 70,000 taels, it dwindled to less than 20,000, which he finally produced after Chang's frantic appeals. Fortunately, Kuei was supported by his friend and fellow official, Yun Hsin-yun, so that their total contribution in the end amounted to some 40,000 taels. Meanwhile, the T'ung-chou directors continued to make slow progress in their capital-raising efforts. They raised another 50,000 or 60,000 taels in 1898, during which time Chang Chien, helped by his loyal friend Shen Hsieh-chün,[45] was actively building the plant and installing the machinery. These activities put a great strain on the company's day-to-day finance. As Chang remembered it, "Often on one day, I would manage a loan of 10,000–20,000 [*sic*] taels, exhaust it by the second, try to borrow more from somewhere else on the third, and then, on the fourth day, need to [find more loans to] return what I had borrowed on the first day."[46] Finally, Chang pleaded his case with Governor-general Liu. The latter was sympathetic and urged the taotai of Shanghai, Chinkiang, Wuhu, and Kiukiang, as well as the transport commissioner of the Huai River, to come to Chang's assistance. They responded by making loans amounting to about 50,000 taels. But inadequate funding continued to plague the company. Later in the same year, Chang made a second appeal to Liu, who responded again by ordering local officials in T'ung-chou and neighboring Hai-men to transfer their revenue deposits from the local pawnshops to the company. This led to an additional 28,000 taels. Chang remained consistently on the move, soliciting new capital funds, and borrowing from others. His son-biographer has offered a poignant description of how Chang Chien went about promoting capital for the modern industry:

> Although, at the top, the governor-general expressed support, at the lower levels all the officials wanted to ruin his enterprise. Bystanders, too, did not want to see him succeed . . . When confronting an impasse, he would often go to [the Shanghai waterfront] and sigh to Heaven and the Whampoa River, his tears pouring out in torrents. Sometimes, when he did not have sufficient money for his travels, he would sell

his calligraphy, for he refused to use any part of the company's funds.[47]

In May 1899, the first spool of Dah Sun's yarn was finally produced. From then on, the company made a comfortable profit, and Chang, as early as October, was sending Liu K'un-i an optimistic report. The company made a profit of 27,000 taels in 1899 and began paying its shareholders a minimum of 8 percent dividend each year. Some of the official loans were repaid, for in 1899 only 38,500 taels were left. Taotai Kuei tried to take over the company in 1899, claiming that it was a government-owned enterprise. Chang complained vigorously to Governor-general Liu and threatened to resign.[48] Chang was apparently successful, for the company, in spite of its 50 percent government share, became known as a *shang-pan* (merchant management) operation. Chang himself, however, called it *shen-tu shang-pan* (gentry supervision and merchant management), even though he would sometime use the term *kuan-shang ho-pan.* Chang believed he had succeeded in inaugurating a privately managed modern enterprise. It can even be argued he had gone further: he was able to co-opt government capital and use it without state supervision.

In spite of the apparent success achieved by both Chou Hsueh-hsi and Chang Chien, a number of problems remained. Some of Chang Chien's difficulties with his Shanghai merchant supporters were not owing to their distrust of government. Individual merchant investors often did not have ample idle cash ready for investment. They were also easily swayed by the fluctuating ups and downs of the market, for as traders they were in the habit of expecting quick and short-term returns of profit. Chang also failed to convince the merchants that his good intentions, unsullied reputation, and status as an official-entrepreneur were sufficient to warrant their trust. On the other hand, government loans, which ultimately made it possible for Dah Sun to begin operation, came reluctantly and after much frustration. Chang Chien's experience, therefore, offered no easy model for other official-entrepreneurs who wished to tap private and state capital to develop modern industry outside of normal government sponsorships.

As for Chou Hsueh-hsi, he owed his success to tightly controlled management, consistent plowback of profits, and well-chosen political backing. The first two qualities were not too difficult to follow once Chou had shown the way. Reliable and sufficiently powerful political protection, however, was much harder to acquire. This was particularly so after 1916, when warlords who replaced mandarins had only ephemeral power and far fewer scruples. Moreover, Chou's success depended on the capital of only a few men and their ability to control its use. On this crucial issue of capital resources, Chou was no better than the earlier group of official-entrepreneurs.

To sum up, there were two notable areas of success achieved by Chou Hsueh-hsi and Chang Chien. Avoiding the practices of earlier official-entrepreneurs like Sheng Hsuan-huai, Chou and Chang eschewed state control, circumvented all public sponsorship by senior officials, and ran a number of profit-making enterprises with a minimum of bureaucratism. All the official-entrepreneurs, however, failed to attract broad financial support or to mobilize public interest in their projects. Consequently, no modern economic infrastructure was developed to integrate their various individual efforts. It remained for others to arouse national enthusiasm for modern enterprise and to give it another try.

Chapter Seven

MERCHANT AND GENTRY IN PRIVATE ENTERPRISE

During the first decade of the twentieth century, the growth of *shang-pan* type companies was not limited to those organized by official-entrepreneurs like Chang Chien who avoided formal official supervision but preserved close official ties. Several other modern industrial *shang-pan* companies were initiated by merchant and gentry sponsors. These ranged from traditional entrepreneurs, who realized that the use of machinery offered bigger sizes and greater profits, to merchants who acquired political consciousness and sided with gentry members to demand private management out of a mixture of self-interest and patriotic concern. The central government, too, played a part by promulgating private company laws and incorporation procedures. Even though many of these state measures did not work well in practice, they bolstered the merchants' claims to legal protection.

The rising political temper during the last years of Ch'ing China contributed to these developments. In the major urban centers, several merchants began to form their own associations to carry out political campaigns. They followed the practice of students and scholars in forming study groups of their own to examine questions of local government and constitutionalism. In Shanghai in 1906, this led to the formation of the Consultative Committee of Chinese Merchants to agitate for Chinese representation in the International Settlement's Municipal Council.[1] In the following year, politicized merchants in Canton organized the Self-Government Society of Kwangtung Merchants (Yueh-shang tzu-chih hui) to discuss a wide range of political issues and to stage nationalistic demonstrations against Japanese and British imperialism.[2] Already others had demonstrated their readiness to participate in direct political action. Back in 1905, a Shanghai merchant, Tseng Shao-ch'ing, organized the first successful boycott against American goods because of the United States discriminatory immigration policy. From Shanghai, the merchant-led movement spread north and south and was finally suppressed only by the repeated warnings of an embarrassed government.[3] Other Shanghai merchants helped organize the first Physical Exercise Association for merchants. By 1907, they were accepted as a part of the International Settlement's militia and became a model for merchants elsewhere in forming their own local merchant militia.[4] All in all, merchants did not lag behind the other social groups in making the 1900s, in Mary Wright's felicitous phrase, "a period of tidal changes."[5]

Such a politically vibrant milieu generated heated debates on state control of modern enterprise. On one side were senior provincial officials such as Chang Chih-tung who continued to argue for state supervision. On the other were merchants, gentry-merchants, and gentry leaders who demanded *shang-pan* operations, not in the sense official-entrepreneurs had used the term, but complete, unfettered private control and management.

One issue that gave these debates focus and popular appeal was the movement to recover rights in railway finance and construction from foreign companies. In this instance, the nation's political interest and economic well-being were joined. Modern industry had first been promoted because it promised to make China strong. Yet it was being handed over to foreign powers because the state would rather borrow capital from foreign bankers and maintain only nominal state control over what would, in effect, be foreign-owned railways. With this argument, provincial gentry and politicized merchants turned private management into a political issue. Their protest was no longer based on economic arguments challenging the desirability of state intervention in modern industry. Their protest became a political contest in which *shang-pan* was equated with preserving the nation's economic strength against foreign encroachment, and state sponsorships was equated with collusion with Western bankers. Private enterprise free from state and foreign control thus became an integral part of the railways' "Rights Recovery Movement."

Provincial Railways and Shang-Pan

Willy-nilly China entered into the age of railways. The earliest railway died stillborn. Completed surreptitiously by British merchants in 1876, the short Shanghai-Woosung Railway lasted barely a year before local opposition forced the Chinese government to tear it up after compensating its foreign owners. The second railway, less than seven miles long, was sponsored by Governor-general Li Hung-chang to transport coal from T'ang-shan's mine field of the Kaiping mines. When it was completed in 1881, Li avoided opposition by using horses to pull the trolleys.[6]

In 1889, when Chang Chih-tung proposed the first major railway to run between Peking and Hankow, there was general acceptance but little enthusiasm. Its two chief proponents disagreed on how to organize the railway projects. Chang Chih-tung believed that, because of their strategic importance, railways should be financed and run by the state. Li Hung-chang, on the other hand, pleaded for merchant participation and the use of foreign loans.[7] Initially, the throne sided with Chang but reversed itself in 1895, because the railway funds collected had been used up for the empress dowager's sixtieth birthday extravaganza or diverted to the war effort against Japan. The throne asked "wealthy merchants in the provinces to set up companies if they could raise a minimum of 10 million taels," and promised that "all the company affairs will be managed by the merchants, and losses and profits will not be the concern of officials."[8]

The throne's generous intention was not carried out. The Peking-Hankow Railway continued to be supervised by Chang Chih-tung and Wang Wen-shao, the two governors-general through whose provinces the tracks passed. It seems that no officials could envisage any large industrial operation free from official direction. After 1895, Chang supported the throne's view on railway finance only to the extent that state funds were insufficient. He remained skeptical not only about the willingness and ability of Chinese merchants to contribute capital, but also about their moral and civic worth. As he turned to foreign bankers for capital, Chang confided to Wang his low esteem for the Chinese merchants:

> The merchants do not consider the broad issues. Some are knowledgeable about foreign matters, but they do not understand Chinese politics. Some are easily taken in by foreigners. Some others are keen and spirited in the management of affairs, but they lack experience. Finally there are those who are daring and deceitful and who scheme for monopoly rights, yet they will never be able to keep their word.[9]

Chang sought foreign capital loans; but he did not want these loans to come through Chinese merchant middlemen or front men acting on behalf of clandestine foreigners. Chang decided that he himself would contract foreign loans directly from foreign bankers, using the railways as collateral. Then, as the railways were built and began to yield profits, merchants would be attracted to put in capital so that, eventually, they would help repay the foreign loans.[10] From 1896, with the appointment of his nominee, Sheng Hsuan-huai, to be director-general of the newly established Chinese Imperial Railway Administration, Chang began to implement a strategy of building railways with foreign loans.

Apart from his distrusting nature, Chang's emphasis on direct negotiations with foreign bankers was motivated by his desire to retain personal control over the railways built with these loans. Predictably, Chang launched a long and persistent campaign against private management of railways. In an 1896 memorial to the throne regarding another railway, Chang argued passionately and in great detail that railways were uniquely unsuited for fully private management, and how they would affect the interest and sovereignty of the state. Chang pointed out that, in foreign countries, railways enjoyed private ownership and management rights for a specific length of time, perhaps thirty years, after which they would be returned to their governments with or without compensation. He also observed that Chinese merchants lacked managerial skill and technical know-how, and would not be able to acquire land or police the line adequately. Hence genuine *shang-pan* operations in which merchants retained control would be impractical. Chang conceded, however, that private participation was desirable. As a compromise solution, Chang proposed the setting up of *kuan-shang ho-pan* railway companies in which private capital and state revenue, supplemented by foreign loans, would be employed, while official and merchant managers would share managerial rights and responsibilities.[11] He thus reverted to the same formula he was advocating for his textile industry.

The Canton-Hankow Railway (Yueh-Han t'ieh-lu) provided the first serious challenge to Chang Chih-tung's views on state control and foreign loans for Chinese railways. When this route was first proposed by Sheng Hsuan-huai in 1896, Sheng had just assumed the responsibility of building the northern trunk line between Peking and Hankow. To extend it southward to Canton was a natural development. Through Chang Pi-shih, the Chinese consul in Singapore and himself a wealthy merchant, Sheng sought to raise capital from among Chinese merchants in Southeast Asia but had little success.[12] On the other hand, the China Development Company, an American concern, offered money and management skill. In 1898 and again in 1900, Sheng signed two agreements with the American company on behalf of the central government, granting it construction and financing rights.[13]

Already local gentry and merchant leaders had approached Sheng Hsuan-huai with offers to raise money and run the railway themselves.[14] But in 1898 there was no widespread interest or substantial financial backing behind their efforts. If the China Development Company had promptly started work on the railway, no effective opposition could have been mounted against it. But it encountered unexpected delays in raising money following the outbreak of the Spanish-American War. In 1904, the company sold a controlling share of its stock to a Belgian syndicate in violation of Article 17 of the Sino-American agreements.

This change of nationality quickly became known in China, whereupon influential gentry and merchant leaders of the Seventy-two Guilds and the Nine Charitable Halls organized several well-attended meetings in Canton to condemn the American company.[15] Since 1903, its foreign engineers had been accused of creating drunken scenes in public, beating up Chinese guards and laborers, and committing one murder and several attempted rapes.[16] In the summer of 1904, the discovery that the Americans had also broken their contract heightened merchant and gentry sense of grievances. It also provided them with a legal basis on which to demand the recovery of Chinese rights.

Several factors gave this new movement force, persistance, and popularity. By 1904, concessions and loans to foreigners had become commonplace, and public hostility towards them was genuinely intense.[17] Profit-seeking merchants who had tried to build feeder railways in the commercially active Canton delta areas but were unsuccessful because of the trunk line's monopoly rights over the entire region vented their anger against the American company.[18] The provincial governments were no less happy to see the foreign company go, for foreign concessions negotiated and approved by Peking diminished their power and revenue allotments vis-à-vis the central government. In Hankow, Governor-general Chang Chih-tung supported, and perhaps even instigated, a similar merchant and gentry-led recovery movement. He held extensive discussions with its leader, Wang Hsien-ch'ien, a well-known scholar and financier, on the feasibility of transferring some grain and salt revenues to railway construction.[19] In Canton, Chang's counterpart, Governor-general Ts'en Ch'un-hsuan, also chaired similar meetings and discussions in support of the local leaders.[20]

Chang Chih-tung's championship of the rights recovery movement is the more striking because he had long favored foreign loans. But when he realized that he had no control over the China Development Company, since the loan was managed by the central government, he quickly forgot his convictions but added his voice to those of the local groups. For similar reasons, Shang Hsuan-huai fought against the recovery movement, because, in spite of his indebtedness to Chang, he was a central government official dependent on central authority for his political power.[21] Thus, while lofty ideals of patriotism and nationalism played a major role, the Rights Recovery Movement was energized by the mundane, self-centered motives of most of its participants.

During 1905, control over the China Development Company

was regained by another American company. But the campaign had acquired so much popular support that the central government, fearing local insurrection, forced the Americans to accept a redemption agreement. Then, in order to pay them for what they had already spent, Chang Chih-tung borrowed from a British banker, the Hong Kong and Shanghai Banking Corporation in Hong Kong, using the opium revenues of Hupei, Hunan, and Kwangtung as collateral. Since Chang himself negotiated the new loan on behalf of the three provinces, the provincial governments had effectively re-established control, while the local leaders retained their recovered rights because the British creditors could make no claims on the railway.

Chang's and Ts'en's success at keeping Peking and the foreign powers out did not extend to their dealings with the local gentry and merchant leaders. The British loan repaid the Americans but left little else with which to construct the railway. In Hankow, Chang agreed that each of the three provinces through which the railway passed would build its own section, but rejected a number of Hunanese leaders' appeals to pull all the resources of the province into forming a 20-million-tael private railway company. Chang reiterated his conviction that the railway had strategic importance, and proposed instead a *kuan-tu shang-pan* company to be supported by both government and private funds. With approval from Peking, he began to levy a surtax on salt to pay for the government share.[22]

Private support for Chang was low. By 1907, Chang relented by offering any private group who could finance the railway a thirty-year franchise, after which period the government would step in to buy back half the company shares. Chang's retreat was met with open skepticism. One local newspaper reprinted Chang's various statements about railways. It questioned his motives in insisting on eventual state control and his ability not to interfere in company affairs. The central government, too, was unwilling to approve such a company. Consequently, the government-controlled Hunan Railway Company had little money and completed even fewer roadways.[23]

The main cause of Chang Chih-tung's failure in Hunan, however, was the relative lack of commercial activity and private wealth in the province. In commercially prosperous Canton, Ts'en Ch'un-hsuan's policy of raising taxes and running a state-controlled railway for the Kwangtung portion did not lead to passive resistance, but to violent opposition. In January 1906, following Ts'en's proclamation raising the salt and miscellaneous (*t'ai-p'ao*) taxes by 70 percent, several scores of angry merchant and gentry leaders confronted the officials in a heated debate. Led by an impetuous, loud-speaking former county magistrate, Li Kuo-lien, and backed by at least two Hanlin academicians and a retired governor-general, this private-interest group presented a formidable challenge to Ts'en's authority. Two days later, Ts'en arrested Li and the other elected representative, Liang Hsiao-shan, a gentry-merchant, for stirring up dissent.[24]

Ts'en's escalation was a miscalculated move, although it eventually produced unexpected yields. Li became a hero overnight as thousands swarmed to public meetings to eulogize him as the defender of the poor against official exploitation. The meetings passed resolutions to deplore Ts'en's surtaxes, organized delegations of support to visit Li in prison, and voiced threats to call for a general strike. Hsu Ying-kuei, the retired governor-general, offered amid applause to go to Peking himself to lay the case before the throne.[25]

To compound Ts'en's difficulty, there were reports of dissension within the provincial bureaucracy and of unhappiness in Peking over his actions. Spurred on by the court's announcement that a senior official would be sent to Canton to mediate, Ts'en rushed several despatches to Tso Tsung-fan, president of the local chamber of commerce and a *chü-jen* scholar-turned-merchant, offering to make compromises. He re-emphasized, however, the need to raise capital from all available sources and appealed to the merchant and gentry groups to cooperate with him.[26] In the secret negotiations that followed, Ts'en backed down and promised to release Li and Liang and to recall the surtax if sufficient capital from private investors could be raised.[27]

On February 17, 1906, Li was triumphantly escorted out of

prison by a large crowd of well-wishers playing music and sending off firecrackers. Governor-general Ts'en, however, skilfully lessened his own loss of face by declaring that Li's imprisonment had served the purpose of calling public attention to the urgency of raising funds and had contributed to the public's enthusiastic response in subscribing capital to the railway company. Since the public had so responded, his surtax was no longer needed and was therefore withdrawn.[28]

Ts'en's claims were factually accurate even if unanticipated. Since August 1905, the provincial bureaucracy and the private interest groups led by the local gentry, the commercial guilds, charitable halls, and the chamber of commerce had been at loggerheads over the nature of the railway company to be formed once the construction rights were recovered from the Americans. These private parties threatened to withhold all financial support if appointed officials were to run the company. Ts'en's response was unreassuring. He promised to give equal rights to government and private shares and to observe the company laws. On the crucial issue of management control, he declared that state and private parties would have separate powers, but that the official supervisors would arbitrate disputes.[29]

With Ts'en standing firm on state control, Li Kuo-lien and Liang Hsiao-shan refused to launch a capital drive, and it was their recalcitrance on this issue rather than their open clash over surtaxes that prompted their arrest. What Ts'en had not foreseen was that his action reactivated the thousands of students and shop hands who had joined the clamor in the Rights Recovery Movement, but who had since withdrawn from the issue of company organization. Now, by condemning Li Kuo-lien for having stood up against higher taxes, Ts'en made Li's cause against official control more popular. On February 3, with Li still in prison, his associates held a public meeting in which they successfully linked the earlier Rights Recovery Movement with the current campaign to demand management rights for the people.[30]

One crucial decision which emerged from the meeting was the formal endorsement of a low-priced share which even the student or the shop hand making an average of $3 (or 2.3 taels) a month could afford. One reason why none of the modern enterprises enjoyed mass subscription of their shares was the high cost of company shares. From Li Hung-chang's first joint-stock effort, the China Merchants' Steam Navigation Company in 1872, to Chou Hsueh-hsi's latest venture, the Chee Hsin Cement Company in 1906, the price per share was 100 taels. The Cantonese entrepreneurs realized that they needed mass participations to raise the huge sums, and that this might come about if the price per share were sufficiently low. Since late 1905, there had been several discussions on this issue. Proposals ranged from issuing lottery tickets to offering shares of very small value, at $2 each to be paid up in ten monthly installments.[31] The scheme finally adopted was a slightly larger $5 (or about 4 taels) share to be collected in $1, $1.50, and $2.50 installments over a twelve to eighteen months' period. Between February 3rd and 5th, pledges amounting to over $4 million were made as tens of thousands responded. By the end of February, $1,648,788, representing a like number of shares, had been collected as first installment payments. The campaign to raise a $20 million capital for a privately owned and run railway company was well on its way.[32]

The Kwangtung Canton-Hankow Railway Company formally petitioned Peking for *shang-pan* status. To keep up pressure on the government, all the new pledges that kept pouring in from Cantonese merchants residing overseas, in Hong Kong, and the other provinces were conditional on the company's receiving such a grant.[33]

Governor-general Ts'en Ch'un-hsuan, impressed by the popular response, helped overcome residual opposition from Peking. He supported the granting of *shang-pan* status as soon as the pledges on the first installment payments were honored and reputable directors and officers elected.[34] On April 25th, Cheng Kuan-ying, the well-established comprador and industrialist, was elected chief manager (*tsung-pan*). On June 21st, following the official grant of *shang-pan* status for ninety-nine years, Cheng announced that over $8.8 million had been received as first installment payments.[35] In just over four months, the railway company in Canton had raised an unprecedentedly large amount of capital. It had doubled its original goal of $20 million. Contrasted with Chang Chien's difficulties only a few years earlier in raising 250,000 taels—or about $300,000—without mass support, the scheme devised in Canton was an astounding success.

But the acquisition of private management rights through the forceful assertion of a popular movement did not end the controversy over the issues of control and direction of the company. During the next five years, the company was run as a *shang-pan* company, but those five years were filled with continual crises. First it was the legality of its elected officers. Factionalism among its shareholders and the contest between gentry and merchants followed. All these contributed to shareholder militancy and public disenchantment. And when allegations were made that the company accounts were not properly kept, and that corruption was rife among company officers, the provincial governments were provided with opportunities to reassert control. In mid-1911, the central government nationalized all private and semi-private railways partly because the Canton railway, like the other major private railway between Hankow and Szechwan, was a dismal failure. At the time of the takeover, the Canton company had received some $16 million, about $10 million of which had gone to build a mere forty-five miles of tracks.[36]

The first crisis was in full swing even as the company was officially granted *shang-pan* status. A group of Hong Kong shareholders, led by two comprador brothers and one *chü-jen* scholar, claimed that Cheng Kuan-ying and the other five managers forming the senior staff were not properly elected. Because they were chosen by the founders' committee composed of merchant leaders of the local guilds and charitable halls in Canton, the general body of shareholders had not been consulted.[37] Their campaign to oust Cheng Kuan-ying gained momentum when several Canton gentry joined forces with them. It appears that, of the six elected officers, only Hsu Ying-hung, a relative of the retired governor-general who had earlier fought for the company, was a gentry member. Hsu refused to serve, and his post went to another gentry, a former acting county magistrate named Chou Lin-shu. Neither of the two imprisoned gentry leaders, Li Kuo-lien or Liang Hsiao-shan, was offered any post, even though Li had once been proposed to head the company.[38] Little wonder then that the Canton gentry thought they were ill-served by the wealthier merchants.

Cheng Kuan-ying, in spite of his several ritualistic offers to resign, stayed on for another year as chief manager. The three Hong Kong leaders who tried to dismiss him were stripped of their shareholder membership by a general shareholders' meeting convened in July 1907.[39] Cheng's support came from Governor-general Ts'en and the Canton merchant community, especially the powerful leaders of the local charitable halls. Ts'en turned against the Hong Kong group and the local gentry because they attempted to by-pass his authority by appealing directly to Peking.[40] Ts'en also looked to the merchants to serve as a bulwark against Chang Chih-tung, for he feared that Chang might use his strong views on greater state control to interfere in the affairs of the Kwangtung company. Thus, he rejected British protests over the company's hiring of Belgian engineers by arguing that he was not bound by the loan agreement Chang had made with the Hong Kong and Shanghai Banking Corporation.[41]

Cheng's tenure as chief manager weakened considerably after Ts'en was replaced by Governor-general Chou Fu. The latter, who had close ties with Yuan Shih-k'ai, could not trust Cheng, for Cheng was a supporter of Yuan's industrial rival, Sheng Hsuan-huai. The same meeting that punished Cheng's detractors also elected Liang Ch'eng to replace him. Liang was a bureaucrat without any experience in industrial management. But he won the support of the shareholders because he was a Cantonese, and he successfully negotiated for the return of Chinese railway rights while serving as Chinese minister to Washington. Liang soon began, however, to doctor company accounts for his own benefit. Revelation of this and other scandalous activities within the company won support for the government's insistence upon closer supervision.

The immediate cause for official intervention, however, was

the increasing militancy of the shareholders. Traditionally, merchant and gentry owners who had delegated management responsibilities to others tended to be passive, uninvolved bystanders in the operation of the enterprise. But the "owners" of the Canton railway company were unique. Their number was literally in legions; and most of them had only a few shares. They also possessed a high level of political activism: they had been involved with the Rights Recovery Movement and had then agitated over Li Kuo-lien's arrest. They took seriously their newly won rights entitling them to vote and to introduce motions at company meetings. Many of their tactics were legal and commendable. They lobbied, they caucused, and they filibustered. But they also formed factions by setting up numerous shareholders' associations, which then became organs for articulate, literate leaders with self-serving motives to sway and influence the views and actions of small shareholders. Thus, in the several struggles between factions and with the management, their large number was employed to intimidate the opposition, to falsify ballot sheets, to cast votes several times over and, when all else failed, to pack the meeting halls in order to outshout and outfight the opposition.[42]

In early 1910, following a particularly noisy confrontation which effectively prevented the election of new officers, the government stepped in and worked out an amended set of rules, plugging up loopholes and restricting the shareholders' rights and privileges. Small shareholders were particularly affected when votes were limited only to those with one hundred shares.[43]

Government intervention, however, had begun much earlier. In December 1906, within days after Chou Fu had assumed his office as governor-general, he set up a Railway Bureau (T'ieh-lu kung-chü), ostensibly to coordinate all official dealings with the company. Then, taking advantage of complaints by the Hong Kong dissident shareholders about company finances, he ordered the bureau to audit the company's accounts.[44] This first audit exonerated the management, but barely had it been completed when Chou clashed again with the company over his right to appoint officials to become the next chief and associate managers. This involved a central issue in management control, and, when he prohibited the company from holding a shareholders' meeting originally scheduled for May 1907 to elect these new officers, government and company seemed set on another confrontation course. Fortunately, this was averted when Chou Fu was suddenly reassigned, and the two officials recommended to the throne declined the offer.[45]

But Liang Ch'eng, who was elected chief manager after the delayed meeting was reconvened, was unable to control the different factions within the management. As drawn up in 1906, the company organization was deliberately decentralized, with different managers in charge of contracts, land purchases, accounts, and engineering. The resulting confusion and inefficiency grew worse under the inexperienced Liang Ch'eng, for individual managers had already established their own fiefdoms of power by appointing their own staff and writing up their own budgets.[46] The founders' committee representing the Nine Charitable Halls became so discouraged that, for a time, it refused to use its influence over the local merchant community to collect the long overdue second installment payments of company shares. Although the committee relented in the end, the railway company never regained public enthusiasm, and managed to collect some 70 percent of the second payments only after a great deal of effort.[47]

Throughout 1908, there were also frequent allegations of corrupt practices. In one of the sessions held in December, the meeting broke up in disorder after one shareholder accused the management of graft, using concrete detail. He alleged that bidders with higher prices were given contracts because some of the directors were business partners of these contractors. According to one local reporter, the accusation "created a great sensation. Everyone present became angry, and the noise was deafening. Many rolled up their sleeves, prepared to participate in a melee with the directors."[48]

Internal chaos of this sort provided Governor-general Chang Chih-tung with the legitimacy to intervene openly in the affairs of the company. Since July 1908, Chang had been officially appointed Director-general of the entire Canton-Hankow Railway.[49] Several merchant leaders were already in favor of an official investigation.

Opposition came only after it was known that Chang intended to do much more. Early in 1909, Chang ordered the setting up of a Canton branch office of the Canton-Hankow Railway Administration. At first sight, this seemed to be a continuation of Chou Fu's short-lived and ineffective Railway Bureau. Chang's branch office, however, posed a far greater threat to the company's independence. As director-general, Chang already had theoretical power of supervision over the company. Now, by opening up an office in the same city as the company, whoever he appointed as head of the office would be in a position to turn that theoretical power of official supervision into practical one. Being close at hand, Chang's representative could exhort and direct the company on a day-to-day basis. Public suspicion that the branch office would indeed institutionalize official control increased when Chang ordered a pro-state control official who in 1906 had backed Ts'en's surtaxes to take charge of the Canton office. And his first order of business was to begin a thorough investigation of all company accounts and records.[50]

Taotai Wang Ping-en's appointment was confirmed in spite of vehement protests from Canton. Wang's report, released in August 1909, roundly condemned Liang Ch'eng and his staff of managers and engineers for gross mismanagement and embezzlement. Wang discovered among several abuses that the company accounts did not match those of the banks, that land purchases were recorded at inflated prices or replaced by bogus land deeds to cover up unaccountable expenditures, that many bridges and supporting walls were poorly constructed, and that officers were given outrageously large salaries.[51]

Wang's investigation was followed by two others conducted by Peking's Yu-ch'uan pu (Ministry of Communications and Posts) in 1910. The new commissions exposed more corrupt and inefficient practices.[52] However, the ministry failed to acquire merchant consent for the government to take over the railway. Meanwhile, Liang Ch'eng was indicted for embezzlement. But he fled to Peking and, through the influence of several Manchu princes, was never brought back to Canton to face his accusers.[53] The discredited *shang-pan* company dragged on for another year. When it was finally nationalized in mid-1911, most protestors in Canton were less agitated over the loss of private management than they were over the government decision to repay their investments by a mix of 60 percent in cash and 40 percent in bonds.

The Shanghai-Hangchow-Ningpo Railway's (Hu-Hang-Yung t'ieh-lu) record as a *shang-pan* company during the same period is in many ways strikingly similar to Canton's.[54] In late 1907, after mounting a massive, at times violent, campaign, the local gentry and merchant leaders recovered the rights of construction from a British company. Chinese legal arguments, based on the foreign company's delays in beginning work on the line, were less solid. The central government, however, was caught between two equally powerful forces: British diplomatic pressure on the one hand, and the threat of local insurrection on the other.[55] In the end, the government compromised by accepting a foreign loan while forcing the British company to return the management and ownership rights of the railway to the Chinese company.

Canton also provided a model for this lower Yangtze railway to raise capital. Initially, it tried to sell shares at $100 each, with some fractional shares at $10. In late 1907, as the two provincial companies picked up public support in the Rights Recovery Movement, they switched to $5 shares to be paid in five equal annual installments.[56] Consequently, Chekiang raised some $9 million and Kiangsu $4 million from wealthy gentry and merchants, workers, and school girls in modern schools.[57]

There were other parallels with the Kwangtung company. The Chekiang company was hit by corrupt practices, shoddy engineering work, management squabbles, and declining public support. In July 1909, after two years of glowing reports about its work in progress, the company's shareholders met to discuss its operating losses, allegations of land purchase abuses, and the growing number of delinquencies on installment payments. There were also numerous complaints about its chief manager, T'ang Shou-ch'ien, a scholar-official elected to the post in 1905 through his persistently outspoken leadership in the Rights Recovery Movement. Without denying that T'ang was hardworking and often effective, his critics complained that he was also crafty, arrogant, and inflexible. A factional attempt within the company to oust him, however, probably led by his associate manager, Liu Chin-tsao, failed. T'ang's powerful personality and his reputation as a progressive official who actively involved himself in the constitutional movement won him many loyal supporters, especially from among the provincial gentry already antagonistic to Peking. When T'ang offered to resign in order to appease his critics, they raised a vigorous campaign to retain him.[58] Thus reconfirmed, T'ang's eventual dismissal a year later by the central government once again brought into sharp focus the problem of state control in railway management. At issue was the meaning of *shang-pan* as understood by both the company and the state.

Government actions against T'ang Shou-ch'ien first took the form of gentle persuasion. In August 1909, barely two months after his reconfirmation by popular acclaim as chief manager, an imperial decree ordered him to resume full-time official duties and promoted him to be the provincial judge in faraway Yunnan. As this effectively took him out of the company's management, T'ang declined the offer, while his board of directors refused to hold a new election to select his replacement.[59]

It seems that T'ang had incurred Peking's displeasure as a result of his growing opposition to the British loan, in exchange for which the Chinese had recovered their railway rights. Under the 1908 agreement, money from the loan would go to the two provincial companies through the Yu-ch'uan pu, whose intermediary role was to ensure that the foreign bankers had no direct contact with, and hence could raise no issues of foreign control over, the railway companies. T'ang's company, however, had received less than one-fifth of what had been promised, for the Yu-ch'uan pu had skilfully diverted some of the funds into other projects. The British bankers, frustrated over their inability to control the use of the loan money, were withholding payment.[60]

Throughout the next twelve months, T'ang used a series of

delaying tactics to forestall Peking's efforts to transfer him. His declinings of reassignment were followed by ritualistic resignation offers in public. His supporters, in turn, took the cue by staging demonstrations pleading with him to stay.[61] Meanwhile, shareholders of the company forced the Yu-ch'uan pu to a showdown by voting to terminate the loan agreement and directing T'ang to proceed to Peking to settle the issue. Since the death of Chang Chih-tung in the summer of 1909, the recently established Yu-ch'uan pu had grown in power and influence because it now not only controlled huge sums of foreign loans but also supervised several railway companies. In August 1910, seizing upon T'ang's telegram to the Grand Council opposing the appointment of Sheng Hsuan-huai as Junior Vice-President of the Yu-ch'uan pu, an imperial edict summarily dismissed him as chief manager.[62]

T'ang Shou-ch'ien complied with this imperial decree. Over 1,200 shareholders then met in special session in Shanghai to discuss how the company should respond to this new form of state interference by imperial fiat. They decided that not even the throne could legally dismiss a company officer who had been properly elected. They cited Article 77 of the state's Company Laws, promulgated only a few years before, giving the rights of election and dismissal of company officers to each company's board of directors. Other meetings were held throughout September, some turning into mass demonstrations. One, reported in Ningpo, had over 10,000 people attending. It was evident that the local gentry and merchants viewed the central government with growing distrust. During the campaigns in 1907 and earlier, they were generally motivated by anti-imperialism and by a belief that Peking was too conciliatory to foreign powers. After 1908, denunciations at these mass meetings took on strong anti-Manchu sentiments; there were increasing suspicions that the court's interference in company affairs and the use of foreign loans were motivated by the desire to consolidate Manchu power at the capital.[63]

In 1910, backed by these popular expressions, the company approached the Chekiang governor, Tseng Yun, and the Provincial Assembly. The latter, the province's preparatory legislative body, agreed that no government could ignore its own statutory laws, especially at a time when the throne was encouraging constitutional government. The governor, who had first tried to stop the assembly from debating the issue, finally consented to transmit its resolution officially to the Yu-ch'uan pu. The assembly had threatened to stop all its official business.[64]

But the ministry had already responded to the company's public declaration challenging the state's right to intervene so directly in the affairs of a *shang-pan* enterprise. Its reply, dated September 24th, reiterated Chang Chih-tung's standard argument that the railways involved sovereignty rights (*kuo-ch'üan*); hence even those railway companies with *shang-pan* status remained tied to the government in a special relationship. Although Article 77 gave private companies the power to elect and dismiss company officers, yet each of the chief and associate managers of the railway companies, after so elected, received his formal appointment from the ministry. The Yu-ch'uan pu concluded that railway companies were "state-controlled companies" (*kuan-ch'ih kung-ssu*), and that the dismissal order would stay.[65]

The Chekiang company's shareholders in Shanghai met again. They voted to send a delegation to Peking to present their case directly and to resolve the issue of the British loan with the ministry. But nothing was resolved in the meetings which followed between the delegation and the ministry's senior vice-president. The ministry insisted that Article 77 was inoperative because T'ang owed his appointment ultimately to the emperor, who authorized it after the ministry had transmitted the wishes of the company shareholders. The emperor therefore had the authority also to remove him. On the question of the foreign loan, the ministry claimed that it was not competent to discuss terminating it since to do so would require a new round of diplomatic negotiations. Thus the matter had to be referred to the Wai-wu pu (Ministry of Foreign Affairs). But the president of the Wai-wu pu was conveniently away from Peking, and the delegation could find no person of authority to settle the issue with them.[66]

It seems that both the government and the company opted

for the rule of law when it suited them. Under the circumstances, only power mattered. But the only form of power—popular support—the company could claim was petering out. As the contest dragged on, the provincial gentry and merchant leadership became even more alienated from the central government. What prevented the mass meetings from breaking into violent demonstrations was the release of new unsavory information about the company. It changed the public mood from support to cynicism. During 1909 and 1910, similar conflicts were also going on in Canton. As more became known about company mismanagement and individual managers' criminal practices, more and more people came to view *shang-pan* not as a right to be won for the public good, but as a license to enrich company directors and managers. Although T'ang Shou-ch'ien was not another Liang Ch'eng—T'ang's sin was trying to acquire more power rather than more personal wealth—both his and the company's reputation suffered. The Chekiang Railway Company retained its fuzzy *shang-pan* status for a while longer. Then it was taken over by the state as part of the nationwide nationalization of railways.

Merchant-Owned Private Enterprises

One might argue that the Kwangtung and the Chekiang railways failed because they could not sever their links with officialdom. In this respect, *shang-pan* railway companies were no different from the other types of modern enterprises which also claimed *shang-pan* status. There were, however, a few modern industries that had no direct connection with the official world. Instead, they owed their origin and spirit to forces outside the traditional society. They included the phenomenal rise of such department stores as the Sincere Company and the Wing On Company, as well as the equally successful Nan-yang Brothers' Tobacco Company. All of them started on "foreign soil," first in Hong Kong and then in the International Settlement in Shanghai. Their original promoters, the Mas, the Ts'ais (Choys), the Kuos, and the Chiens (Kans), were all Cantonese who had made money and learned their entrepreneurial skills as overseas merchants trading in Australia, Vietnam, and

Japan. The Wing On Company, founded in Hong Kong in 1907 by Kuo Lo (James Gocklock) and his brother Kuo Chuang (Philip Gockchin), was modeled upon an Australian department store they had seen while running a fruit shop in Sydney.[67] During this period, these entrepreneurs had no contact with the Chinese official-entrepreneurs and needed none of their support. These two groups of men lived in different social worlds. Even their economic worlds rarely overlapped. Much interaction came later, as these companies expanded into the hinterland and branched out into a host of other businesses such as insurance and banking. Both these developments took place from the late 'teens onward, when the vastly different political context meant a generally different relationship between officials and merchants.

The Mou-hsin Flour Mill (Mou-hsin mien-fen ch'ang) represents one other group of private modern enterprises that successfully minimized official contacts. It is also the more typical because it grew on native Chinese soil from the traditional merchant background. Begun in 1901, this mill owed its origin to two brothers, Jung Tsung-ching (1872–1938) and Jung Teh-sheng (1875–?1950s) of Wusih, Kiangsu. Basically merchants, they had some official affiliations. Their father was a minor tax collector in Kwangtung in the employ of a kinsman and patron, Chu Chung-fu, a junior official in the provincial likin bureau. Teh-sheng purchased the minor gentry title of *chien-sheng* and spent some four years in Kwangtung holding a minor bureaucratic post through the help of his father. In their outlook and inclination, however, the Jungs were not members of the gentry or official class. The father sent the older son to a blacksmith's shop to be an apprentice and the younger one to school. The latter preferred learning a trade; ultimately, both of them spent three years as apprentices in two local banks (*ch'ien-chuang*) in Shanghai.[68]

Upon completing their apprenticeship, Jung Teh-sheng went to Kwangtung to be a minor bureaucrat, while the older brother, Tsung-ching, continued to work in a local bank in Shanghai. Then sometime during 1897–98, while in Shanghai together, the senior

Jung and the two brothers decided to invite a few friends to open a local bank of their own. But it made little profit during the first few years. The father died soon after the bank was opened, and the two brothers, both only in their twenties, could not command the respect of their colleagues or gain the trust of their clients. Eventually, the other investors sold all their shares to the Jung brothers. In 1899, their family patron, Chu Chung-fu, recommended Jung Teh-sheng as chief accountant at a supplementary tax bureau in Kungtung. This re-entry into the bureaucratic world lasted only briefly, for Jung lost his job when the tax collection was assigned to merchant tax farmers.[69]

This resorting to tax farming apparently affected Chu Chung-fu as well. He retired to Shanghai where he told his friends that he was tired of looking for another official post and that he would like to go into some modern industry. The Jung brothers quickly responded by persuading him to help them raise money for a flour mill. Jung Teh-sheng had discovered that, although there was a growing market, flour was still tax exempt because it was still regarded as an imported item strictly for foreigners' consumption. There was little competition, only four mills having been founded: one each in Tientsin and Wuhu, two in Shanghai (one American-owned and the second owned by Sun To-shen). Chu and the Jung brothers were, however, complete outsiders (*wai-hang*), not knowing what machinery was needed and how much the whole operation would cost. None of the mills they approached would allow them to inspect their plants. They made inquiries at one foreign firm importing American machinery and were told that they would need some 80,000 taels for machinery alone in order to start a small-sized factory. This was far too expensive for a competitive venture. Finally, they found some British-made motors to run four French-made stone grinders. Altogether, they cost less than 20,000 taels.

Although the machinery was modern, the management structure followed the traditional mode. It was a partnership of ten shares of 3,000 taels each. Chu and one of his friends, Wu Yung-mou, supplied 15,000 taels, or half the total. The two Jung brothers provided money for two shares. A relative, Jung Pin-chih, accepted another share, and a small number of other relatives and friends took up the remaining two shares split up into fractions. The total 30,000 taels capital, however, was found to be inadequate even before the mill was launched. Late in 1901, three more shares were added, and they apparently came from the Jung brothers themselves. Their banks in Shanghai and Wusih had become very profitable, and all their profits, 4,900 taels for 1901 and 5,000 taels for 1902, were invested in the mill. Thus, from their original two shares, they had, by 1902, become the mill's largest partners.

In 1903, with the banks again making good profits, the Jung brothers had another opportunity to increase their share. Chu had lost his son, and he decided to return to Canton where the provincial government had resumed the tax collection. Since he wanted to be rid of his shares, the Jung brothers bought the entire 15,000 taels' worth. Then with the help of other friends, they raised the capital by another 11,000 taels to a total of 50,000 taels. The name of the company, which had begun as Pao-feng, was changed to Mou-hsin. These reorganizations were just completed when the Russo-Japanese war began. That increased the demand for flour, and the mill began to make money.[70]

The Jung brothers' entrepreneurial talents were a mixture of the old and the new. Jung Teh-sheng acknowledged that he aspired to be a tax collector because he believed that he could earn more in that capacity than as a small traditional banker. He confessed that his initial interest in modern industry was aroused after he had read a translation of the biographies of "Ten Wealthy Men in America."

Both brothers were extremely superstitious. No major business decisions were made without consulting their trusted fortunetellers. Part of their traditional make-up, however, was simple honesty. After a bad flood in 1911, they threw away all their mildewed flour, absorbed the loss, then gradually won a larger and larger clientele while their competitors lost out because they had mixed their bad flour with some fresh.[71]

They were also not beneath bribing a foreman of a rival company to take Jung Teh-sheng in disguise to find out the type of machines used. Teh-sheng had apparently acquired some basic knowledge of flour-mill machinery. In 1904, the company was ready to buy something better than the original stone grinders. After Teh-sheng had seen his competitor's machines and had memorized what they could do, he then went on to get six new British steel grinders at a bargain price. The model was new, and the British importers were anxious to try them out in China. They turned out to be a great success, for the improved and increased product in 1905 yielded the mill a profit of 66,000 taels for that year.[72]

This profit, together with some more earnings from their banks, was again plowed back into the mill. On January 11, 1905, when the Mou-hsin Flour Mill became the fourth enterprise to register with the central government as a private corporation of limited liability, it had already announced its intention to raise its capital to 60,000 taels.[73]

The Jung brothers then tried to branch out into another field of modern enterprise. Around 1906 and 1907, they invited their friends and relatives to set up a cotton mill in Wusih. Their investment capital came from their flour mill profit for these years. The market fell, however, following the end of the Russo-Japanese War. Faced with an uncertain future, they quickly withdrew and then transferred their money back to the flour mill. They then waited until 1915 before they launched a second, and this time successful, venture into the cotton-spinning industry. Meanwhile, their flour enterprise continued to prosper. In 1908, they established a second factory in Wusih. It was expanded in 1910 and again in 1914. With the outbreak of World War I, flour imports ceased, and the mill grew by leaps and bounds, branching into Shanghai and Hankow. By 1929, the Jung brothers controlled some twelve factories, which turned out 100,000 bags a day, representing one-sixth of China's total flour output produced by machine-run factories. In 1902, when it first began operation, it had produced only 300 bags a day.[74]

The Jung brothers were the first traditional merchants to make a successful switch into modern industry with a bare minimum of official sponsorship and financial support. Back in 1883, Chu Ta-ch'un had successfully set up a $100,000 privately owned and run machine shop in Shanghai called the Yuan-chang Machine Factory. He then went into other industries, including textiles, paper, rice, and flour mills. But Chu was a comprador.[75] On the other hand, the Jung brothers built up their mill from money they had saved from their local bank, as well as from the mill's profit which they plowed back consistently.

They had, however, some help from bureaucratic sources. First, Chu Chung-fu, a minor official, supplied half the mill's original capital even though he took it all back two years later. Chu's funds were crucial in that initial period when the brothers had very limited resources. More important, Chu's participation probably gave the venture that needed lift of prestige and assurance so that the Jung brothers could persuade their friends and relatives to put in their investments. Second, they ran into bureaucratic opposition while building their plant. Local gentry, supported by local officials, complained about its tall chimney which, by the rules of geomancy, might bring disaster upon the community. Although available records do not tell what role Chu played in the negotiations that followed, it would be safe to assume that he helped considerably in drawing up the final settlement, which allowed the plant to be built with only small restrictions.[76] Third, there was the minor bureaucratic background of the Jung family itself. Both the father and the younger brother had been minor bureaucrats for some time. The money they acquired as tax collectors presumably made up some, if not most, of their initial investment in the local bank and then in the flour mill.

After these "bureaucratic influences" are taken into account, however, one must conclude that the success of the Mou-hsin Flour Mill represents a new departure for traditional Chinese merchants. Perhaps even more important than the Jung brothers' entrepreneurial behavior, both traditional and new, was the chemistry that existed between the two brothers while working as a team. Jung Tsung-ching was slow, less imaginative, but solid and a good and honest manager. On the other hand, Jung Teh-sheng was quick of mind, highly imaginative, aggressive, and ready to learn new ways. They also provided long-term stability and a lack of factionalism for the management at the top, thus avoiding two problems that plagued so many of the other industrial and commercial ventures in China at this time.

The Jung brothers' type of unfettered private modern enterprise was not common during the late Ch'ing, but it set a pattern for others to follow later on. It is questionable whether it provided a real breakthrough on the issue of state control. The Mou-hsin Flour Mill during these years had rather insignificant capital–in tens of thousands of taels as opposed to Chang Chien's Dah Sun, ten times larger, or Chou Hsueh-hsi's Chee Hsin, a hundred times larger. In the political context of the time, running a large modern enterprise required official protection. But protection almost invariably meant some form of state control. The few exceptions were a small number of enterprises managed by a few official-entrepreneurs like Chou Hsueh-hsi and Chang Chien. Each succeeded by practically merging his several identities as official supervisor, manager, and investor into one. But even they did not totally escape official–as opposed to state–control. Chang Chien constantly needed the support of Governor-general Liu K'un-i, while Chou Hsueh-hsi was able to carry on only so long as he enjoyed the confidence of Governor-general Yuan Shih-k'ai. Moreover, there was one other major limitation. Although Chou and Chang with their extensive official connections were able to raise far more capital than the Jung brothers, neither group attracted a sufficiently broad base of investors to participate in modern enterprise.

For a while during the 1900s, it appeared that the promoters of private railways had stumbled upon a strategy which, in one stroke, would eliminate both hurdles–excessive control and inadequate funding. By appealing to an aroused populace's sense of national pride and outrage against Western encroachment, these promoters successfully organized widespread public subscription campaigns, raising several millions of taels as investment capital.

The same campaigns also generated such a popular movement of potentially revolutionary force that the state was driven out of the railways.

Unfortunately, the new private management did not produce good managers. Many shareholders, already politicized and very concerned about their ownership rights, turned factious and meddlesome. Corruption among managers and directors followed, and, as the private railways lost public support, the state stepped in to re-impose control. Consequently, all major modern industries attempted during the late Ch'ing, irrespective of whether they were *kuan-tu shang-pan, kuan-shang ho-pan,* or *shang-pan,* remained in the hands of the state or of individual officials.

One feature of state control that remained constant throughout this period was its exercise by the provincial authorities. For example, it was Yuan Shih-k'ai's authority and power as Governor-general of Chihli and Superintendent of Trade for the Northern Ports that permitted Chou Hsueh-hsi to benefit his own industry. However, during the last few years of the Ch'ing dynasty, the central government began adopting a radical overhaul of the central bureaucracy. Among the several new ministries established between 1902 and 1907, three specifically dealt with commerce and modern industry. After a century of gradual decline vis-à-vis the provinces, the central government's attempt to reassert supremacy through regaining control over the direction of modern enterprise highlights the persistent problem of conflict and competition between the center and the region.

PART THREE

THE CENTRAL GOVERNMENT: AN UNSUCCESSFUL CHALLENGE

Chapter Eight

THE FOUNDING OF NEW MINISTRIES

The domination of modern enterprise by provincial authorities functioned under a number of inherent limitations. First, most provincial officials rotated from post to post. Li Hung-chang was able to promote many modern industries because he did not have to move about for a crucial quarter of a century—between 1870 and 1895. But Li, and to a lesser extent Chang Chih-tung, were major exceptions. Most industrial sponsors had no long-term tenure, and their efforts were often repudiated by those who succeeded them. Second, although the central government did not have the money to promote large industries on its own, it retained the authority to approve how the various categories of revenue collected in the provinces were to be spent or distributed.

To take the case of the Hanyang Ironworks, Chang Chih-tung between 1890 and 1894 made various appropriations from the revenue resources of Kwangtung and Hupei. Each time, he submitted his request to the Hu pu (Ministry of Finance) for approval. However, once permission was given, the actual disbursement and all the patronage that went with it were under Chang's authorization. Such a diffusion of authority between the central and regional governments led to an inability of all participants to plan a list of priorities on a national scale for the various industries to develop in an orderly manner.

It is doubtful that the central government was aware of this kind of weakness in its overall drive for modern industry, for the concept of economic planning was not a topic of intellectual debate at this time. There were, however, persistent efforts to reclaim state control from the provinces. These attempts were regarded as a means of restoring the balance of power between central and regional authorities. But the central government throughout the nineteenth century was heavily dependent on the provincial leaders for military defense and fiscal solvency. Moreover, given the progressively worsening quality of their personnel during the late Ch'ing, the ministries in Peking could not have performed better in sponsoring modern industry than the provincial authorities.

After 1900, the contest was renewed with energy and ingenuity. Almost by chance, the political leadership in Peking stumbled on a new way to confront provincial officials when it turned inwards to question its entire bureaucratic structure.

The Bureaucratic Structure: Trauma of Change

Since the Opium War, the Chinese had responded to the challenge from the West by making a series of adaptations. The gradual acceptance of guns and gunboats, spindles and railways was followed by the adoption of institutional changes to accommodate the new technology. These activities required no drastic revision of the value system and were rationalized, in Chang Chih-tung's epigrammatic phrase, as "Chinese learning for the essence; Western learning for practical use."

Between 1895 and 1900, however, China was successively defeated on the battlefield by Japan, threatened with political extinction by Western imperialism, and punished ignominously for sponsoring the anti-foreign Boxers. These events put an end to the old complacency about the Chinese political structure and forced the central government to introduce fundamental reforms on two levels. First, it authorized discussions for a constitution; and second, it launched a major overhaul of the central bureaucracy.[1]

While the first program seemed radical, the second was even more so. Constitutional reform promised to change the Chinese political order drastically in the long run, yet to the men in power in Peking at the time the creation of new ministries and the reorganization or abolition of old ones had the greater immediate impact. Constitutionalists and government officials debated the actual content of a new constitution which would not come into force until some future time. Meanwhile, hundreds of officials in Peking were being reassigned to new posts where they would have to find new bases of power and influence. Hundreds of others felt uncertain as they waited for reassignment. In 1906, when the reorganized Nung-kung-shang pu (Ministry of Agriculture, Industry, and Commerce) absorbed some of the jurisdiction of the old Kung pu (Ministry of Works), which then ceased to exist, some 400 officials were not reassigned. Many memorials on their behalf petitioned the throne to authorize their transfer to the Nung-kung-shang pu. Most of them were presumably reassigned, but all had to wait for the deliberation of its president, Tsai-chen.[2]

In addition to the real fright and confusion the overhaul created among officials, its ideological commitment was also radical. For the first time since the T'ang dynasty, the "Six Ministries" (Liu-pu) model was dismantled to make way for a different bureaucratic system modeled after Japan and the West. This new bureaucracy, by acquiring new areas of management, promised to direct national policies from a new orientation. The old Six Ministries were concerned with coordination. Ordinarily, they left the initiatives in provincial affairs to the governors-general and governors.[3] But now, the new ministries were asked to be much more assertive, to affirm the authority of command for the central government. Implicit also was a general shift away from the traditional ideal that the state ruled in order to maintain peace and order, and to collect taxes. The new state sought to play a more active and managerial role by centralizeing control. It looked to the new and expanded ministries to provide a more efficient institutional means for achieving this ideal.

These new directions of the central bureaucracy soon became a part of the central government's efforts to counter the predominance of the provincial authorities. In the area of commerce and industry, it organized a new ministry of commerce, set up specialized agencies, launched branch bureaus in the provinces, and encouraged private merchants to form chambers of commerce. In these activities, conflicts between Peking and the provinces were inevitable. There was no open defiance; that came a decade later with the rise of warlordism in China. But many provincial officials, in spite of their strong sympathy with bureaucratic modernization, allowed their personal interest in retaining power to get the better of them. They remained entrenched in their old bureaucracy through administrative delays, or they turned the new bureaucracy to their own benefit by means of the revenues they still controlled. Moreover, the new ministry's power and influence were circumscribed by opposition from the older ministries in Peking.

The first break from the Six Ministries bureaucratic model was the creation of the Wai-wu pu (Ministry of Foreign Affairs) on July 24, 1901. In the past, foreign affairs were conducted by either the Li-fan yuan (Bureau of Dependencies) or the Li pu (Ministry of Rites). After 1861, as a result of Western demands, a committee called the Tsungli Yamen was organized under the Grand Council, composed of senior officials all of whom had concurrent posts in the government. But, despite its prominent membership, it was by nature an ad hoc organization. As late as 1890, its existence was ignored by the authoritative *Ta-Ch'ing chin-shen ch'uan-shu* (Complete directory of the Ch'ing officials and titled notables). The Tsungli Yamen's jurisdiction also was limited. It handled only those foreign matters that occurred in the capital, while those from the provinces were still largely left in the hands of a number of governors-general, especially the two in Tientsin and Nanking, who held concurrent posts as the Pei-yang and Nan-yang commissioners.[4]

In the nineteenth-century context, the institutional justification for the Tsungli Yamen may be found in another ad hoc committee called the Reorganization Bureau (Shan-hou chü) at the provincial level. These bureaus were created during times of war or natural calamity to draw together the senior officials of a province for concerted action. One example is the powerful Kwangtung shang-hou chü which began during the Taiping Rebellion and persisted till almost the end of the dynasty. In this sense, the Tsungli Yamen represented a reaffirmation by the state not to tamper with the traditional political structure. In 1901, its demise and substitution by the Wai-wu pu, a full-fledged ministry, represented the state's acceptance that the traditional bureaucratic structure was no longer adequate to cope with foreign demands. But just as this first break was made in an area where the Chinese state felt most vulnerable—its relations with foreign powers—a second innovative ministry, the Shang pu (Ministry of Commerce), established two years later, was created in another area of equally pressing concern to the state.

The Founding of the Shang Pu

Following the failure of the Boxer uprising, a mollified court from Sian called upon high provincial and metropolitan officials to come up with suggestions for a program of reform. On January 8, 1901, an imperial decree asked for a deeper understanding of European methods in the art of government. By April 23rd, a Board of State Affairs (Cheng-wu ch'u) was set up to collect reform proposals and to make selections for implementation.[5]

Many memorials in response stressed the need to protect mercantile enterprises. Hsu Ying-kuei, the Governor-general of Fukien and Chekiang, argued that, while foreign merchants played a central role in their national finances, Chinese merchants "are everywhere given the lowest status, . . . even though they do not lag behind their Western counterparts in their contributions to public service." Because they feared official exactions, they hid their accumulated wealth and dared not speak out. Hsu suggested that a survey of merchant capital should be made. All would be given protection while those with sizeable capital should be given various official titles.[6]

Hsu's memorial, representative of much of the official thinking from the provinces, is more significant for what he left out than what he put in. No provincial officials, in spite of the universal concern for "encouraging commercial and industrial affairs," suggested the setting up of a ministry to direct these affairs from the capital. Yuan Shih-k'ai reportedly discussed with Chang Chih-tung the possibility of establishing a Bureau of Commercial Affairs (Shang chü) with rather specific responsibilities in Peking. Presumably, as Governor-general of Chihli, Yuan expected that such a bureau would be under his control.

The notion of a national ministry of commerce had been expressed for quite some time. Cheng Kuan-ying, the merchant-intellectual, had so advocated in his book *Sheng-shih wei-yen* (Warnings to a seemingly prosperous age), published in the 1880s.[7] In 1895, Ho Ch'i and Hu Li-yuan, two intellectuals closely affiliated with the merchants in Hong Kong, had also discussed the need to increase the traditional six ministries to eight, the two new ones being for commerce and foreign affairs.[8] These discussions, however, received no official response. When the court was finally won over to this idea, the encouragement came from members of the imperial clan and a central government official.

Sheng Hsuan-huai, whose official position and court rank were rising rapidly in the first months following the Boxer uprising, contributed some of the initial impetus. Sheng's interest in such a venture is understandable. From the beginning of his official career under Li Hung-chang, he had been involved with the new textile, shipping, telegraph, and railway industries. But he had no independent power base, while the good graces of Chang Chih-tung, his other patron, were not always dependable. In 1901, as a Vice-Director of the Imperial Clan Court (*tsung-jen-fu fu-ch'eng*), he was appointed associate imperial commissioner for negotiating commercial treaties (*hui-pan shang-wu ta-ch'en*).[9] Sometime in 1902, while in Shanghai as imperial commissioner, he pointed out that the kind of appointment he was holding, which dealt with specific issues of trade, was totally inadequate. He suggested the setting up of a permanent ministry at the nation's capital to direct industrial and trade affairs.[10]

Sheng might have done no more than simply second Prince Ch'un, the brother of the Kuang-hsu Emperor and later regent. Between June and November 1901, the prince headed a mission to Germany to apologize for the Boxer uprising. On his way, he met many overseas Chinese merchants. They apparently had a great impact on him, for he began to champion a pro-mercantile policy. Before he made the trip, his attitude toward commerce and industry was not known. On the eve of his arrival in Hong Kong, the local newspaper *Hua-tzu jih-pao* issued an editorial inviting the prince to receive local merchants. Until then, the editorial observed, high officials while passing through a place received only local officials and did not care to meet with local merchants. It reminded Prince Ch'un that Western merchants entertained and were entertained by high officials of their own countries. This practice, the editorial added, had even been extended to Chinese merchants and foreign dignitaries. Prince Ch'un needed no further reminders. Two days later, the same newspaper enthusiastically reported the prince's courtesy call on the premises of the Chinese Merchant Association.[11]

From Singapore and Malaya came similar reports of mutual good will between the prince and the merchant community.[12] While in Malaya, Wu T'ung-lin, a Szechwanese merchant, presented Prince Ch'un with a lengthy proposal of reform. Wu had become an expert on many Western skills through extensive travels in Southeast Asia. The prince was apparently impressed by him and later corresponded with him about the setting up of the Shang pu. In 1902, Wu was asked to return to Peking to work for the Ministry of Foreign Affairs and later for the Shang pu.[13] The prince also stopped at Shanghai on his way home. He met more merchant leaders, visited some silk, cotton, and paper-making factories, then attended a banquet held in his honor by the merchant community.[14]

Soon after his return to the capital, Prince Ch'un proposed that the throne set up the Shang pu. The case was referred to the Grand Council which in turn consulted Sheng Hsuan-huai. Meanwhile, Prince Ch'un was supported by another member of the imperial clan, Tsai-chen, who submitted a similar proposal, complete with suggested regulations to the Board of State Affairs. Tsai-chen, the son of the powerful Prince Ch'ing, spent a good part of 1902 abroad. First, he represented China at King Edward VII's coronation ceremony, then traveled to Japan via America at the invitation of the Japanese Foreign Ministry. He was most impressed by Japanese industrial development.[15]

The *Hua-tzu jih-pao,* which normally represented the Cantonese merchants' viewpoint, supported these proposals. Its editorial of April 8, 1902 observed that the Pei-yang and Nan-yang commissioners had assumed office without making a careful examination of trade. It applauded Prince Ch'un for having realized the importance of commercial affairs in the nation's economy, and noted that his proposal would stimulate trade. The Foreign Ministry's agent in Vladivostok reported equal enthusiasm from the Chinese merchant community there. From Malaya, Wu T'ung-lin wrote to Prince Ch'un, letting him know that he had received many inquiries from his merchant friends in Shanghai, Hankow, Amoy, Swatow, Hong Kong, Singapore, Kuala Lumpur, and Penang. They all wanted to learn more about the government's intentions in this matter.[16]

Many officials in Peking, on the other hand, were skeptical. Led by Grand Councillor Jung-lu, they argued that the ground had not been sufficiently prepared to improve relations between merchants and officials. China still lacked a blueprint for commercial and industrial development. Such an institutional change would only create new sinecures at a time when revenue was running low. Another line of attack pointed out that the new Shang pu, if set up, would infringe upon the jurisdiction of the two Pei-yang and Nan-yang commissioners, as well as of the imperial commissioner in charge of commercial treaty negotiations. These criticisms persisted, reaching a crescendo a few months after the ministry was opened.[17] But proposals for the new ministry had gained two powerful supporters—the empress dowager and Prince Ch'ing. Also symbolic of the times was the financial support of Chang Pi-shih. Chang, a wealthy overseas Chinese merchant and one-time Consul-general at Singapore, had returned to China at Sheng Hsuan-huai's invitation to invest in a variety of industries. In 1903 he apparently promised to contribute the princely sum of 200,000 taels for a commercial school to be run by the new ministry. It was also understood that he would receive the rank of vice-president (*shih-lang*) of the ministry.[18]

On April 22, 1903, eleven days following Jung-lu's death, the court suddenly ordered Tsai-chen, Yuan Shih-k'ai, and Wu T'ing-fang to form a preparatory committee. They were to lay down a set of industrial and commercial regulations and to make proposals on how to promote industry and commerce.[19] Wu T'ing-fang, a legal expert educated in England, was immediately put to work. They soon realized that too much time would be needed to compile a system of commercial laws. In order to get the ministry started, the committee decided to draw up its structural and regulatory rules first. These preliminaries were quickly worked out, and, on September 26, 1903, the Shang pu was officially launched.

The New Ministry Under Challenge

The haste with which the Shang pu was set up was a true reflection of the state of mind of its proponents. Their main interest was in executing what appeared to them to be reform measures, and little time was given to anticipating the consequences that these measures might bring. There was little debate, and differences were not thrashed out. According to one report, the empress dowager expressed impatience when, during the summer of 1903, the Board of State Affairs wanted to study the matter further. She then personally gave the order to expedite the ministry's establishment proceedings.[20] As a result, the Shang pu was bogged down by conflicting claims of jurisdiction and the lack of sufficient funding almost as soon as it began operation.

The jealousies and criticisms it triggered can be better understood when one examines the size, scope, and manner of its operations as authorized by the September 26th imperial edict. The Shang pu had four departments (*ssu*) with the following functions:

1. The Department of Trade (Pao-hui ssu) would manage commerce and commercial schools, give protection to merchants, and award patent rights and monopolies.
2. The Department of Agriculture and Forestry (P'ing-chün ssu) would promote and manage all land utilization and reclamation, farming, sericulture, and afforestation.
3. The Department of Industry (T'ung-i ssu) would manage all industrial projects, machinery, railways, steamships, mining, and road construction.
4. The Department of Auditing (Hui-chi ssu) would manage tax, revenue, banking, currency, trade and industrial fairs, standardize weights and measures, and settle commercial and industrial litigations.[21]

Unlike the other new ministry, the Wai-wu pu, whose jurisdiction was better defined, the scope of jurisdiction claimed by the

Shang pu was much more disturbing to a large number of establishments in the capital. Thus, its Auditing Department was presumed to have authority in areas of fiscal policy and management which traditionally belonged to the Hu pu. Equally ominous was its implied mandate to take over all major commercial and industrial programs delegated among the six old ministries. As soon as the Shang pu was opened, its junior vice-president, Ch'en Pi, went to the Hu pu to discuss the transfer of the Salt Administration and the Mint Office. The Shang pu also tried to take over the Maritime Customs which was lodged with the Wai-wu pu. But neither the Hu pu nor the Wai-wu pu agreed to the transfer.[22]

However, these efforts by the Shang pu were not taken lightly. President Tsai-chen had powerful backing from his father, Prince Ch'ing, who, as head of the newly formed Committee of Finance (Ts'ai-cheng ch'u), was writing up a general reform of state finances. It was even rumored that Prince Ch'ing intended to put this powerful committee under the Shang pu's jurisdiction.[23]

The new ministry's overall responsibility for commerce and industry also excluded the need for any more commissioners of trade for the Pei-yang and Nan-yang ports, imperial commissioners to negotiate commercial treaties (*shang-yao ta-chen*), imperial commissioners for commercial affairs (*shang-wu ta-chen*), or imperial commissioners for railways (*t'ieh-lu ta-chen*).[24] Its founders were aware of the jurisdictional overlapping between these offices and the Shang pu, and tried to settle the problem before the ministry was established. Early in 1903, Chang Chih-tung and Yuan Shih-k'ai, the two imperial commissioners of commercial affairs, were consulted on this matter.[25] They could not find a solution; the commission continued as before. As for the specific responsibilities for commercial treaty negotiations, the Shang pu sidestepped the issue by appointing Commissioner Wu T'ing-fang to be senior vice-president in the new ministry. These negotiations, however, continued to elude the control of the ministry since Wu soon returned to the Ministry of Foreign Affairs. With the railways, the ministry fared no better. The various commissioners went on as before. In 1906, a new wave of reorganizations created the Ministry of Posts and Communications (Yu-ch'uan pu) to take charge of the railway enterprises.

The Shang pu's efforts to control salt and customs did not stem merely from a desire for greater power. It had insufficient funding and needed money. After 1900, with many sources of revenue earmarked to pay off foreign debts, the Chinese government was caught in a vicious circle. To reform it needed money. But the normal sources of revenue were already tremendously strained to maintain even the bare minimum of existing administrative needs. Only reform of a major order could tap and increase the national wealth and hence revenue. Yet where was the money for such a reform to be found? This was a problem that confronted the Shang pu from beginning to end.

The Shang pu began to set up its office with an appropriation of only 40,000 taels. Most of these went to remodel the ministry's building and to buy furniture and office equipment.[26] In the following year, the ministry received even less, its major source of income being the interest acquired from the customs deposits in Shanghai banks before they were disbursed for the Boxers' indemnity payments.[27] This practice seems to have persisted. In 1909, the Shang pu's successor ministry complained that its income varied from year to year, depending on fluctuating bank interest rates.[28]

In 1904, the ministry memorialized the throne for a regular annual budget of "several tens of thousands of taels."[29] When that failed, it tried to raise revenue for its own use by asking the court to approve a new stamp duty tax. Although the throne approved it, it was later called off because of merchant protest.[30] In 1905, the ministry's bid for a supplementary source of income was more successful. With Prince Ch'ing's backing, the throne agreed to let the Shang pu manage the Ch'ung-wen Gate Customs and Octroi (Hatamen)–tax collection stations on goods going in and out of Peking. The income from its management, however, was insufficient, and the ministry continued to propose new schemes to increase its income.[31]

The manner of the Shang pu's operations did not endear it to the rest of the bureaucracy in Peking. Its founders, who wanted to give the new ministry a modernistic look, promised to offer easy access to merchants. Gatekeepers were prohibited from receiving bribes as entrance fees, and the staff was paid on a new and raised scale.[32] Indeed, the whole tone of the new ministry, its style, and organization emphasized its new departure from the traditional structure. For a while, the court thought the new ministry should be headed by a controller who would be a senior member of the imperial clan. The president, as chief executive officer, would then be his assistant. This was the institutional format introduced by the newly established Wai-wu pu. This grandiose plan was finally dropped. But within the central government hierarchy, the ministry was assigned a place just behind the Wai-wu pu, and in front of the traditional ministries. At its inception, the ministry's prestige was indeed high. There were reports of officials scurrying and lobbying for positions.[33] It seems that all the Peking bookstores were stripped of any books on international trade, industry, geography, and accounting. So many persons were apparently cramming for the entrance examination given by the new ministry.[34]

The Shang pu's personnel was the subject of some concern to its founders. Early in 1903, Tai Hung-tzu, President of the Ministry of Rites, recommended Chang Pi-shih to a senior post in order to counter the attack of those critics who believed the new ministry lacked men who were knowledgeable in industry and trade.[35] Chang received the rank of vice-president, but it was not a substantive post. Similarly, Sheng Hsuan-huai was mentioned for the presidency because of his senior rank and long involvement in industrial supervision.[36] But after October 1902 he fell into political disfavor, losing his posts as Imperial Commissioner and Vice-President of the Ministry of Works. The imperial clansman Tsai-chen was named president, while Wu T'ing-fang was made senior vice-president. Wu, however, soon left to return to the Wai-wu pu.

Between 1903 and 1906, much of the routine work of the ministry was carried out by T'ang Wei-chih, who rose from senior councillor to acting president. In 1902, T'ang accompanied his patron, Tsai-chen, to Japan, and encouraged him to enter into the debate on commercial and industrial matters.[37] Another senior post went to Ch'en Pi, who began as junior vice-president, then succeeded Wu as senior vice-president. Ch'en, a Fukienese, had been the prefect of the metropolitan area, Shun-t'ien fu. Another appointee was Yang Shih-ch'i, who rose from junior secretary to vice-president by 1906. Yang stayed on until 1911 when Yuan Shih-k'ai chose him to be president of the Yu-ch'uan pu.

These appointments point to an interesting pattern. Except for Tsai-chen and Yang Shih-ch'i, all these senior officials came from the south and the lower Yangtze Valley. T'ang came from Kiangsu, Ch'en from Fukien, and Wu and Chang from the Canton delta via Penang. Yang, however, belonged to a prominent Anhwei official family—his elder brother, Yang Shih-hsiang, succeeded Yuan as governor-general of Chihli (1907–1909). He was chosen because Yuan had entrusted him with the supervision of the China Merchants' Steam Navigation Company and the Imperial Telegraph Administration, two enterprises Yuan Shih-k'ai had taken over from Sheng Hsuan-huai in 1902. Since the Shang pu claimed jurisdiction over these two companies, but failed to control them because of Yuan's objections, Tsai-chen did the next best thing. He appointed Yang to the ministry, so that through him the ministry had some control over these modern enterprises.

The Shang pu had been founded without the support of the provincial governors-general, who realized that any strong ministry in Peking directing the nation's commerce and industry would diminish their control over the same fields in their own provinces. They therefore did not resolve with the ministry the issues of jurisdiction. The various trade and industrial commissions they held concurrently went on as before. Moreover, the Shang pu was challenged by the other ministries at the capital. They, too, could not agree on conflicting jurisdictional claims. Thus, the Shang pu was weakened not only by the uncooperative provincial hierarchy, but also by a central bureaucracy confused and troubled with the trauma of change. In 1906, the throne ordered a general overhaul affecting all ministries. The Shang pu was drastically reorganized. It assumed a new name and lost a major portion of its jurisdiction.

The Nung-kung-shang Pu: Reorganization and Decline

On September 1, 1906, following the return of the four commissioners who had been abroad to study constitutionalism, the throne decreed that it would adopt the constitutional form of government as soon as the nation was sufficiently educated about its meaning. Meanwhile, the government would further revise its bureaucratic structure. On the next day, it appointed a committee headed by Prince Ch'ing to draw up the new bureaucracy.[38]

On November 6th, the committee announced its recommendations. It proposed to add new ministries, to reorganize or merge others in an effort to distinguish between executive, legislative, and judicial functions, and to make more logical divisions of responsibility among them.[39] Thus, the old Ministry of Punishments (Hsing pu) was reorganized into the Ministry of Justice (Fa pu) with only judicial responsibilities. The Shang pu, which had a Department of Industry and a Department of Agriculture, was considered misnamed. It merged with the Ministry of Works and became the Ministry of Agriculture, Industry, and Commerce (Nung-kung-shang pu). The Ministry of Works, however, had accumulated large areas of responsibility that had nothing to do with what its name implied. Thus, the Nung-kung-shang pu took over only those parts that were relevant to its concern: river works, drainage, construction and repair of coastal harbors, mining, measurement standards, and technical innovations. Other responsibilities like public construction went to the Ministry of the Interior, military provisions to the Ministry of the Army, and rituals or state functions to the Ministry of Rites.[40]

In theory, all these changes were based upon rational principles. In practice, however, the same principles, Ch'ing style, were open to various interpretations. In the case of the reorganization of the Shang pu, an unnecessary distinction was made between industrial efforts in the transport and communication system and those in other areas. Consequently, all matters concerning the railway, shipping, telegraph, and the postal service[41] went to a new Ministry of Posts and Communications (Yu-ch'uan pu).

The real reason behind this kind of jurisdictional gerrymander is still unclear. Undeniably, power politics and expediency rather than principle dictated these changes. At the time, railways, shipping, and telegraphs formed a major part of China's industrial enterprises. By taking them away from the Nung-kung-shang pu, the ministry was left with little else to manage, for the manufacturing and mining industries were solidly in the hands of the provincial officials. With so much of its power and authority at stake, Tsai-chen and his father, Prince Ch'ing, must have opposed it, for both of them sat on the committee recommending the change. But of this there is no record. It was probably a compromise solution between the central and the provincial government.[42] Thus, while imperial clansmen like Tsai-chen, and later P'u-hsu, retained control over the more limited Nung-kung-shang pu, Yuan Shih-k'ai assumed various degrees of control over the Yu-ch'uan pu between 1907–1911.

It has been suggested that by elevating the Yu-ch'uan pu, the central government was shifting away from the earlier emphasis on general promotion of modern enterprise—almost all of which eluded its control—to a new concerted effort in railway enterprises. Railway construction had a special appeal to the central government because an efficient communication network had strategic importance and required national planning. It also involved such an enormous capital outlay that only the central government, by borrowing from foreign bankers, could raise sufficient funds to sponsor it. Consequently railways became the crucial area for Peking to reassert its leadership in modern enterprise.[43]

If this was in fact the case, the central government failed badly. For the Yu-ch'uan pu did not become a stronghold of either the central bureaucracy or the Manchu princes. A brief listing of the ministry's senior officials would suggest that Yuan Shih-k'ai had far better control over it throughout the last years of the dynasty. Thus, among its presidents were Yuan's protégés Ch'en Pi, Hsu Shih-ch'ang, and T'ang Shao-i. The important railway department was headed by his protégé Liang Shih-i. The first president, Chang Po-hsi, was not under the influence of Yuan or other provincial interest groups. But he was counterbalanced by T'ang

Shao-i as his active senior vice-president.[44] Moreover Chang's term was short-lived; he apparently died of chagrin following a running feud with T'ang, who wanted to appoint wealthy Cantonese merchants to senior posts in the ministry.[45] Chang's successor, Ts'en Ch'un-hsuan, was also not indebted to Yuan or to any provincial interest. He was appointed by the empress dowager as her confidant. But Ts'en's term was equally brief. He left after he clashed bitterly with Prince Ch'ing.[46]

Prince Ch'ing's enmity toward Ts'en reminds one of the other central government officials' jealousy toward the Shang pu. In both cases, the central bureaucracy could not collaborate among themselves to form one single power bloc against the provincial authorities. Their disunity further weakened the Nung-kung-shang pu.

Contemporary observers were not slow to point out that the division of responsibilities between the Nung-kung-shang pu and the Yu-ch'uan pu was both inappropriate and illogical. As the progressive monthly magazine *Tung-fang tsa-chih* pointed out, railways, telegraphs, and shipping which the Yu-ch'uan pu controlled were, strictly speaking, commercial and industrial affairs.[47] This was borne out later in 1907 when the two ministries quarreled over the control of the China Merchants' Steam Navigation Company. The Yu-ch'uan pu claimed it was shipping and therefore under its jurisdiction; the Nung-kung-shang pu demurred, arguing that the company was under merchant management and, therefore, within its sphere of influence. The final compromise allowed the former to have supervision over the company's transportation policies such as operation routes, and the latter over its business operations–a decision that was full of confusion and patently unworkable.[48]

In the ensuing several months, reports were circulating that the Nung-kung-shang pu was trying to bring the Yu-ch'uan pu under its wing. One report describes how Prince Ch'ing, as head of the Board of State Affairs, argued that the two ministries should be amalgamated.[49] But shortly after that, his son, Tsai-chen, was forced out of the presidency. Tsai-chen had been accused by Censor Chao Ch'i-lin of accepting bribes for himself and for Prince Ch'ing.

Late in 1906, while passing through Tientsin on a mission to Manchuria, Tsai-shen apparently allowed a member of his retinue, Tuan Chih-kuei, to buy him a songstress at 12,000 taels. He was also accused of accepting 100,000 taels as a gift for the prince's birthday. Immediately thereafter, Tuan was promoted from taotai to acting governor of Heilungkiang without any apparent merit or cause. Although an imperial commission set up to look into these charges covered up for both father and son, Censor Chao and Acting Governor Tuan were cashiered. Then, on May 17, 1907, Tsai-chen bowed to official pressure and resigned.[50]

Even prior to his appointment as president, Tsai-chen had already acquired great notoriety as a dissolute and corrupt man. Undoubtedly his personal behavior and attitudes affected adversely the performance of the ministry. However, Tsai-chen had powerful political backing, which his successor P'u-hsu, although also an imperial clansman, did not have.[51] P'u-hsu emerged from obscurity in 1906 when he was appointed the first president of the newly formed Ministry of Finance. From 1907 to 1911, he stayed on as the Nung-kung-shang pu's president, competent but unable to arrest the ministry's decline from its initial Olympian heights.

One major source of its weakness was inadequate funding throughout the whole period. The Shang pu's tight budget persisted. In 1909 the Nung-kung-shang pu memorialized the throne for permission to sell "lottery-bond tickets." The first in the series was called "The Nung-kung-shang pu's Industrial Lottery" and had a goal of $10 million at $1 per ticket. One idea behind it was new. There would be cash prizes up to a total of $3 million. Those who received no cash prizes could, however, keep their tickets as bonds at 2.4 percent nominal annual interest until maturity in sixty years.[52]

Such an effort, aimed at sidestepping the usual moral criticism against lotteries, was still opposed by both the Censorate and the merchant-oriented newspaper *Hua-tzu jih-pao,* which argued that the lottery would encourage gambling and further drain the resources of the poor. In the end, the court did not come to a decision and, by delaying, killed the lottery.[53]

While the lottery-bond ticket was being debated, the Nung-kung-shang pu, in order to meet day-to-day administrative needs, asked the different chambers of commerce in the provinces to circulate three contribution books, at $300, $200, and $100 respectively. Each merchant member could then pledge a voluntary contribution by entering his name in one of the three books.[54]

Resorting to such begging-bowl-in-hand tactics in order to meet its routine expenses seems a far cry from the spirit in which the ministry was first conceived. As the 1909 memorial petitioning for the lottery-bond ticket sale pointed out, the ministry had never had the use of any ample and unrestricted funds to initiate industrial projects, or to help floundering industrial projects already underway. The tone of the memorial was set by its rhetorical opening statements: "Why is industry growing so slowly? Because capital is short. Why can't the Nung-kung-shang pu help? Because it, too, is short of funds."

Finally, one can trace the rise and fall of the Shang pu and the Nung-kung-shang pu by the various issues of the *Complete Directory of the Ch'ing Officials and Notables*—the authoritative official guides published every three months in Peking. Between 1903-1906, the Shang pu's roster consisted of the twelve office holders for the four departments plus a quota of thirty-six supernumerary officials. That quota was never more than two-thirds filled. For the period 1906 to 1911, these quotas were slightly increased as the reorganized Nung-kung-shang pu absorbed displaced officials from the Ministry of Works. But the new quotas were never met. When compared with the other ministries, they were far smaller. Small size was understandable at the beginning. But when the original quotas continued to be unfilled, much less expanded, then it became apparent that the ministry had little distinction. Between 1911 and 1912, the roster of officials expanded enormously. But this was also true of all the other ministries, and the extra personnel must be attributed to the unstable political order at the time and not to actual growth.

The same *Complete Directory* for the summer of 1907 also shows a new hierarchical positioning for the Nung-kung-shang pu.

Until then, this ministry and its predecessor, the Shang pu, had always been placed second, right below the Wai-wu pu. It was now put almost last, below all the reorganized traditional ministries. It may be argued that the Shang pu, by merging with the old Ministry of Works to form the Nung-kung-shang pu, came to assume the traditional place of the latter, which had always been last among the Six Ministries.[55] In fact, this was a clear acknowledgment that the Nung-kung-shang pu had fallen into relative insignificance.

Chapter Nine

PROGRAMS AND EXPERIMENTS AT THE CAPITAL

The Shang pu and the Nung-kung-shang pu did not succeed in their attempt to assume commanding roles in the nation's program of modern economic development. But they were not failures. That they were established and kept operating as full-fledged ministries was an important accomplishment. Their existence represented the state's acknowledgement that commerce and industry had a proper place in Chinese society. Their decline within the central bureaucratic structure did not mean that the state thought any less of modern enterprise. Rather, it reflected competition within the national government and Peking's inability to wrest control of modern industry from the various official patrons in the provinces.

Between 1903 and 1911, the two ministries organized and initiated a great many experiments and programs, which irrevocably brought many modern ideas of business and industrial practice to the Chinese entrepreneur. Many of these activities were channeled through innovating institutions modeled upon the West and Japan. Although they created no dramatic changes in the Chinese merchant's mentality, they prepared him for a greater awareness of the nature of modern business and the role governments could play in partnership and as protectors. Furthermore, the ministries' programs provided greater opportunities for officials and merchants to meet openly and to form relationships sanctioned by the state. In the long run, the programs helped to promote greater social equality between the two sides.

Two types of programs and experiments to be considered here are the numerous specialized agencies established at the capital with specific tasks to perform, and the series of official awards as incentives to investors and managers of modern enterprises. Both types sought to institutionalize official protection for the merchant. Indirectly, they also hoped to reclaim policy initiative for the national government.

Specialized Agencies

The Commercial Law Office (Shang-lü Kuan). This office predated the founding of the Shang pu. Authorized by an April 22, 1903 imperial decree, its initial task was to draft a comprehensive legal code for commerce and industry and to map out an organizational framework for the Shang pu. In this way, it served first as a preparatory committee for the formation of the ministry, then as a specialized agency under Wu T'ing-fang to compile and translate foreign commercial laws for possible use in China.[1] It was staffed with returned law graduates from Japan and other countries. On January 21, 1904, it promulgated the Shang-jen t'ung-li (General rules for merchants) in nine articles and the Kung-ssu shang-lü (Company law) in 131 articles. They were enlarged in 1910. Other laws it published or helped to draw up included the laws on company registration (1905), bankruptcy (1906), patent rights (1906), regulations governing government awards (1906, 1907), newspaper publications (1906), and the chamber of commerce (1904).

The Commercial Law Office's relationship with Shen Chia-pen's Bureau for the Compilation of Law (Fa-lü pien-tsuan-kuan) is unclear. It apparently enjoyed independence under the Shang pu until Shen's own broad program of legal reform was reorganized in 1906 into the Codification Committee (Hsiu-ting fa-lü-kuan). The latter then assumed some supervisory control over it. Although the Commercial Law Office failed in the end to recommend a comprehensive system of commercial and industrial laws, it introduced the modern concept of law to Chinese business practices.[2]

The Patent Bureau (Shang-piao Chü). Chinese merchants knew about patent rights and had discussed the subject long before the founding of the Shang pu. In theory, a Chinese entrepreneur could establish patent claims by registering his trademark with the Maritime Customs Service or with its supervisory office, the Nan-yang or the Pei-yang Commissioners' Office. After 1901, these registrations were transferred to the Wai-wu pu.[3] In practice, however, there were no rigid rules, since items not directly involved in import or export were often registered with the provincial authorities.

Besides, many of the items were, strictly speaking, not eligible for patent rights, since they were exact copies of Western models. But because they were new to the Chinese market, and usually involved a machine-making process, they were given what amounted to monopoly rights in the provinces. During the late nineteenth century, there was much confusion at the provincial level between monopolies and patent rights.[4]

Soon after the Shang pu was founded, the Patent Bureau acquired its responsibility from the Wai-wu pu.[5] But when its organizing committee tried to set up some minimum standard for patent rights, it ran into strong opposition from foreign powers, who threatened not to recognize it. Finally, through lengthy negotiations, an agreement was reached, and on July 23, 1906, the Patent Bureau was opened.[6]

The Commercial Newspaper Office (Shang-pao Kuan). This was organized by Ch'en Pi, Vice-President of the Shang pu, almost as soon as the ministry was established. It published a weekly newspaper called *Shang-wu pao* (Commercial affairs). It had columns for imperial edicts relating to commerce and industry, the ministry's policies, editorials, reports of investigations on local products in the different provinces, translations of foreign literature on commerce and agriculture, advertisements, and short stories in the vernacular. Its editor was Prince Ch'un's merchant friend, Wu T'ung-lin.[7] Like its parent ministry, it immediately ran into financial difficulty. It did not get the 10,000 taels appropriation originally promised. Even a monthly subsidy of 300 taels did not materialize. Wu tried a capital-raising campaign, asking merchants to take up 200 shares at 100 taels each. But that, too, proved abortive. By early 1904, while subscriptions remained low, its running expenses reportedly came from Wu's own pocket.[8]

For the next two years, the newspaper managed to go on with very little money. Since it received informal support from outside the government, it became less and less an official paper, until in the spring of 1906 the ministry decided to regain control.[9] The bureau was reorganized and renamed the Bureau of the Commercial

Gazette (Shang-wu kuan-pao chü), and a new publication, *Shang-wu kuan-pao* (Commercial gazette), was published on every 5th, 15th, and 25th day of each Chinese calendar month. The aims remained roughly the same, but the contents were amplified. It did not, however, become an official mouthpiece entirely. Individuals whose names did not appear on the ministry's roster of officials occasionally wrote for the essay section, expressing divergent views. Its espoused aim was to educate the Chinese merchants. Thus, the *Gazette* published many articles on English and European chambers of commerce as well as on the American and European equivalents of the Ministry of Commerce. Other articles of like nature discussed the development of university-level commercial education in the West.

Once launched on April 28, 1906, the *Gazette* reported almost instant success. It was selling so well that the early numbers had to be reprinted. Probably because of its commercial success, the *Gazette* suffered none of the financial difficulties of its predecessor. Without showing any unevenness of quality, it came out consistently to the very end of the dynasty.[10]

Company Registration Bureau (Kung-ssu Chu-t'se Chü). This bureau was foreshadowed by Article 22 of the Company Law, which stated that all companies that conformed to it might register with the Shang pu. The Company Law recognized five broad types of commercial and industrial enterprises: 1) partnerships of two or more persons with unlimited liability; 2) similar partnerships with limited liability; 3) joint-stock companies of seven or more shareholders with unlimited liability; 4) similar joint-stock companies with limited liability; and 5) sole proprietorships with unlimited liability.[11] Hence, all companies would qualify for registration. On June 15, 1904, the court approved the "Regulations for the Registration of Companies" in eighteen articles. The opening of the bureau then followed.

The results were quite impressive. Some 272 companies with a total authorized capital of approximately $133,000,000 or Tls. 100,000,000 registered with the bureau between 1904 and 1908.[12]

Table 1—Types and Sizes of Authorized Capital (in Taels) of Companies Registered with the Nung-kung-shang Pu 1904–1908

	1904–5		1906		1907		1908		
	No. of companies	Average size	No. of companies	Average size	No. of companies	Average size	No. of companies	Average size	Total
Partnership-unlimited	2	158,000	17	43,303	2	14,300	1	50,000	22
Joint-stock unlimited	2	133,000	2	25,000	1	100,000	0	0	5
Partnership-limited	18	83,806	7	55,450	14	155,098	9	105,113	48
Joint-stock limited	36	407,668	39	177,453	38	438,595	40	2,229,410	153
Sole proprietorships	13	12,408	13	19,394	11	102,118	7	25,000	44

Source: Calculated from data in *Nung-kung-shang pu t'ung-chi piao, ti-i-tz'u* (Peking, 1909), hereafter cited as *NKSPTCP-I*, ts'e 5; also 2nd collection: *NKSPTCP-II*, ts'e 5.

Table 1 shows the average size of these companies according to their different types. It should be noted, however, that the figures are deceptive in the sense that not all the authorized capital was ever fully paid. One example is that of the Kwangtung Canton-Hankow Railway, whose $44,087,810 authorized capital, computed in full for Table 1, was about one-third paid. Thus, if allowance for it is made, then the average size of joint-stock limited companies for 1908 should have been under 1,000,000 taels, instead of the more than 2,000,000 taels shown.

Table 1 also shows that over half the companies registered were joint-stock companies of limited liability.[13] They were by far the largest in the amount of authorized capital. This group made up practically all of China's modernized enterprises: cotton spinning and weaving, flour milling and rice husking, tobacco, cement and soap, railways, steamships and mining, and the like. The government's modernizing efforts, by promising legal guarantees under a set of commercial laws, appealed to them as much as the Western concepts of business organization–joint-stock formation and limited liability–which they borrowed.

Since 1875, Britain had recognized Shanghai as a port where ships on the Chinese coastal and inland waters could be registered as British owned. This, in turn, had led to the founding of British joint-stock shipping companies of limited liability in Shanghai under the protection of British law. Many compradors and other Chinese merchants subscribed heavily to these foreign firms, so much so that, by 1900, at least 130 of them had become directors.[14] The many Chinese who had a good working knowledge and years of experience in these types of companies presumably contributed to the popularity of the joint-stock companies of limited liability.

On the other hand, companies of unlimited liability, both partnerships and joint-stock, were much smaller in size. During the five years' period under review, only 27 of them ventured forth to be registered. A check of the Nung-kung-shang pu's *Statistical Tables* will reveal that all of these 27 were pawnshops and other traditional enterprises (for example, 16 out of the 17 partnerships with unlimited liability registered in 1906 were pawnshops from Kiangsu).[15]

The 44 sole proprietorships and 48 partnerships of limited liability were also mostly traditional businesses. They included local banks, herb medicine shops, and wholesale and retail commerce.

Although single-owner and partnership companies were most numerous in China, only a negligible fraction registered with the ministry. This reconfirms the fact mentioned earlier, that traditional merchants disliked to reveal their ownership to the government. It would be more pertinent to ask why these 119 companies applied for registration.

The simplest explanation may be the receptiveness of these entrepreneurs to their official friends' persuasion. The central government had promised legal protection to any registered company. This had apparently impressed many merchants who had little to hide from any official investigation. Between August 3 and 7, 1905, 2 local banks and 9 other general wholesale and export-import companies registered with the bureau. They all came from Swatow and were partnerships of limited liability.[16] At about the same time, 20 other commercial houses in the same city expressed their interest in registering after they had learned from their fellow provincial, Chang Pi-shih, that registration would afford them government protection.[17] Similarly, in 1906, when 16 pawnshops registered with the ministry, they came from the neighboring districts in Kiangsu, and they made their applications in groups.[18]

Bureau of Industry (Kung-i Chü). Two officials, Huang Shen-chih and his son, Huang Chung-hui, formed the first Bureau of Industry in Peking about late summer of 1901, to help provide relief work for the many unemployed in the capital following the Boxer uprising. The central project of the bureau was a technical school for young unskilled workers who would be paid a nominal wage while learning a skill from master craftsmen and technicians. It was small, and financial support came from the metropolitan prefect's yamen. By the end of 1902, the school had succeeded so well that some of its work sent to a trade fair in Hanoi was awarded prizes. The Huangs planned to set up a branch in Shanghai. But they received no support, for the relationship between the prefect's yamen and the bureau had become so tenuous that, during the summer of 1903, even the Peking bureau was temporarily closed. Fortunately, with the founding of the Shang pu at about this time, they found a new sponsor.[19]

Transferred to the Shang pu, the Bureau of Industry continued to thrive as a training center. In 1905, it branched out to take on women trainees, including some doing embroidery work. Its size, however, remained modest, for its parent ministry did not have sufficient funds to support a large training program. There was much discussion of building a large polytechnical college in Peking under the bureau's jurisdiction, but it did not go beyond the planning stage. In its later years, the bureau became important by serving as an institutional model for the provinces to organize their own bureaus.

Display Center for the Promotion of Industrial Products (Ch'üan-kung Ch'en-lieh So). Since the 1870s, Chinese officials had been aware of the many international expositions held in the West. Through Robert Hart's encouragement, China had been represented in a number of them. But such representations were made by officials; few Chinese merchants attended these fairs in person. Early in 1903, one secretary from the Grand Secretariat in Peking asked the court to offer incentives in the form of tax exemptions and transportation subsidies to any merchant who wished to attend the forthcoming St. Louis Fair in the United States. Their participation, he argued, would promote direct contact between Chinese and foreign merchants, thereby increasing the amount of the nation's export.[20]

The Shang pu had similar ideas. Just prior to his appointment as its first president, Tsai-chen had traveled to Japan to visit a trade fair. Soon after he assumed office, Tsai-chen issued a number of incentives for merchants who would display their products at these international fairs. They included awards, tax exemptions, and free freight for those exhibits which were not for sale.[21]

This favorable attitude toward international fairs led officials at the Bureau of Industry to suggest that a national display center should be set up to instruct Chinese merchants in the benefits of displaying their products. Provincial authorities and local chambers of commerce would be asked to submit entries of local produce and manufactured articles. In this way, the center would keep a record of the different items available from each region.

In 1905, the Shang pu sought and received imperial sanction for the project. By late 1906, it completed building a new display center in three stories and proceeded to hold its first successful exhibition. At the end of the third day, it was reported that over 8,000 people, including many foreigners, had visited the center and made purchases worth over $1,000 from the third floor, which alone had items for sale.[22] A second exhibition took place the following year. Then interest lapsed, probably because of the large-scale exhibition being planned by Governor-general Tuan-fang in Nanking.[23]

The Advanced Industrial School (Kao-teng Shih-yeh Hsueh-t'ang) *and the Apprenticeship School* (I-t'u Hsueh-t'ang). These two educational centers were opened by the Shang pu in the fall of 1904 and the spring of 1906 respectively to offer two levels of technical training to some 540 students. They emphasized technological education like chemical engineering, mechanics, mining, electricity, and metallurgy, as well as the humanities, ethics, and physical education. A number of the Industrial College's graduates were sent abroad for further training–probably to Japan since some twenty or almost half of the instructors were Japanese. The Apprenticeship School also aimed at improving the method of production in the handicraft industry and in imitating foreign designs.[24]

Early in 1905, the Shang pu took over a commercial school in Shanghai which had begun in 1897 under Sheng Hsuan-huai's sponsorship. Sheng had subsidized it by using funds from the Imperial Telegraph Administration and the China Merchants' Steam Navigation Company. Around 1903, when Sheng lost control of the two enterprises, money for the school was cut off and was not resumed until the Shang pu became its new sponsor. Significantly, the name of the school was changed from the Nanyang Advanced Commercial

School (Nan-yang kao-teng shang-wu hsueh-t'ang) to the Advanced Industrial School (Kao-teng shih-yeh hsueh-t'ang).[25]

Here is an example of officials putting industry above commerce. Up to the founding of the Shang pu in 1903, the general educational efforts had emphasized *shang-hsueh* (commercial and industrial learning), which was understood broadly as a skill to be used when confronting the Western powers in "commercial and industrial warfare" (*shang-chan*). This was Sheng Hsuan-huai's intention when he supported the commercial school in Shanghai. It was also Chang Chih-tung's aim. Back in the 1880s, he had sponsored a commercial program in mathematics and economics in his provincial high school for forty students from merchant families. In 1891, Chang even raised the quota to fifty, and added foreign language and practical commercial courses to the program.[26] In 1902, Chang pursued this further by opening a Commercial Affairs School (Shang-wu hsueh-t'ang) in Wuchang.[27]

After 1903, industrial and technical education assumed dominance over the broader commercial and economic education in much the same way that the new term *shih-yeh* ("modern" industrial enterprise) gained acceptance and became a distinct and greatly favored department of the broader term *shang-yeh.*

Besides the industrial schools the ministry sponsored in Peking and Shanghai, it also made some efforts to open a commercial school. One proposal even suggested that the school could be set up inside the ministry's compound so as to save some running expenses.[28] But nothing came of it. Another proposal was to leave commerce for the national university, whose prospectus at the time projected eight faculties, one of which could be commerce. That, too, did not materialize.[29]

Modern commercial education was left to private efforts. By the end of 1908, fifteen schools, mostly sponsored by the local chambers of commerce in Kiangsu, were registered with the ministry.[30] Meanwhile, the ministry continued to show the government's concern for industrial education by investing a considerable part of its total expenses, some 100,000 taels annually, in its two industrial and technical schools at the capital. As its official *Commercial*

Gazette pointed out in 1906 (and repeated in 1911), "If a state is to seek prosperity and strength, there can be no other way but to encourage industrial education (*shih-yeh chiao-yü*) which provides a key to utilizing science for practical use." It went on to cite the case of Germany, which was fast catching up to England because the Germans had developed a better technical educational system.[31]

Official Awards

Apart from the specialized agencies discussed above, the Shang pu and its successor, the Nung-kung-shang pu, also initiated a series of administrative devices to encourage commerce and industry. One such device was the formulation of an elaborate system of official awards. This practice predated the Shang pu. The Tsungli Yamen officials who began it were attracted by similar British and Russian practices. What prompted them in 1898, however, was the widespread fear of the increasing number of foreign-owned factories and the threat these developments posed for domestic handicraft products.[32]

Hence, in this first set of regulations, the emphasis was on rewarding master craftsmen and inventive mechanics who could devise new or comparable techniques of production for armament and items for daily use. Other awards were promised to those who could introduce copies of Western inventions still unavailable in China. A third area of awards went to those who could write treatises on technology and those who would contribute to the founding of schools, museums, or libraries, or the dissemination of scientific concepts. These awards came in five broad categories: hereditary titles, substantive posts, brevet ranks, monograms, and citation tablets.[33]

Approved and promulgated by the Kuang-hsu Emperor on July 12, 1898 as part of the "Hundred Day Reform" program, these regulations were probably never put into effect. There is no record of any award that had actually been made, or of any mechanism set up to run it. In 1903, within months after its own founding, the Shang pu drew up a new set of *Chiang-li Hua-shang kung-ssu chang-ch'eng* (Regulations to award and encourage Chinese companies). The emphasis, however, was no longer on technology, but on the size of capital investment (see Table 3 below).[34] Although it was not clearly spelled out, it seemed that the awards were for both investors and promoters. But this set of regulations was found to be impracticable. First, no investor stood a chance of getting an award because the size of capital was so inflated that the smallest amount an individual needed to invest in order to win the lowest award was half a million dollars (the highest being at least 50 million). Since the model for the new companies was the joint-stock company of limited liability, the emphasis should have been on attracting more investors of moderate means than the few wealthy individuals who could make substantial capital contributions. Second, even for promoters, anyone who could raise half a million dollars would have such high social standing in the first place that the corresponding award, that of an "advisor (*i-yuan*) fifth class," would be downright unattractive, if not demeaning.

By 1904, the Shang pu, having made no award under these regulations, must have recognized their flaws. It ignored the award provisions altogether when it recommended that the throne appoint Chang Chien a "counselor (*ku-wen*) first class" of the Ministry. On April 16th, Chang Chien became the first to receive the honor for having organized "eleven companies with a combined capital of over $2 million and an annual profit of between $300,000 and $400,000."[35] Had the ministry followed the 1903 provisions, the same award (plus a "button of first rank") would have required the raising or an investment of over $20 million. Chang's "pitiful" $2 million would have entitled him to become an "advisor second class" of the Ministry. Indeed, it seems that, like the 1898 regulations, the 1903 regulations were never put into effect, because when three other persons were similarly honored (one each of first, second, and third class), their awards were not based entirely on their promotion and capital-raising efforts for new industries. Two of them were officials holding substantive posts and known for their general promotion of merchant interests.[36]

At any event, from then on, the role of even the small promoter of capital investment was formally recognized. Thus, in the prospectus of the Szechwan-Hankow Railway Company dated January 1905, Article 17 offered an honorable mention in a memorial to the throne for anyone who was able to raise 1,000 shares at fifty taels per share. Others who could raise ten times more, at half a million taels, would have separate individual memorials sent to the throne on their behalf.[37]

In 1906, as the Shang pu experimented with these various ideas of giving awards, it scrapped all past measures, then worked out a comprehensive system of awards. This policy was continued by the Nung-kung-shang pu. On October 15, 1906, the first set of new regulations was approved by the court. The Nung-kung-shang pu proposed to renew the 1898 practice to honor master craftsmen and inventive mechanics (see Table 2). And, in order to assure success, it asked provincial officials and the various chambers of commerce to submit candidates.[38] Two other sets of regulations followed in 1907 to reward the promoters and the investors of industries (see Tables 3 and 4). First, the 1903 regulations were revised by lowering the unrealistically inflated amounts of capital required for each award.[39] They were then reserved for the promoters of industry. Second, an entirely new kind of award, based on the conferring of nobility titles, was set up for investors. The nature of these awards for technicians, promoters, and investors of industries are summarized in Tables 2, 3, and 4.

Except for the new order of *shang-hsun* decorations given to technicians, the other awards of ranks and titles were transferable to a family member if the recipient had already had comparable official recognition. Similarly, shareholders or partners of a company might relinquish their claims in favor of their largest shareholder or partner. As for counselors and advisors, they would not be required to attend to official duties at the ministry. They were given, instead, the privilege of having direct access to it at any time for consultation or for airing their grievances. Viscounts and barons so awarded received their titles as a kind of life peerage. Nonhereditary and without an emolument, their nobility titles could be passed on to their sons only if the sons maintained their investment holdings.

Table 2–Awards for Technicians (1906)

Awards	*For technological and other results achieved*
"Shang-hsun" Decoration 1st class; Official Button of 2nd rank	Building steam ships, railways, automobiles comparable to the Western counterparts, railway bridges of several hundreds of feet, electrical generators
"Shang-hsun" Decoration 2nd class; Official Button of 3rd rank	Building steam engines and having expertise in locating mines
"Shang-hsun" Decoration 3rd class; Official Button of 4th rank	Building new machines to manufacture domestic products efficiently, better methods of making steel; new farming tools, improved seeding and irrigation methods, planting 5,000 trees per person, and setting up vineyards worth $10,000 each
"Shang-hsun" Decoration 4th class; Official Button of 5th rank	Making improvements on domestic handicraft products and imitating foreign ones for export
"Shang-hsun" Decoration 5th class; Official Button of 6th rank	Imitating foreign products for the domestic market

Sources: "Chiang-chi shang-hsun chang-ch'eng," in *Nung-kung-shang pu hsien-hsing chang-ch'eng; NKSPTCP-I,* ts'e 6:18a–b.

The elaborate system of both awards and qualifications indicates the government's order of priorities. Table 2 shows that the late Ch'ing government's primary concern was for an independent heavy industry related to strategic hardware–ships, railways, mining, and arsenals. On the other hand, it made no specific mention of the textile technology which remained the staple item of Chinese industry for the next few decades. Presumably, it was subsumed under the desire for "new machines to manufacture domestic products efficiently," and was lumped with the desire to improve agricultural technology. Another emphasis was on the export market, reflecting the dominant economic theory that

Table 3—Awards for Promoters (1903 and 1907)

Awards	1903	1907
	For a promoter having raised a minimum amount of	
Counselor (*ku-wen*) of the Nung-kung-shang pu, 1st class; Button of 1st rank, Double Dragon Gold Medallion; hereditary counselor 4th class to 3rd generation	$50,000,000	$20,000,000
Counselor 1st class, Button of 1st rank, hereditary counselor 1st class (*sic*) to 3rd generation	40,000,000	15,000,000
Counselor 1st class, Button of 1st rank, hereditary counselor 2nd class to 3rd generation	30,000,000	10,000,000
Counselor 1st class, Button of 1st rank	20,000,000	8,000,000
Counselor 2nd class, Button of 2nd rank	10,000,000	6,000,000
Counselor 3rd class, Button of 3rd rank	8,000,000	4,000,000
Counselor 4th class, Button of 4th rank	5,000,000	2,000,000
Advisor (i-yuan) 1st class, 5th brevet rank (1903 and 1907)	3,000,000	1,000,000
Advisor (i-yuan) 2nd class, 5th brevet rank (1903)/Button 5th rank (1907)	2,000,000	800,000
Advisor (i-yuan) 3rd class, 6th brevet rank (1903 and 1907)	1,000,000	600,000
Advisor (i-yuan) 4th class, 6th brevet rank (1903)/Button 6th rank (1907)	800,000	400,000
Advisor (i-yuan) 5th class, Button of 7th rank (1903 and 1907)	500,000	200,000

Sources: Wang Ching-yü, ed., *Chung-kuo chin-tai kung-yeh shih tzu-liao, ti-erh-chi, 1895–1914 nien* (Peking, 1957), I, 640–646; *Tung-fang tsa-chih,* hereafter cited as *TFTC,* Shang-wu, 411: 117–120 (1907); "Chiang-li Hua-shang kung-ssu chang-ch'eng," in *Nung-kung-shang pu hsien-hsing chang-ch'eng.* Imperial approvals on 10/20–11/18, 1903 and 9/20/1907.

Table 4—Awards for Investors (1907)

Awards	*for an investor having invested a minimum amount of*	*and employing a minimum working force of*
Viscount (*tzu*), 1st class	$20,000,000	1,000 persons
Viscount (*tzu*), 2nd class	18,000,000	1,000 persons
Viscount (*tzu*), 3rd class	16,000,000	1,000 persons
Baron (*nan*), 1st class	14,000,000	1,000 persons
Baron (*nan*), 2nd class	12,000,000	1,000 persons
Baron (*nan*), 3rd class	10,000,000	1,000 persons
"*Ch'ing*" (court rank), 3rd rank, Single-Eye Peacock Feather	8,000,000	500 persons
"*Ch'ing*" 3rd rank	7,000,000	500 persons
"*Ch'ing*" 4th rank; Single-Eye Peacock Feather	6,000,000	500 persons
"*Ch'ing*" 4th rank	5,000,000	500 persons
"*Ch'ing*" 5th rank; 2nd brevet rank	4,000,000	500 persons
"*Ch'ing*" 5th rank	3,000,000	500 persons
"*Ch'ing*" 4th brevet rank, Button of 1st rank	2,000,000	—
"*Ch'ing*" 4th brevet rank	1,000,000	—
2nd brevet rank	800,000	—
3rd brevet rank	500,000	—
4th brevet rank	300,000	—
5th brevet rank	100,000	—
Medallions of 7th–9th ranks*	10,000	—

Sources: *TFTC*, Shih-yeh, 4.12:175-8 (1907-1908); *Hua-tzu jih-pao*, 9/18/1907; "Shih-yeh chueh-shang chang-ch'eng" in *Nung-kung-shang pu hsien-hsing chang-ch'eng.* Imperial approval on 8/2/1907.

*This was added to the list in a separate edict dated September 20, 1907, in recognition of the difficulty for many Chinese investors to invest in more substantial amounts.

China must export more and import less in order to regain her strength. The government's concern for the domestic market was by and large limited to finding domestic replacements for foreign products.

More significantly, the awards of nobility titles to investors in modern industry in Table 4 show the government's bias toward industrialists. Such a bias was already evident in scholar-officials' debates and in the Shang pu's preference for industrial and technical schools over commercial schools. Now, as the state singled out individual entrepreneurs for special recognition, it specifically stated that nobility titles would be awarded "only to those in industry (*shih-yeh*) or those who can open up the sources of wealth and enrich the people's livelihood. Those who make profit by the exchange of goods or of currencies will not be included in the awards."[40]

Requests for these awards proved to be minimal. As the *Tung-fang tsa-chih* and the *Hua-tzu jih-pao* were quick to point out, Chinese enterpreneurs did not want brevet ranks and empty titles, but real enforceable measures of protection from the government.[41] One might go further and suggest that, since the brevet ranks and titles could be bought, and were in fact bought by merchants in large numbers, such awards must have lost a good deal of their prestige value and other awe-inspiring qualities.[42] By 1900, hardly any Chinese merchant who was anybody in the merchant communities both in China and overseas was without some kind of official title. While the desire for glory and an external symbol of success no doubt came into the mind of these merchants, yet the larger factor which motivated them was sheer necessity. For without such titles they could have no contact with officials.

The government was probably not entirely without misgivings. For the first time, nobility titles were offered as awards. This idea was first suggested by Feng Kuei-fen back in the 1860s when he deplored the increasing number of officials who acquired their offices through purchase. He felt that it had led to mismanagement, and favored a return to a practice in Chou times when noble ranks were awarded to commoners for meritorious deeds. During the

Table 5—Awards to Technicians

	Shang-hsun Decorations				
	1st class	2nd class	3rd class	4th class	5th class
1907	0	0	0	2	1
1908	0	0	0	0	0

Source: *NKSPTCP-I,* ts'e 6:18a-b.

Table 6—Awards to Investors

	Viscount			Baron			Ch'ing			Ch'ing-Brevet		Brevet			
Class	1st	2nd	3rd	1st	2nd	3rd	3rd	4th	5th	3rd	4th	2nd	3rd	4th	5th
1907	0	0	0	0	0	0	0	0	0	0	0	1	0	0	0
1908	0	0	0	0	0	0	0	0	0	1	1	0	0	1	0

Source: *NKSPTCP-I,* ts'e 6:17a-b; *NKSPTCP-II,* ts'e 5:18a-b.

Table 7—Awards to Promoters

	Counselor				Advisor				
Class	1st	2nd	3rd	4th	1st	2nd	3rd	4th	5th
1907	0	0	0	0	1	1	2	6	9
1908	0	0	1	0	2	0	0	0	1
1909	0	0	0	1	0	0	0	0	0
1910	0	0	0	0	2	0	1	1	0

Sources: *NKSPTCP-I,* ts'e 6:19-23b; *NKSPTCP-II,* ts'e 5:19a-b; *Shang-wu kuan-pao* (1909), No. 27 (10/28), pp. 3-4; (1910), No. 28 (11/26), pp. 7-8.

1900s, Chang Chien not only echoed Feng's concepts; he also pointed to precedents in the West.[43]

However, in spite of the 1907 formula, no industrialist became a nobleman, since no single person made the minimal $10 million investment required for a "baronetcy, third class." In 1909, the Nung-kung-shang pu memorialized the throne to discontinue the measure entirely.[44] Similarly, the newly created *shang-hsun* decorations for technicians were allowed to lapse almost as soon as they began. In March 1911, when a committee appointed specially to present a new national scheme for decorations published its recommendations, no mention was even made of this category of decoration.[45] Tables 5, 6, and 7 summarize the number of recipients of various awards who qualified under the 1906 and 1907 sets of regulations.

The two ministries' systems of awards, like their numerous agencies, may also be seen as efforts to increase their ability to direct economic policies in the provinces. When applied judiciously, awards could establish beneficial links between the central government and local merchant leaders. But the policy of giving awards was not vigorously pursued. As Tables 5, 6, and 7 show, there were few recipients. The specialized agencies were more successful. The Bureau of Industry became a model for the provinces. Its control over company registration and patent rights, as well as the promulgation of a rudimentary code of commercial laws, all helped to enhance the central government's role in determining the economic policy of the nation. The specialized agencies also made the central government more visible to the average merchant on the local scene. However, they did not take any jurisdictional rights away from the provincial governments. The contest between the provincial governments and the ministries was joined on other issues.

Chapter Ten

THE SEARCH FOR SUPPORTING INSTITUTIONS IN THE PROVINCES

It would be simplistic to blame the central government's overall lack of revenue or faltering confidence in the reform program for the weakness and decline of the Shang pu and the Nung-kung-shang pu. Even an impoverished government like the Ch'ing government in the 1900s could, if it would, put together a rather sizeable sum of money for some project if there was a sense of urgency for that project. As for its commitment to the reform of the central bureaucracy, drastic changes continued through the decade as new ministries like the Ministry of Interior (Min-cheng pu), the Ministry of Finance (Tu-chih pu), and the Ministry of Justice (Fa pu) were formed or amalgamated from old ones.

One must look elsewhere for the failure of the Shang pu and the Nung-kung-shang pu. To begin with, the Chinese political leaders were ignorant about the dynamics of change. Initially brought about by the requirements of sheer survival, the changes made in the central government gradually instilled in the leadership an almost unshakeable faith that the new institutional structure could of itself miraculously bring forth improvements. Leaders did not understand that the new facade could not function within the traditional political and social setting. Each new purpose and function created a chain reaction that demanded corresponding changes elsewhere in the bureaucracy, in the capital and the provinces. When wielders of related powers refused to cooperate by redrawing their jurisdiction, or by agreeing to a common program of reform, then no amount of dedication and hard work practiced by one sector would make that sector function properly.

This was what happened to the Shang pu and the Nung-kung-shang pu. They represented that sector of the bureaucracy which was new. But in order to bring about the kind of change they envisioned they needed the help of the provinces which for many years had been dealing with the problems of economic modernization.

But the desired help did not come. Provincial governments which had been gaining military power and economic resources throughout the nineteenth century already felt threatened by these new bureaucratic reforms. They had acquired their growing strength through the use of personnel, revenue, and office not subject to central control. Now, by demanding that these men follow ministerial directives and that old institutions be replaced by branch bureaus of the ministries, the central government was cutting at the roots of regional power. Such threats to reclaim industrial direction were particularly menacing because they would affect an important source of revenue and personal wealth for the provincial officials.

The result was neither open flouting of central authority nor compliance. Provincial authorities responded by offering token compliances in a variety of ways. As the ministries tried to impose their programs on the provinces by setting up their own agencies at various administrative levels, the provincial governments pushed forward comparable institutions they had already developed and put them under Peking's nominal control.

There was at least one other compelling reason for the lack of effective authority from Peking. The provincial governors and governors-general did not enjoy unchallenged leadership among their own subordinate officials or the local gentry elite. In a recent study on regionalism, K. C. Liu has skillfully analyzed the limits of their power.[1] Peking still retained the power of withholding rewards, such as promotions, and of dispensing punishments, such as dismissals or reassignments, to all the regular officials in the provinces; non-compliance or token compliance with Peking's directives was as likely owing to the provincial officials' inability to enforce them as to their unwillingness to carry them out. As the numerous political agitations led by local gentry and merchants have indicated, provincial governors and governors-general were often powerless to act against popular demands. They were also at the mercy of their own staff and subordinates whose own private interests probably had a much greater impact on determining what programs would be enforced or dropped. At a time when the court's standing among the public was declining because of a growing belief that Manchu princes were maximizing power to themselves, local interest groups had even more reasons for dissuading governors from following Peking's orders.

The Bureau of Commercial Affairs (Shang-wu Chü)

Before Prince Ch'un and Sheng Hsuan-huai had discussed the desirability of a national ministry of commerce, there had been many proposals for such a centralized bureau at the provincial level. The first suggestion for a provincial office came from Governor-general Chang Chih-tung.

In July 1895, following the signing of the Treaty of Shimonoseki, Chang submitted a memorial to the throne proposing various reform measures. Ghost-written by Chang Chien, the governor-general's memorial included an analysis of China's economic weakness. Chinese merchants were weak, he contended, because the government offered no protection, leaving each merchant to fend for himself. As a result, each merchant tried to connive with the foreign merchant for his own selfish interest. He proposed the setting up of a Shang-wu chü (Bureau of Commercial Affairs), where a select group of merchant leaders from the different trades could meet regularly to plan trade strategies and to advise the government on how it might best help merchants. The bureau's staff members, however, would be regular officials. They would compile data on local products and encourage merchants to invest their money in large joint-stock companies.[2]

A few months later, a censor, Wang P'eng-yun, followed up with another memorial urging explicitly that such a bureau be established in the provincial capitals under the direction of the governors-general. Under Wang's plan, a governor-general would appoint an official bureau chief, and ask the local trade guilds to select or elect one director to meet regularly with the bureau. Their deliberations would then be transmitted to the governor-general and, for important issues, ultimately to the throne through a new coordinating office in Peking.[3]

The Tsungli Yamen, having been asked to comment on Chang's and Wang's proposals, agreed that some kind of organization at the provincial level to support the merchants was indeed necessary. It felt, however, that these proposals presupposed a working bond between officials and merchants which did not yet exist. Instead, the Tsungli Yamen recommended that the provincial Shang-wu chü should be staffed and run by the merchants themselves, and be organized at all levels down to the county level. The Tsungli Yamen was also not in favor of a coordinating office in Peking, arguing that it was already performing such a role.[4] Thus, while Chang and Wang wanted a bureau controlled by the provinces, the Tsungli Yamen was interested in diffusing that power and maintaining the tradition of non-interference with merchant organizations.

However, the Tsungli Yamen's proposal came too late. Chang Chih-tung, as Acting Governor-general of Liang-Chiang, had already ordered his model of the Shang-wu chü to be opened in Nanking, Shanghai, Soochow, Chinkiang, and Chang Chien's home town, T'ung-shou.[5] Although the throne endorsed the Tsungli Yamen's plan, Chang's bureaus continued to function, then gave token compliance to the imperial decree by asking gentry merchants (*shen-sheng*) to serve as directors.

Chang's abrupt action without waiting for the throne's approval resulted from his pressing need to have a new institution like the Shang-wu chü to help him raise capital for industry. In September 1895, Chang Chih-tung, supported by the Kiangsu governor, Chao Shu-ch'iao, wrote to the Tsungli Yamen proposing to convert 2,260,000 taels raised in Kiangsu as government bonds into merchant capital for modern industrial projects. The bonds had been issued to meet some indemnity payment deadlines but were no longer needed for that purpose. Chang and Chao thought the Shang-wu chü could become a finance corporation by withholding reimbursement and transforming the 2,260,000 taels into merchant capital. It could then process loan applications by local merchants who wanted to start industrial projects like the making of pottery, matches, cement, needles, spirits, carpets, and the like. Chang and Chao further claimed they had won the gentry's and rich merchants' endorsement, and that those who did not wish to have their money transferred could cash in their bonds. By their own assessment, they were only "using the local gentry's and merchants' money to help themselves."[6]

Chang Chih-tung's published correspondence does not include a copy of the Tsungli Yamen's reply. Probably it cautioned restraint, for its later report to the throne failed to mention the role of the Shang-wu chü as a finance corporation. Chang, however, carried out his plan on his own authority. In the next few years, in spite of persistent local opposition, the management of private capital became the bureaus' main activities.[7]

Peking remained unaware of, or chose to ignore, these developments until a censor complained that Chang had forced holders of government bonds to transfer their cash rebates into capital for the Shang-wu chü. Chang's successor, Liu K'un-i, was ordered to investigate. Liu's report defended Chang's action. But it also showed clearly that Chang used high-handed tactics. For example, Chang pledged to honor every bond-holder's decision not to transfer his cash repayment to the Shang-wu chü. In practice, he allowed only those with less than 200 taels' worth of bonds to do so.[8]

By 1901, Governor-general Liu K'un-i informed the court that the several Shang-wu chü in Kiangsu needed drastic reform to rid their officials of arrogance. The merchants, Liu observed, thought of them as "wolves and tigers." As long as officials continued to exalt themselves and degrade the merchants, they could accomplish little.[9]

Liu's characterization indicated that the average Shang-wu chü had become very unpopular. Following Chang Chih-tung's model, their main business was to devise new means of raising funds and not to enforce the original goal of developing modern economic policies.

The Bureau for the Protection of Merchants (Pao-shang Chü)

While the Shang-wu chü languished for lack of merchant support, a similar institution was established in Amoy around 1899, then spread to Canton in 1900 and Swatow by 1902. Organized under the name Pao-shang chü (Bureau for the Protection of Merchants), it was set up with the specific purpose of protecting Fukienese, Cantonese, and Teochiu merchants when they returned home from abroad. In 1893, Huang Tsun-hsien, the Chinese Consul-general at Singapore, wrote a letter to Hsueh Fu-ch'eng, the Chinese Minister in London, to describe the plight of Chinese merchants upon returning home:

> When the subject of returning to their native land is touched upon, [the overseas Chinese merchants] shake their heads with a frown, and tell me how, if they do, they are examined by the officials, worn out by the yamen runners, and pestered by their relatives and neighbors. People call them absconding pirates who have made friends with foreigners, accuse them of importing arms to aid the bandits in slave-dealing, etc. Some even go to the length of breaking open the boxes and tearing down the houses of those who return, in addition to suing them for imaginary debts which, it is alleged, were contracted prior to their departure and of which they avoided payment by absconding. From these false charges they had no way of escape, and that is why they are afraid to come back. Others again of these returned emigrants pretend to be of foreign nationality, and on the strength thereof practice deceptions of a kind which is past finding out.[10]

Huang's account prompted an imperial declaration that the old ban against going to live or travel abroad had been abrogated, and that returning merchants would be accorded every protection. Huang tried to formalize official protection by issuing passports to these merchants.[11] However, they proved ineffective and the practice was stopped. It was Huang's successor, Liu Yü-lin, who finally secured the support of the Governor-general of Fukien and Chekiang to set up the Pao-shang chü at the ports of disembarkation for returning merchants. The responsibilities assigned to it were: 1) to receive and settle overseas Chinese merchants' complaints about local officials' squeeze and oppression, 2) to protect these merchants and their families against kidnapping, and 3) to foster and promote enterprises financed by overseas Chinese capital.[12]

However, the new bureau seemed unable to stem the tide of official extortion. Instead, more incidents of harassment were reported. The increases probably meant that more Chinese merchants were returning home, and more of them were making their complaints known to the authorities. In 1901, the Governor-general in Kwangtung conceded that the bureau in Canton was not functioning well, and ordered the Chinese Consul-general in Singapore to supply him with details of all returning merchants before their arrival.[13]

In Amoy, the bureau reported satisfactory results for the first few months when a number of merchants were running it. It was then turned over to the officials, who subjected it to so much bureaucratic bungling that the governor-general's office was flooded with complaints. In 1901, the provincial government conducted an investigation, then brought in a new director. But these measures apparently produced little change.[14]

In March 1903, the throne reaffirmed its intention to render protection to all overseas Chinese who returned on visits. In a tone that contrasted sharply with the traditional warnings against Chinese merchants' going abroad, this edict praised the overseas merchants' loyalty and continued attachment to their ancestral land. It observed that the state laid the greatest emphasis on the promotion of trade, and that the success of such a national policy depended upon the officials' ability to attract the kind of talent overseas Chinese merchants possessed. The throne then exhorted governors-general to treat these merchants with care, and to punish severely any local officials who dared to subject them to extortion.[15]

The court's strong statement led some provincial officials in Amoy to try to redefine their control over the Pao-shang chü. But various proposals to merge it with the provincial Shang-wu chü or to turn it over to the local chamber of commerce were never resolved. It continued to function as an independent office until 1911. Apparently, the Amoy bureau had become a new source of considerable income for the provincial government and its officers. For it charged a fee when it issued passports to both incoming and outgoing merchants. Meanwhile, merchant complaints continued unabated.

In February 1911, the Singapore Chinese General Chamber of Commerce issued a resolution on behalf of the various Chinese chambers of commerce throughout Southeast Asia. It singled out Amoy's Pao-shang chü for special condemnation, then declared that the overseas Chinese would no longer apply to its office for passports. Instead, each returning merchant could pay a $1 fee to the semi-official Overseas Chinese Association (Hua-ch'iao kung-hui), which would make the necessary arrangements, and render protection for his safety.[16]

Two more Pao-shang chü were established in Swatow and Canton, because they were the two other important ports of entry for the overseas Chinese. Practically nothing is known about Canton's Pao-shang chü other than that it existed during this period. As for the one in Swatow, it was founded in 1902 by the local taotai, Ting Pao-ch'uan. From the beginning, it was entrusted to the local merchants, and enjoyed good relations with both the ministry and the overseas Chinese. The founding of the local chamber of commerce in 1906 only reconfirmed this arrangement. The chamber, which provided the legitimacy to supervise a bureau of this nature, was controlled by the same men who ran the bureau as merchant directors.[17]

The Bureau of Industry (Kung-i Chü)

The third related institution in the provinces was the Kung-i chü (Bureau of Industry). Although modeled after the Peking bureau, some of these provincial offices were larger than their parent organization. Probably the most impressive of these provincial bureaus was the Pei-yang kung-i chü at Tientsin. Headed by Yuan Shih-k'ai's able assistant, Chou Hsueh-hsi, it gradually acquired a number of agencies until it developed into Yuan's own miniature Nung-kung-shang pu.

The Tientsin bureau's chief agency was the Industrial Promotion Workshop (Ch'üan-kung ch'ang), which had one section to display products, another to carry out research, and a third to offer fortnightly public lectures. It also encouraged trade guilds to set up their own study groups, some of which were actually formed. Another agency of the bureau encompassed its experimental shops teaching technical skills to special types of workers. A number of these shops were set up in prisons to train convicts. There were two technical schools at two different levels. Many of the graduates from the advanced-level school were sent to Japan for further studies.[18]

Thus, by its own research, lectures, and workshops, the Pei-yang kung-i chü sought to create new interest in industry and to compile data on the province's produce and market condition. During 1905–1906, over sixty sub-prefectures and counties applied for branch offices throughout the province. Others brought their mechanical inventions and improvement models to the bureau to apply for patent rights.[19]

Much of the Tientsin bureau's success must be attributed to Chou Hsueh-hsi, who was its founding director in 1903, and who stayed on until 1908. Besides his considerable skill as an official-entrepreneur, Chou was equally competent as a bureaucrat. An admiration for modern business practice led him to impose a new set of rules upon his subordinate officials. Thus, in the regulations drawn up for the Pei-yang kung-i chü, he insisted that appointment to an office must depend on one's ability, not influence. He asked every official to discard the traditional air of pomposity and arrogance, especially in his attitude toward the merchant. He encouraged his subordinates to express their views, to suggest new ideas, and to do more than simply follow routines. No one, the regulations went on, should remain silent when an issue was being discussed. He also insisted on regular office hours: from 7:30 a.m. (or 8:00 a.m. in the winter) to 5:30 p.m., with a generous three-hour break at midday. During office hours, no official could entertain private visitors for more than one hour. Junior officials who had occasional free time should use it for reading; they were particularly warned not to congregate for jokes and gossip.[20] Such a litany of *dos* and *don'ts* reveals many aspects of the life led by lesser mandarins in their yamens.

On a less elaborate scale, other Kung-i chü were established in other provincial capitals. In many cases, they were supported by local government funds. In a few cases, local merchants helped with money and even ran a few bureaus of their own.[21] In Kwangtung, two bureaus were established by about 1906. One was apparently run by the provincial government. The second one was sponsored by Cheng Kuan-ying, who rallied the combined support of the Canton General Chamber of Commerce and nine local private charitable organizations. It was named the Industrial Charitable Halls (Kung-i shan-t'ang), and it successfully ran two technical schools at different levels as well as a workshop.[22]

Problems of Central Control

During the first few years of the 1900s, the Shang-wu chü probably became even more unpopular. In October 1902, the Governor-general of Liang-Kuang proposed closing the Canton bureau because it had so little business. It was in fact closed for a few months in 1903.[23] The bureau in Shanghai, the other major commercial center, was also shut down for parts of 1904.[24] The total number of Shang-wu chü, however, actually grew during these years. One reason was that many provincial governments preferred using them to raising sundry new taxes and loans to meet the Boxer indemnities. An example of this was the Shang-wu chü founded in 1903 in Kiangsi's provincial capital.[25] The more important reason was the intention of provincial officials to propose these bureaus as the most logical choice for the Shang pu's (Ministry of Commerce's) provincial offices.

President Tsai-chen did not want to revive the Shang-wu chü as the ministry's branches. They were already part of the provincial bureaucracy, and for the most part they had a bad reputation. Tsai-chen had drawn up an entirely new bureaucratic network to serve his ministry in the provinces. He would appoint new officials for the different administrative levels down to the county level.[26]

The provincial authorities, on the other hand, rejected this, for a new institution so conceived would owe its allegiance to the ministry. It would also give the ministry considerable voice in its operation. Furthermore, the Shang pu, by creating its own provincial offices, would upset the traditional administrative rule that prevented any provincial bureau from falling under the direction of any of the Six Ministries at Peking. In 1904, the Shang pu, although a very young ministry, laid claim to being a kind of "super-ministry." The provincial authorities viewed its intentions with great suspicion. Understandably they preferred the Shang-wu chü—an institution which was their own and which they could exploit to do their bidding. Thus, while conceding that the bureau had been unpopular, they argued that its new responsibilities as the ministry's branch office would give it a new lease of life.

By the summer of 1904, the Shang pu succumbed to these arguments, and a compromise solution was forged. Under the regulations drawn up by it and approved by the throne in August 1904, the Shang-wu chü were accepted as the ministry's branch offices to direct all commercial and industrial developments in the provinces. Each would be headed by a commissioner for commercial affairs (*shang-wu i-yuan*), who would be selected by the governor-general and governor, but approved and appointed by the ministry. The commissioner, an official with the rank of prefect or expectant intendant (taotai), had to be conversant with commercial and industrial affairs. Among his duties, he would make periodic reports, compile statistics, conduct investigations, and provide protection to the local and returned merchants. He was allowed direct access to the ministry by writing, but a copy of such reports had to go to the offices of the governor-general and the governor.[27]

The ministry was thus given the face-saving device of appointing the commissioners, while the provinces held the actual power of selecting their own candidates. The provinces were further assured of retaining the commissioners' allegiance, since a copy of any report they might independently make to the Shang pu went to their provincial superiors as well.

The new arrangement between the central and provincial government led to the opening of new bureaus or the reopening of old ones. By the end of 1908, forty-four commissioners of commercial affairs had been appointed to office.[28] The merchants' response was less enthusiastic. In Canton, the old Shang-wu chü had been so unsuccessful that the merchants there virtually boycotted its reopening on August 1, 1904. Although the provincial financial commissioner tried to pump up support by making personal calls on the leaders of the various guilds, he had scant success. Only a few merchants showed up for the opening ceremony.[29] During the next few years, it continued its unimpressive existence as succeeding governors-general tried in vain to resuscitate it.[30] For most of the time, the bureau did not even have a commissioner; its work was probably too little to warrant one. In October 1905, Tso Tsung-fan, President of the Canton Chamber of Commerce, was persuaded to take the post. But Tso resigned shortly thereafter. Eighteen months later, the office was filled again, this time by a regular official who served concurrently as an acting circuit intendant in Kwangtung.[31]

While the Cantonese merchants were merely uninterested in the Shang-wu chü, officials at the Shang pu discovered that the provinces would not allow the ministry to direct the bureaus' activities. The following administrative maneuvers between Peking and the provincial capitals are revealing; they show both the ministry's plight and its ineffectiveness in dealing with the provincial authorities.

In late 1904, the Shang pu complained to the throne that the provinces were not choosing commissioners of commercial affairs carefully. They did not follow the regulation which required that these commissioners have a knowledge of commerce and industry. The ministry's memorial observed that "although many governors-general and governors are conscientious in selecting good men [for the posts], many others regard them as routine appointments [for anyone on their staff]." It then requested the throne to command the governors-general to be more careful in their recommendations of commissioners in the future. It further demanded that the provinces present as candidates for its approval only those knowledgeable in commerce and industry, and that the provinces provide the ministry with details of candidates' experience in each case. After their appointment, commissioners should be permitted to communicate directly with the ministry, and be subject to the Shang pu's periodical checks.[32]

This is a good example of the difficulty encountered when a ministry from the central government tried to enforce executive directives upon a non-complying provincial government. The roundabout tactics and the resorting to imperial authority were methods regularly employed by the traditional central and provincial bureaucracies in their relations with each other. In the past, the system had functioned adequately, since both sides would normally have a sufficiently large area of mutual acceptance of each other's rights and responsibilities. Where differences arose, a strong emperor like the Yung-cheng Emperor could step in and play the role of an arbiter. In the late Ch'ing period, however, appeals to the throne were more likely to be cover-ups for some hard bargaining between the two sides.

The founders of the Shang pu had hoped that it would be able to do more than the traditional ministries in carrying out national policies in the provinces. Yet in its efforts to bring the Shang-wu chü under its control, it found that, instead of giving commands to the provincial authorities, it could not even develop an area of mutual agreement between itself and the provinces. There is no evidence that the governors-general even tried to compromise with the ministry, which had the misfortune to arrive on the scene at a time when the central government was becoming more dependent on the provinces for new sources of revenue to pay off the national debt. Thus, the Shang pu's efforts in the provinces could only be regarded as an undesirable intrusion on the provincial government's jurisdiction.

The provincial authorities were particularly anxious to control the Shang-wu chü since it was often involved with the supervision of the tax structure. In fact, there is evidence of inter-bureau rivalry between the Shang-wu chü and the Reorganization Bureaus (Shan-hou chü) in provinces where the latter were present. Reorganization bureaus had begun in the 1850s as coordinating committees to pull the financial resources of each province together to support the war efforts against the Taipings. In Kwangtung, the conflict was resolved in favor of the Reorganization Bureau: any tax reforms the weaker Shang-wu chü might undertake had to have the prior approval of the Reorganization Bureau.[33]

With so much working against the Shang pu, the old machinery which had served well for the Six Ministries was unable to function properly for the Shang pu. Its appeal to the throne only elicited token compliance by the provinces.

Early in 1905, the Shang pu launched its attack on Amoy's Pao-shang chü. It informed the throne that this bureau had not even acknowledged receipt of its regulations sent out a year earlier on the subject of protecting the merchants. The regulations elaborated on the throne's strong statement in 1903 asking provincial governors-general to take particular care of overseas Chinese merchants on home visits. The Shang pu now admitted that it did not have any information about the operations of the Amoy bureau[34] and that only the Liang-Kuang governor-general had made copies of the regulations available for circulation.[35]

In the summer of 1905, the Shang pu submitted another lengthy memorial to the throne on the difficulty of enforcing its directives in the provinces. It complained that the Shang-wu chü did not carry out its orders. While the ministry took the initiative in settling many bankruptcy claims made on defaulting local banks in Kiangsu, Kiangsi, and Shantung, it managed to enter one case in Shanghai only after the provincial government, responding to its repeated appeals, finally allowed it to perform a part in the settlement. The Shang pu's memorial contended that the other provinces "refused even to acknowledge receipt of letters from us for the last four to seven months. As for our telegrams, they were met with similar delaying tactics."[36] Sometime later, a contributor to the Shang pu's *Commercial Gazette* expressed the frustration that must have been shared by all the officials at the ministry. While discussing the subject of protecting the merchants, he pointed out that, even with the best of intentions, the ministry could do nothing unless the provincial governors-general and their subordinates enforced its policy.[37]

In 1907, following the reorganization of the Shang pu into the Nung-kung-shang pu, the new ministry tried again to control the provincial Shang-wu chü. It made some headway when the latter in turn were reorganized into Nung-kung-shang-wu chü, with a rearrangement of departments to correspond with those in the ministry. In 1908, more progress was made when the new bureaus were regularized and elevated to the same level as the provincial salt or police administration. A regular official with the title of "intendant (taotai) for the encouragement of industries (*ch'uan-yeh tao*)" headed the Nung-kung-shang-wu chü. As specifically required by the imperial decree creating the new post, the intendant was responsible to both the Nung-kung-shang pu and the Yu-ch'uan pu (Ministry of Post and Communications).[38] Presumably, as a regular and senior provincial official, he was no longer selected entirely by the provincial authorities. By the end of 1908, nine intendants were appointed to the new bureaus.[39]

Such an institutional innovation would seem to be a great victory for the Nung-kung-shang pu. There is, however, no evidence that, from 1908 on, the ministry had any more impact or control over the industrial and commercial activities in the provinces. A number of reasons may account for this. First, after 1908, the Nung-kung-shang pu itself lost much of its zest or sense of mission. The new president, P'u-hsü, lacked imagination and strength of character. He also did not have the kind of political backing his predecessor had been able to provide. Second, during these last years of the dynasty, the central government was preoccupied with its own factional struggles for power. This apparently led senior provincial officials to identify their interests more and more with the provinces in which they held offices. If the career of Chou Shan-p'ei was at all representative, it would appear that the new intendants behaved in this way. Chou, a Chekiangese, had been the intendant in Szechwan from October 1908 to the summer of 1911. When the crisis over the nationalization of the Szechwan-Hankow Railway came in 1911, he opposed the central government's policy.[40]

Third, the same years saw a further deterioration of the central authority over the provinces. The throne, by permitting the expression of popular sentiment through the formation of representative assemblies in the provinces, had hoped to bring the local gentry and gentry-merchants more to its side. But the result was to unbalance even further an already tenuous relationship between the gentry elite and the regular bureaucracy headed by governors-general and governors. The power and authority of the provincial government became so eroded that when the 1911 Revolution came most governors simply had to follow the gentry's lead in supporting the revolutionists or run for their lives. Representative assemblies, by legitimizing popular sovereignty, also denied Peking's monopoly on legitimate authority. As they preferred stronger regionalism and localism, ministerial directives from Peking had even less chance of gaining acceptance in the provinces.

The Shang pu's efforts to set up branch offices in the provinces down to the county level failed because they ran into the strong opposition of provincial governments. The provinces successfully blocked this move by offering the Shang-wu chü instead. But the latter were already a part of the provincial bureaucracy. Thus, the ministry was never able to control them.

However, the central government's attempts to by-pass the provincial hierarchy represented a new departure from the established system of control. The problems of control between the different levels—national, provincial, county, and municipal—have been continued up to the present. Since the 1950s, the Communist Chinese have endeavored to use "dual lines of control" to resolve the problem of conflicting jurisdictions between the central and provincial governments. Thus, they set up, with varying success, certain organizations in the provinces that are under both the provincial hierarchy and some specialized ministry in Peking.[41]

The new Nung-kung-shang-wu chü established in 1908 paralleled in concept these more recent developments. But, although it provided the Nung-kung-shang pu with some measure of institutional control, the latter was no longer able to offer either forceful or imaginative leadership toward a new national program of modern enterprise.

Chapter Eleven

THE CONTINUING SEARCH: THE CHAMBER OF COMMERCE

The phenomenal rise of chambers of commerce (*shang-wu hui*) into a national network of some eight hundred associations and branches during the last years of the Ch'ing dynasty was an outgrowth of several complex social changes that went beyond the narrower requirements of modern or reformist developments in Chinese merchant organizations. During the nineteenth century, merchant institutions underwent major organizational changes, but the trend did not necessarily point to the creation of chambers of commerce. Instead, forceful sponsorship by the central government was crucial to their initial establishment, first in Shanghai in 1904 and then in Canton the following year. They came at a time when the Shang pu, having failed to set up its own branch bureaus in the provinces, was looking for some other ways of establishing direct contact with the merchants. As a result, the ministry pushed vigorously for a national system of merchant associations under a uniform set of rules.

However, the interest of the state often did not coincide with that of the merchant leaders who ran the chambers. Consequently their development, reflecting their many sponsors' aims and aspirations, was not entirely the result of an authoritarian imposition from above, or of spontaneous activities by the merchants. Some chambers continued the tradition of geographically based group domination. Others co-existed with other merchant organizations like guilds and charitable halls. Contrary to the central government's efforts, the larger chambers alternately asserted independence and sided with the local authorities. Their commitment to modern reform went beyond the setting up of market survey teams; they plunged enthusiastically into civic activities that ranged from installing street lights and sponsoring muscle-building physical exercises to organizing merchant militia. Like so many other social groups whose organizations mushroomed during this period, the merchants made use of the chambers to emphasize their roles not only as entrepreneurs, but also as citizens and patriots.

Traditional Organizations: Guilds and Charitable Halls

Traditionally, Chinese merchant organizations were based on trade and common geographical origin. When merchants from the same area but engaged in different trades dominated a commercial city, they formed separate trade guilds (*kung-so, t'ang,* etc.) which collectively were known as a "band" (*pang*). The Szechwan band in Hankow, consisting of at least the herb medicine and boatsman guilds, is an example. More often these guilds became constituent members of a larger Landsmann guild (also called *kung-so* or *t'ang*). Examples are the powerful Ssu-ming kung-so of Ningpo merchants and the Kuang-ch'ao kung-so of Cantonese merchants in Shanghai.[1]

These Landsmann guilds were offshoots of the provincial clubs or Landsmannschaften (*hui-kuan*) which, since the fifteenth century, had been serving as boarding houses and mutual aid organizations for traveling gentry, students, officials, and stranded persons from each different province or region. The commercial counterparts sprang up as early as the sixteenth century because the older establishments generally excluded or discriminated against merchants.[2] By the nineteenth century, however, the Landsmann guilds gained great prominence because their members, as merchant sojourners, commanded enormous wealth and influence.

These guild organizations often impeded social and economic integration of a community. If a certain line of trade was dominated by traders of different geographical origins, there would likely be as many guilds of the same trade as there were merchants from the different places. Even though such fragmentation was sometimes mitigated by the guilds' relief work that bridged class differences, their central concerns were regional, traditional, and seldom community-oriented. The well publicized struggle between the Ssu-ming kung-so and the French Consulate in Shanghai for half a century (1849–1898) was not over some commercial or city-wide interest. It was over the Ningpo merchants' insistence on maintaining their cemetery grounds and the French equally stubborn insistence on leveling the area. That the merchants won ultimately only shows the power of their organization and the tenacity with which they fought to protect their interests.[3]

A major new development in merchant institutions took place sometime in the mid-nineteenth century. Civil war and economic decline had greatly increased the need for social services. While the gentry continued to manage public welfare and relief work in the countryside, urban merchants organized themselves to offer similar services for their cities. Several of these organizations, modeled upon gentry-run charitable halls (*shan-t'ang*), began to appear in Shanghai during the 1850s and the 1860s.[4] In Canton, merchant-run charitable halls were not founded until the 1870s, and they were set up according to the Shanghai model.[5] By 1900, at least nine had been inaugurated to form the "Nine Great Charitable Halls" (Chiu-ta shan-t'ang) of Canton.[6] Together with another steering committee representing all the local guilds—the "Seventy-two Guilds"—they were a powerful voice in local affairs on behalf of the Canton merchants.

Charitable halls facilitated the development of broader community concerns, for, at least in theory, they should not have limited their beneficiaries to their own kinsmen and native villagers. In practice, however, the management of these merchant charitable halls still preferred those from their own areas. In Shanghai, where the merchant community was dominated by several geographical groups, the charitable halls did not grow into truly large or powerful institutions. In Canton, the merchants were overwhelmingly Cantonese natives. Their charitable halls had no major regional barriers to overcome and became far more community-wide institutions with great power and prestige.

Canton's lack of a sizeable number of merchants from other areas also led to the relative weakness of Landsmann guilds vis-à-vis the trade guilds. By contrast, of the fourteen largest merchant organizations in Shanghai during the 1900s, seven of them were Landsmann guilds, while none of the rest were charitable halls.[7]

Central to the change in direction of these charitable halls and guilds was a new group of merchant directors. Many were men with quasi-official and gentry background. Others were wealthy merchants who had purchased official ranks for prestige and easy access to the mandarins. Their leadership facilitated the shift from the narrow or self-serving guild regulations to more integrated and broader orientations.[8] These new leaders, no longer limited to a traditional background, made use of their official ties and knowledge of Western models to push for a greater voice in the political and economic life of the whole community. Their organizational model was the foreign chamber of commerce found in the treaty ports.[9]

It is no accident, then, that Yen Hsin-hou, a gentry-merchant with both new skills and traditional roots, was first active in the banking guild and later took the lead in the formation of the Shanghai General Chamber of Commerce. In Canton, Cheng Kuan-ying, a comprador who left his foreign employer to work for several modern enterprises, and Tso Tsung-fan, a *chü-jen* scholar who became a merchant, followed a similar route. While serving as officers of the Kuang-jen Charitable Hall, they worked energetically for the inauguration of the Canton General Chamber of Commerce. Yen in Shanghai and Tso in Canton became the first presidents of their respective chambers. Such a continuity in leadership personnel contributed immeasurably to a relatively smooth transition from late traditional to early modern merchant institutions.[10]

The Official Initiative

During the 1890s, as both conservative and progressive literati became convinced that the promotion of commerce and industry could enrich China and so strengthen her, many began to champion the founding of chambers of commerce. For them, the thriving and powerful foreign chambers on the China coast represented symbols of the strength and unity of the Western entrepreneurs. Proposals came from men like T'ang Shou-ch'ien, a scholar-official, railway promoter, and later a constitutionalist from Chekiang; and Wu Maoting, one time comprador of the Hong Kong and Shanghai Banking Corporation at Tientsin. Liang Ch'i-ch'ao observed that a chamber of commerce could become a school for self-government, while a fellow social critic, Ou Chü-chia, emphasized its role as an institution to reform the merchant class.[11] Given these objectives, they clearly felt that the guilds were inadequate and that the new institution must be radically different.

Nothing was accomplished, however, until 1903 when the Shang pu was established. In a memorial seeking imperial approval for a national network of chambers of commerce, the Shang pu stressed the deplorable state of disunity not only between officials and merchants but also among the merchants themselves. It cited other weaknesses: the general lack of commercial knowledge, and the poverty of capital accumulation. It then proposed a detailed set of guidelines to govern the form and functions of the chamber.

Under the ministry's plan, all provincial capitals and major commercial centers would have general chambers of commerce, to be supplemented by branch chambers in all the secondary commercial centers throughout the country. The functions of the chambers were broadly stated. They consisted of 1) seeking improvements in commercial matters; 2) finding out conditions of trade, compiling statistical surveys, and reporting them each year to the ministry for reference; 3) sponsoring commercial exhibitions and running commercial and technical schools; 4) protecting merchants by notifying the ministry of any grievances inflicted by the local authorities; and 5) presenting merchant opinions to the local and central government authorities.[12]

Each chamber would draw up its own regulations following these general guidelines. Once approved, it would be given an official seal. Similarly, its officers were to receive the ministry's approval before being properly installed in office. In other words, the Chinese chamber of commerce was not only officially inspired; it was seen as a quasi-official institution subject to the Shang pu's control and guidance. On January 11, 1904 this proposal was approved by the throne.[13]

The Shanghai General Chamber of Commerce

Back in Shanghai in January 1901, Sheng Hsuan-huai had sought imperial sanction for a similar kind of chamber of commerce.[14] Although his proposal was not acted upon by the court,

Sheng set about to found the first officially sponsored commercial organization. Modeled upon the foreign chamber of commerce in Shanghai and the provincial Shang-wu chü, it appears to have been educational, preparatory, and consultative in nature—a kind of forum for the different merchant groups to meet and discuss problems of mutual interest. Yen Hsin-hou, general manager of Sheng's Imperial Bank of China in Shanghai, organized his group into the Shanghai Commercial Consultative Association (Shang-hai shang-yeh hui-i kung-so) in early 1902, and became its first president (*tsung-li*).[15]

The association's vice-president (*hsieh-li*) was Chou Chin-piao, whose qualifications were very much like Yen's. Both came from Ningpo, working as partners in banking and in the textile industry. Both bought official ranks, held official posts for a period, and remained closely connected with official enterprises.[16] Its declared intention notwithstanding, the association's membership was not representative of the Shanghai merchants. Yen and Chou drew support mainly from their fellow Ningpo merchants.

In less than three months after the imperial decree authorizing the founding of chambers of commerce, Shanghai became the first to comply. The Commercial Consultative Association quickly raised 12,000 taels, drew up a new constitution, and changed its name to Shanghai General Chamber of Commerce (Shang-hai shang-wu tsung-hui). There was only a slight change in leadership. Yen remained in the presidency. Chou stepped down to become the junior vice-president, while the well-known Cantonese ex-comprador and entrepreneur, Hsu Jun, assumed the senior vice-presidency.[17]

At the time, Hsu and Chou were in charge of the China Merchants' Steam Navigation Company and the Imperial Telegraph Administration respectively—two state-controlled organizations which provided half of the chamber's founding expenses. Hsu's appointment was noteworthy because he was the only Cantonese among the chamber's leaders in Shanghai. Although he and Yen were partners of the Hua-hsing Insurance Company in Shanghai, they were in opposing factional groups. Hsu was closely connected with Yuan Shih-k'ai, who had just engineered Hsu's return to the

China Merchants' S.N. Company after having first forced Sheng Hsuan-huai to relinquish his control. This must have been particularly sweet to Hsu because, in the mid-1880s, Sheng had pushed him out of the same company.[18] On the other hand, Yen and Chou worked closely with Sheng and probably did not invite Hsu to join the leadership. As Hsu himself said, he owed his post to the Shang pu, which was interested in bringing in some Cantonese merchants to widen the Shanghai chamber's base of support and to check the Ningpo domination. Hsu had impressive credentials. Besides his long involvement in modern enterprise, he had been very active in relief work the year before, and was a founder of the Kwangtung Landsmann guild.[19]

Any such efforts to broaden the base of support of the Shanghai chamber were futile. For the next twenty years, the chamber remained a preserve of the Ningpo merchants.[20] Hsu was not reelected. In 1905, Yen retired and Tseng Shao-ch'ing, a native Shanghai merchant (whose family originally came from Fukien), was elected president. Tseng had become well known for his leadership in the anti-American boycott and anti-opium campaigns earlier in the year.[21] He was the only non-Ningpo merchant to be president until the 1920s. In 1906, another Ningpo man, Li Hou-yu, took over for one year. Then from 1907 to 1915, when he was appointed the Shanghai prefect, Chou Chin-piao assumed the presidency with only one brief interruption. Chou's successor was Chu Pao-san, another Ningpo merchant who had been vice-president in 1905-1906 and again in 1914-1915. During the 1911 Revolution, Chu also headed a pro-revolutionary splinter chamber.[22] The vice-presidents were also from Ningpo, the only exceptions being Hsu Jun, already mentioned, and Sun To-shen in 1906. Sun, the owner of a successful flour factory in Shanghai, came from one of Anhwei's most prominent official families. His father was Grand Secretary Sun Chia-nai.[23]

Other prominent Ningpo merchants who became directors in the Shanghai General Chamber of Commerce at this time included Yü Hsia-ch'ing, comprador, banker, and shipowner; Fu Hsiao-an, comprador and shipowner; Fang Chiao-po, sugar refiner; and Shao Ting-sung, broker. In theory, the chamber had 50 directors representing the different guilds. In practice, the management fell into the hands of the officers and a board of directors which varied between 12 and 21 members. The Ningpo merchants' domination over the chamber was exercised by their majority number on this board. In addition, the chamber's membership was purposely kept small. As late as 1919, it had 300 members, consisting mostly of guilds and well-established firms, as well as a few individual members. The board of directors had successfully resisted various demands for a larger membership. In 1907, when a branch chamber was set up in the Chinese or southern part of Shanghai, the new organization was similarly dominated by the Ningpo group. Its president was Wang I-t'ang, a comprador, painter, and steamship entrepreneur from Ningpo. This branch chamber, however, played no independent role, but followed the general chamber in the International Settlement on important issues.[24]

The Canton General Chamber of Commerce

In Canton, preliminary plans for a chamber of commerce began in August of 1903, when the governor-general asked the five largest charitable halls—Kuang-jen, Kuang-chi, Shu-shan, Ai-yü, and Ch'ung-cheng—and the Seventy-two Guilds to discuss the question. Over one hundred merchant representatives answered the governor-general's call and congregated at the Kuang-jen Charitable Hall for the first meeting on October 20th. There was, however, little enthusiasm, and less than half of them attended the following two meetings.[25]

Throughout 1904, with renewed government pressure, preparations continued under the direction of an organizing committee of twelve elected directors. According to Cheng Kuan-ying, one of the elected twelve, the merchants were suspicious of a centralized and government-backed association that might threaten their own independence. Finally, it was agreed to raise an endowment fund for the chamber at $10 a share. Each guild and each company would, according to its size, subscribe a large or small number of shares. The capital would be deposited in local banks, and the interest accrued would then be used to run the chamber. That this was done with great reluctance is evident from the fact that the organizing committee was not given any funds or allowed to touch any of the capital until there were enough members to make the chamber operable. Official pressure continued, so that, when the Canton General Chamber of Commerce was finally opened on July 3, 1905, over half the guilds had registered; its endowment funds exceeded $100,000.[26]

The guilds' opposition had apparently been neutralized by a special arrangement built into the chamber's constitution. Article 4 stated that, besides following the ministry's guidelines of one president and one vice-president, the Canton chamber, "having regard for the unique condition of Kwangtung province, the thriving state of her handicraft industry and commerce, and the pioneering nature of the institution, decides to add and appoint seven resident managers (*tso-pan*) to be filled from among the directors and elected by the Seventy-two Guilds. These resident managers will be on duty in rotation." The Shang pu consented, and the seven resident managers were recognized one month after the chamber was officially opened.[27]

The two top posts went to officers of the Kuang-jen Charitable Hall. The chamber president, Tso Tsung-fan, was a director. Cheng Kuan-ying, elected vice-president, was another. Cheng's credentials were impressive. Besides his fame as an articulate political commentator, he had been closely associated with Sheng Hsuan-huai in modern industry. In 1905, he was the chief manager of the Kwangtung Canton-Hankow Railway Company. It seems that he deferred to Tso as the choice for president simply because Tso was one of those rare merchants whose gentry rank was not purchased. He was a *chü-jen* degree holder.

Leadership and Authority

While both Canton and Shanghai retained the old established leaders by making them officers of the new chambers of commerce, the chamber in Shanghai became far more dominant in its respective merchant community than the Canton chamber. In Canton, leaders of the charitable halls, supported by the guilds, overshadowed and even controlled their local chamber. Edward Rhoads, in his study of merchant associations in Canton, and Mark Elvin, in his study on political institutions in Shanghai, have observed the different behaviors of the merchant elite in their respective cities. For example, the Canton leaders vehemently disagreed among themselves over matters the Shanghai leaders combined to promote.[28] In part, this was because of the different native place ties of the commercial elite in these two cities. In Canton, where no serious rival geographical groups existed, the leadership was less cohesive, with various group leaders identified with their own guilds or charitable halls. In Shanghai, because the Ningpo group was pre-eminent, leaders of the Ningpo Guild simply took over the Shanghai Chamber of Commerce and made it the most prominent merchant organization. The chamber consolidated and legitimized their domination because, unlike the old guild, the chamber could claim community-wide jurisdiction, and was backed by imperial endorsements giving the individual officers and directors quasi-official status.[29]

In Shanghai, Canton, and elsewhere the traditional leadership was able to maintain their strong hold on the chambers of commerce by restricting membership to the representatives of guilds and proprietors of the large commercial and industrial houses. In terms of the proclaimed ideals behind the founding of the chamber of commerce, this in effect was a step backward in comparison with the traditional guilds, where proprietors, master craftsmen, journeymen, and shop hands were all allowed membership.[30] The central government did not intend to encourage shop hands, salesmen, or factory workers to participate actively in the affairs of the chamber. Such encouragement might turn it into a forum for the social mobilization of the merchant and working classes. But neither did it plan for an exclusive membership. The Shang pu was, however, partly responsible, since it failed to spell out the qualifications of membership in its general guidelines for the establishment of the chamber of commerce. Significantly, the constitutions of the Canton and Shanghai chambers were equally vague on this point. Presumably the criterion was determined by the officers and their boards of directors. Thus, although Mark Elvin's study suggests great variations in determining chamber membership in the different provinces—so much so that Shansi province, which had far less economic activity than Kiangsu province, had more chambers and more members per chamber than Kiangsu—the fact remains that only the locally prominent merchants in each place were accepted for membership.[31]

However, unlike the question of membership, the authority of the chamber of commerce as conceived by the ministry was quite explicit. Article 15 of the ministry's regulations for all chambers of commerce gave the president, when acting in concert with the directors, the authority to hear and decide cases involving merchants' disputes. Local officials might review the case only after the chamber had passed judgment and if the parties concerned were still unsatisfied.

In practice, however, the chamber of commerce did not have such power of arbitration over its members. It seems that only the traditional guilds retained such a strong hold over their own members, and they had acquired it by force of custom rather than by law.[32] Given the nature of the chamber leadership in Canton and Shanghai, one can readily see how they could not enforce their authority to arbitrate cases. In one case, the leadership existed at the sufferance of the charitable halls and the traditional guilds; in the other, the leadership was not sufficiently representative to warrant compliance from the entire merchant community.

The regulations of the Canton General Chamber of Commerce, without openly contradicting the ministry's guideline, implied that the chamber did not intend to enforce any arbitration. Article 11, which promised to *mediate* cases involving merchants in disputes, was followed by a qualifying Article 12. It declared that, while it would comply with the ministry's guidelines in all matters, it would first "attune itself to local conditions." Only after the various merchants had met and agreed on a course of action, it continued, would the chamber decide what could be done. Article 20 then called upon each guild, according to its size, to appoint one to four representatives to attend any such consultations. Already, the Canton chamber had seven resident managers representing the interests of the guilds.

In spite of its limited power, many cases of arbitration were in fact brought to the chamber of commerce. First, many came before the branch chambers in the smaller commercial centers where their prestige in the community loomed high and their authority was relatively uncontested. Second, there were cases which came from disputants who voluntarily approached the chamber themselves beforehand. Third, there were the bankruptcy cases. The new bankruptcy law of 1905 envisioned that each chamber would set up its own committee to enforce the law and to settle claims.[33] It seems that, at least in the commercially prominent province of Kiangsu (which included Shanghai), the chambers carried out this authority regularly, even after the law itself was repealed in 1908. Fourth, there were cases involving Chinese and foreign disputants. The constitution of the Shanghai chamber made a specific pledge to perform such services when so requested by the foreign chamber of commerce (Article 2).

The chamber of commerce's decisions, however, were not final. Even the bankruptcy law, which at first glance gave the chamber sweeping judicial powers, required local officials to give final clearance and to order such minor executive actions as the sealing up of the properties in dispute. Thus, the actual power remained largely with the provincial Shang-wu chü, and later the Nung-kung-shang-wu chü, where special arbitration committees were set up to hear cases whenever the chamber's decisions were challenged. Similarly, the Mixed Court in Shanghai, whenever it referred a case to the Shanghai chamber, declared that it reserved the right of review, for it felt that the decisions of the chamber were not always above suspicion.[34]

The chamber of commerce, therefore, depended on local officials for the enforcement of its decisions. More often, the chamber would refuse to decide on a case, except for those where consensus among the merchant leaders could be reached. This was quite different from the traditional guilds, whose "non-binding" decisions were in almost all cases effectively enforced.[35]

Peking and the Chambers of Commerce

One other factor which could influence the authority of the chamber of commerce was the amount of support it received from the central government. From the Shang pu's viewpoint, the chamber of commerce was meant to operate as a mechanism of administrative and political control over the local commercial communities, and to serve as a supporting institution that by-passed the regular provincial bureaucracy and carried out the ministry's directives at the local level. Article 7 of its guidelines gave the general chambers of commerce the right of direct appeal to the ministry against local excesses. Early in 1904, new regulations were issued inviting chamber directors to make personal calls on the ministry with a minimum of fuss and formality.[36] Then, to assure its close supervision over the management of the various chambers, the ministry confirmed the office holders, checked their regulations before approval, and set up a bureau to deal specifically with their affairs. It also pushed hard for a national network of chambers so that even the less commercially prominent provinces would be well represented. Thus peripheral provinces like Yunnan and Kweichow were found to have set up a number of chambers of commerce.

Given the ministry's interest, it would appear that maximum support would be offered the chambers of commerce. The actual situation, however, was more complex. The ministry's conception of the chambers' functions required an effective chamber leader to serve both as agent and leader. He had to represent merchant interests ably to the officials and, at the same time, relay the government's policies and make them palatable to his merchant colleagues and followers. The timing of the chambers' founding compounded his difficulty, for, during this period, many self-government associations and constitutional preparation study groups were active in many cities, including Shanghai, Tientsin, and Canton.[37] Even though the chambers of commerce never became another school for the constitutionalists, much less the political radicals, many of their members became assertive about their own views. The fact that Tseng Shao-ch'ing was elected president of the Shanghai chamber in 1905—soon after his organization of the boycott movement against American goods—indicated the mood of the chamber.

Tseng's election did not have the support of the central government; his movement had been discouraged by it, and maligned by officials like Yuan Shin-k'ai.

Many merchants suspected both the central and local government's intentions in espousing the cause of the chambers of commerce. In 1903, while the Cantonese merchants debated on whether to have a chamber, one merchant demanded that the government promise not to interfere with the work of the chamber. If the supervision of an official was agreed upon on any occasion, then his role and the limit of his power was to be clearly stated in the chamber's regulations.[38] One newspaper's editorial actually prejudged the government's intentions pessimistically. Chinese merchants, it informed its readers, knew nothing about collective efforts, while individual merchant leaders could be manipulated easily so that chambers of commerce would simply help the government raise more money and force the merchants into greater dependence on official directives.[39]

Such skepticism was partly responsible for the resistance in Canton. The merchants in Peking, too, resisted the Shang pu's pressure, which had been applied since early 1904. Finally its local and draft remittance banks were persuaded to organize miniature trade chambers of commerce (*shang-hui*) themselves.[40] This practice was borrowed by the tea, cloth, medicine, books, foreign goods, and brocade guilds which reorganized themselves into individual chambers until 1907, when they agreed to merge into the Peking General Chamber of Commerce. In Hankow, the merchants were "not very enthusiastic," and again required a good deal of persuasion by the local taotai and the commissioner of the Shang-wu chü before "the various merchants agreed to come together to elect two directors" to initiate preparatory proceedings.[41]

On the other hand, the overall result of Peking's efforts in pushing for a national network of chambers of commerce was a success. Nationally, by 1908, there were 58 general chambers of commerce (19 of which were founded overseas), and 223 branch chambers.[42] In 1912, the total number rose to 794, and in 1915, 1,262.[43]

Evidently the central government's program was popular in the smaller commercial centers, and this accounted for the large increase in the total number of chambers in later years. In 1905, there were only 13 branch chambers. In 1906, the number reached 58. Two years later, it was 88. The huge numbers in the 1910s represent mostly branch chambers, for major commercial centers worthy of a general chamber were limited in number. The traditional merchant leaders in these smaller centers, with their relatively low social status and fewer institutional supports like the charitable halls, were keen to assume leadership in the new chambers of commerce, for the chambers had the appeal of imperial sanction. Joining the chamber became a new prestige symbol.

Thus, chamber leaders developed diametrically opposed attitudes toward the central government, depending on whether they came from a major or a subsidiary commercial center. While the subsidiaries welcomed Peking's efforts and sought its help and influence, the majors were skeptical and assertive of their independence. In Canton, the Cantonese merchants clashed with Peking over the control of the provincial railway. In Shanghai, the chamber's past record of independence led the central government to ignore it during the bank failures of 1910.[44] It was not until the second wave of bank failures that it was forced to call on the chamber to negotiate a loan with the Hong Kong and Shanghai Banking Corporation, for the bank would only accept what the chamber directors could put up as collateral. Then in December 1910, after the loan was concluded, the president of the chamber, Chou Chin-piao, was forced to resign by another ministry, the Yu-ch'uan pu, in Peking. Chou was accused of filing false reports about the financial crisis, favoring foreign debtors, and colluding with the local taotai, Ts'ai Nai-huang, who had also been cashiered for his misappropriation of public funds.[45]

Marie-Claire Bergère has suggested that Chou's fall was precipitated by the chamber's close identification with foreign interests, and that it meant a victory for the guilds which were against the policy of repaying foreign debtors first.[46] There is little doubt that the chamber was susceptible to foreign influence. It was situated inside the International Settlement, and in 1911 seven of its directors were compradors.[47] It is, however, unlikely that the guilds, in spite of their public protests, did not support Ts'ai's and Chou's policy of repaying foreign debtors first. For the guilds most affected by the crisis were themselves directly connected with foreign trade—the two Chinese bankers' guilds, the cotton yarn guild, the piece goods guild, to name only a few. They also participated fully all summer in the chamber's deliberations. Much as they disliked the policy, they were hardly in a position to argue with the foreign bankers, who threatened to curtail or stop all credit facilities extended to Chinese banks.[48] As the customs report pointed out, foreign trade in Shanghai was largely financed by the credit facilities foreign banks extended to Chinese bankers, importers, and exporters. In 1910, there was really no shortage of money in Shanghai, for, once the foreign bankers agreed to the loans guaranteed by the Chinese government, cash and credit were immediately made available, and the crisis disappeared.[49]

It is more likely that Chou and the Shanghai chamber had been punished by the central government because of their attempts to be independent. Since 1907, the chamber had been encouraged by the Preparation Committee for Constitutionalism (Yü-pei li-hsien kung-hui) to sponsor a series of discussions on commercial law. As various chambers sent delegations to Shanghai to discuss the issue, studies were made about how to organize themselves into a permanent nationwide association of chambers of commerce. Cheng Kuan-ying, who led the Canton delegation, expressed great enthusiasm, and even began planning for a large commercial bank and a shipping company with capital to be raised by the different provincial chambers and the overseas Chinese. Also interested in the project was a group of American merchants who apparently had been the first to propose it.[50] These inter-chamber activities had not been authorized by Peking, which saw them as a threat to its authority.[51]

Factionalism might also have accounted for Chou's dismissal. Chou, who had been president of the Shanghai chamber since 1907, was a protégé of Sheng Hsuan-huai. In 1910, Sheng had just resumed his post as the Junior Vice-President at the Yu-ch'uan pu. Almost immediately, he ran into a feud with its president, T'ang Shao-i. Chou was probably one of the casualties of the feud, for, soon after Sheng won his fight in early 1911 and succeeded T'ang into the presidency, Chou was restored to his office in the Shanghai chamber.[52] Therefore, clashes between Peking and individual chambers were not always the result of conflicting interest between the two levels. They also occurred because of factional feuds or incompatible personalities among the power holders.

Local Government and the Chambers of Commerce

In contrast to its relationship with the central government, the chamber's relationship with local and provincial governments was often rather harmonious. If the chamber could ignore the central government, it needed to cooperate with local authorities for its day-to-day operations. When a community was hit by an economic depression or a financial crisis, the chamber and the local government would usually work hand in hand. In 1910, as the Shanghai financial crisis spread to other cities, the chambers in Hankow and Tientsin cooperated with the local authorities. In Hangchow, a loan of 300,000 taels was secured from the provincial treasury and the salt commissioner through the local chamber's intervention.[53] In Shanghai, the chamber worked closely with Taotai Ts'ai Nai-huang from the beginning of the crisis. Although it was ignored by the central government, it laid the groundwork for the first foreign loan. Even the loan proposal to the central government was made jointly by the taotai's office and the chamber. Cooperation of this kind was common in many other financial crises—for example, 1906 and 1911 in Shanghai, 1909 in Tientsin, and 1912 in Hankow.[54]

Personal interests were often another factor that influenced such cooperation. In 1910, Taotai Ts'ai Nai-huang and President Chou Chin-piao were charged with collusion in misappropriating public funds. There was some basis for this charge. Ts'ai's office received all the public money from the provinces earmarked to pay the foreign indemnity before it was transmitted to Peking. While the money was under his care, Ts'ai deposited large sums with Chou's Imperial Bank of China and apparently made personal use of them to invest heavily in rubber stock, whose falling prices led to the bank failures. At one point during the financial crisis, Ts'ai's account reportedly showed he had overdrawn more than one million taels. Chou was undoubtedly aware of Ts'ai's activities.[55] However, mutual interest like this between Ts'ai and Chou could only favorably affect the leadership between the two institutions they represented.

But cooperation did not occur in all cases. In 1906, when Governor-general Ts'en Ch'un-hsuan's railway policy proved too unpopular for the Cantonese gentry and merchants, the Canton chamber joined the campaign to get rid of Ts'en by making direct appeals to Peking.[56] In the 1910 financial crisis, in spite of personal collaboration between Taotai Ts'ai and President Chou, the Shanghai chamber apparently had little influence with the local government over issues about which they disagreed. As Kotenev observed, "It is very doubtful whether the chamber exercised any considerable influence over the government, except in cases where the government made use of the chamber to express official opinions which were otherwise liable to be disregarded."[57]

Reform and Growing Self-Assertion

Even as the relationship between the chambers of commerce and the government remained in flux, the chambers were experimenting with new reform projects which took the merchants' activities into new areas of social concern. Their leaders strongly believed that chambers could become catchalls for all sorts of progressive ideas then current. In this way, the chambers of commerce quickly acquired an image and a style of their own, quite independent of what was intended by their official sponsors. They were attuned to the social activism of the day; they shared the same qualities of inventiveness and reforming zeal that characterized the new social and political institutions of this period.[58] It was in the 1920s that the chamber of commerce began to acquire the image of a stodgy, establishment-oriented institution.

One chamber leader who formulated a comprehensive plan was Cheng Kuan-ying. In 1905, as the newly elected vice-president of the Canton chamber, Cheng corresponded with the Shang pu and the Governor-general in Canton on the functions of the chambers of commerce. In Cheng's view, the chambers' primary role should be educational. What China needed most urgently, he contended, was "the opening up of commercial and industrial knowledge" (*k'ai shang-chih*). More concretely, the chambers should sponsor commercial and technical schools, industrial workshops, commercial newspapers with free circulation down to the county level, and centers to display local products and to do research. The chambers should also raise capital and organize agricultural, industrial, and commercial banks of the modern type. At the various general chambers, capable and honest merchants and technicians would be appointed to tour the branch chambers. Their role would be to spread new concepts of business and modern technology.[59]

A second area of the chambers' roles was to promote a modern system of legal rights and responsibilities in commercial and industrial practices. Cheng pointed out that prominent men often did not have to be responsible for their debts in bankruptcy cases because their ownership was never revealed. On the question of legal rights, Cheng expressed concern over the independence of the chambers. He felt that the government should refrain from sending officials to supervise and intervene in the affairs of the chambers.

Many of Cheng Kuan-ying's proposals were discussed by the organizing committee of the Canton chamber.[60] By 1906, the chamber had an industrial workshop, a commercial school, a display center, and a newspaper. Cheng failed, however, to realize his more ambitious plans. The chamber did not hire competent men to visit the smaller communities to disseminate knowledge. And in spite of the Shang pu's encouragement, not many merchants volunteered information about the ownership of their enterprises.

But the progressive zeal had caught on in many other chambers. In Hangchow, the chamber established a Commercial Studies Association in 1905, with a program to establish a commercial newspaper, a commercial school, and a lecture hall giving periodic lectures on commerce to the public. There were also plans to compile trade statistics and to establish a workshop.[61] Perhaps the chamber's spirit is best represented in the 1906 annual report of the Sung-kiang Branch Chamber of Commerce in Kiangsu. It laid claim to achievements in four areas in which progressive merchants had recently showed increasing interest. The Sung-kiang chamber reported that first it had set up a tuition-free evening school for shop hands. It offered courses ranging from English and commerce to self-cultivation and gymnastics. By the year's end, it had forty graduates. Second, it had opened a Physical Exercise Association to train its young members in arms for self-defense. Third, it had established a Stop Opium-Smoking Association where over two hundred members had signed pledges to stop smoking. The association also sold pills to the poor at a loss in order to cure them of opium addiction. Fourth, in collaboration with the local charitable halls, it had installed street lights, purchased three more fire engines, and kept a company of fifty volunteer firemen.[62]

The Sung-kiang chamber's programs were representative of what the other chambers were doing. Schools, workshops, and display centers were extremely popular and reflected a conscious effort by chamber leaders to imitate the programs already launched by the Shang pu and carried out into the provinces by the provincial bureaus of commerce. While these merchant efforts were publicly applauded by the officials, they were also a source of conflict. For the merchants tried to modify these programs to suit their own needs in the face of the government's attempts to impose some control. In the area of providing municipal services, the chamber's participation was a continuation of similar efforts already undertaken by charitable halls and some of the guilds. However, in Shanghai, this led individual chamber members to argue for representation in the governing councils of the International Settlement. Sung-kiang's Physical Exercise Association and its emphasis on gymnastics in its evening school represented a new departure for merchant organizations. This shows that the Chinese merchants had become aware of contemporary reform literature which emphasized the need for Chinese patriots to grow strong bodies to fight off foreign invaders. It also shows that the merchants saw the need to have their own militia for self-defense. The first physical exercise association for Chinese merchants was launched in Shanghai in 1905. In 1907, one hundred of its members were allowed to join the foreign volunteer corps as one Chinese company. The reorganized association then called itself the Merchant Volunteer Corp (*shang-t'uan*), which became a model for many other treaty ports, including Canton, Swatow, Tientsin, Hankow, and Sung-kiang.[63]

Finally, the Sung-kiang chamber's establishment of the Stop Opium-Smoking Association was an expression of the merchants' new sense of civic responsibility and of nationalism. This association was again an imitation of the one initiated in Shanghai called the Association to Raise the Martial Spirits (Chen-wu tsung-she). Both gentry and merchants participated in the movement, which spread nationwide. For example, in Canton, a major campaign was launched in 1907 by both gentry and merchants with the acting governor-general serving as honorary president.[64] In Tientsin, the chamber not only organized the anti-opium campaign; it also set up a bureau which monopolized the production and sale of opium —the idea being that, for the campaign to succeed, the addicts' source of supply had to be regulated.

The Tientsin chamber's last program reveals one other aspect of these reforms. Merchants often tried to combine reform with profit-taking ventures. The opium monopoly was run strictly as a business enterprise. The capital came from chamber members, and the officers were chamber directors serving by rotation.

In these and other activities, it became clear that chambers of commerce had, by 1912, assumed a style and form all their own. The chambers adopted many progressive ideas and programs, and they were no longer restricted by the old guild structure to achieve those new goals. Many chamber leaders, including the major ones of Shanghai and Canton, supported the revolutionary forces of 1911 with money and men.[65] On the other hand, they were not much different from the traditional guilds, with their clannishness and factionalism. They also reinforced and indeed regularized the mode of collaboration with local authorities. But this was probably as it should be. The new merchant elite, while politicized and pressing for economic and social modernization, did not at this time constitute a united class with common bourgeois goals. The chambers' mix of traditional patterns and modern tendencies was a fair reflection of the mentality of the men who ran them.

The chambers also brought some subtle changes to the relationships between merchants and government at different levels. One reason why the central government sponsored this institution was the prospect of using it as a direct link between Peking and the local communities. In this, it had little success. Instead, by giving legitimacy to such a merchant organization, the state increased the independent strength of the merchants. Furthermore, the chambers allowed provincial and local officials to be more independent of the central government, for part of those officials' growing power vis-à-vis the central government during this period rested on the independent strength of the merchants in their areas. Such a form of support to local or regional authorities persisted into the 1920s and contributed far more to the collapse of the Chinese central authorities than all the short-term support so many chamber leaders openly gave to the revolutionaries of 1911.

Chapter Twelve

CONCLUSIONS

Despite dynamic efforts, late Ch'ing merchants and officials failed to establish modern enterprise in China. This study has examined those efforts from three perspectives: first, the merchants who were undergoing major changes in their roles, class composition, status, and group organizations as a result of the state's decision to push for industrialization; second, the provincial officials, who experimented with various forms of industrial organization in their search for securing state or bureaucratic control; and third, the central government, which, after 1900, formulated vigorous but futile policies to challenge the provincial authorities' domination over modern enterprise.

The key issues affecting these developments throughout were control and who was to exercise it. They became the operating force behind the two main themes—competition between merchants and officials and competition between regional and central authorities. They led to several organizational formats which altered the original character of state control and, consequently, the nature of political influence on industrial development.

During the late nineteenth century, Chinese political and intellectual leaders came to realize that the state's economic weakness was the main cause of foreign encroachment. This was reflected in their preoccupation with using commerce and industry as means of achieving national "wealth and strength" (*fu-ch'iang*). As they looked alarmingly at China's unfavorable balance of trade, they raised these common issues repeatedly to the level of a battle for national survival—their intensity encapsulated in the pithy phrase *shang-chan* (the war of commerce and industry).

The connection between wealth and power, however, had not been obvious at first. The early self-strengtheners at mid-nineteenth century did not understand this. During that earlier period, conservatives preached austerity, self-sufficiency, ethical rule, and a return to traditional social principles, while reformers advocated Western arms and armaments. It was from the 1870s that the self-strengthening movement turned to modern industry as the key to making the state wealthy and powerful. By 1900, with many debates and much theorizing behind them, everyone, progressives and cultural purists alike, was in favor of setting up modern enterprises.

But this new commitment did not mean that the Chinese scholar-officials truly understood modern economics. They continued to use primitive theories to prop up their arguments. Commerce and industry were seen as means of strengthening China; they were not appreciated for their economic and social values.

At the same time, China's political and social elite were engaged in an ideological reappraisal of the merchant class. They looked to the merchants to provide both capital and management skill. As a group, the comprador-merchants responded most actively, probably because of their familiarity with Western enterprise. But the compradors also facilitated the introduction of broadly Western notions of entrepreneurship and the place entrepreneurs should have in society. While none of the comprador-merchants became major political activists demanding social and economic rights for the Chinese merchant, their business contacts and cooperation with the scholar-officials had a liberating impact on merchants and officials alike.

In any event, an increasing number of officials and gentry assumed entrepreneurial roles publicly. They joined the merchant ranks even though their attitudes toward modern enterprise varied widely. Some, like Sheng Hsuan-huai and Nieh Ch'i-kuei, remained primarily officials and only secondarily entrepreneurs. They became the first group of official-entrepreneurs. Others, like Chang Chien and Chou Hsueh-hsi, adopted many modern entrepreneurial values. After 1900, as indicated by the careers of Chang Chien and Nieh Ch'i-chieh, the son of Governor Nieh Ch'i-kuei, careers in modern enterprise had become "respectable" in the eyes of the majority of the scholar-official class.

However, in spite of the accelerating changes in its function, social class composition, and status, this new group of merchants, gentry, and officials engaging in modern enterprise did not form a new Chinese bourgeoisie. New values were still intermingled with the old; the various sub-groups were still tied to their disparate loyalties and traditional symbols. Common place origins, family and clan interests, *t'ung-nien* (same year) affiliations through passing the same state examinations, shared memberships in some guilds or secret society lodges—these forces and others like them still exerted a far stronger pull on their allegiance than reasonable and common interests as members of an emergent bourgeois class. As individual merchants, gentry-merchants, or official-entrepreneurs, many sponsored community-wide reforms expressing their modern social and political concerns. They successfully made use of new institutions such as the chamber of commerce or of their own official positions. But as the efforts of a group or of a new social stratum, their activities remained local and uncoordinated.

Although merchants and officials had agreed on a rationale for industrial development, they reached little consensus on how it should be carried out. Already the central government was too financially dependent on the provinces to take any effective initiative at the national level. All agreed, however, that the government had an important supervisory role to perform, for both the tradition of state intervention in the national economy and the political justifications for building modern enterprise supported the idea of state domination. Thus the provincial officials allocated to themselves the roles of sponsors and supervisors of modern enterprises.

At first, Governor-general Li Hung-chang's *kuan-tu shang-pan* formula required merchants to invest their own capital and some amount of government loans at their own risk and to run the enterprises under his general supervision. Li saw in such an arrangement a means to tap and co-opt private capital because there was not sufficient state capital to start a full range of modern industry. Several private investors responded favorably. For them it was an equitable form of exchange, because Li's promise of state control meant freedom from excessive official squeeze. But Li offered no safeguards against official supervisors who became increasingly ensnarled in conflicting interests of national goals and personal interests. From the very beginning, *kuan-tu shang-pan* was an *ad hoc* arrangement between government and merchants. It had no fixed structure but was meant to be interpreted flexibly to suit the needs of each enterprise. Without any abrupt change of policy, therefore, official supervisors could more and more encroach upon the rights of merchant managers. Then, as the merchants were in many cases unwilling or unable to provide adequate capital, provincial government funds were utilized with increasing frequency. This provided official supervisors with the excuse to turn themselves into official managers and to transform state supervision into bureaucratic control.

But even the few enterprises that enjoyed sufficient private support could not escape such a trend of growing bureaucratization. The China Merchants' Steam Navigation Company lost its merchant managers, Tong King-sing and Hsu Jun, in 1884 when they were found diverting some company funds into their own private business. Sheng Hsuan-huai, Li's appointed official supervisor, took over the company and became its official-manager.

From the late 1880s onward, as less and less private capital went into officially sponsored modern industry, provincial officials tried to offer alternative formulae to recapture the merchants' interest. New terms signifying equal partnership such as *kuan-shang ho-pan* were coined. Governor-general Chang Chih-tung established a number of textile factories of this type. But he and others who offered these formulae refused to delegate authority to their merchant partners, and few private entrepreneurs stepped forward to invest money in them. In 1902, as a result of bureaucratic bungling and deficient funding, Chang's numerous textile plants were leased out to a private company.

This did not mark the end of state control in modern industry. It only led to changes in the nature of control. In the 1890s, several of Li Hung-chang's associates began to experiment with a new form of partnership between *individual* officials and merchants. The official transferred state funds into a private account and, by means of his political power and influence, assured his enterprise of official protection without the need of formal state sponsorship. Thus an official was still in charge, but quietly and unofficially.

After 1900, officials who participated in modern enterprises evolved further refinements to improve their own position, and a new group of official-entrepreneurs emerged to assert their own brand of official control. The earlier official supervisors' and managers' main concern had been to control the use of private capital and provincial funds invested in or loaned to industrial enterprises. The new official-entrepreneurs had very different aims and functions. They invested heavily with their own capital, thus combining the roles of investors, managers, and protectors. They also became more efficient. Since the capital involved was their own, they had a personal interest in preferring good business sense to bureaucratic waste and inefficiency. Chou Hsueh-hsi, who typified this group of official-entrepreneurs, ran two successful enterprises, the Lanchou Official Mining Company Ltd., and the Chee Hsin Cement Company Ltd. He and his small group of official friends put up the capital, plowed back a good deal of their earnings during the early period, and led both companies to spectacular growth without state interference.

Other official-entrepreneurs, like Chang Chien, continued to turn to private capital for support, but without much success. In spite of his unsullied reputation, Chang managed to raise 500,000 taels for a spinning mill only after provincial officials rallied to his support by extending to him government loans. Chang's success, however, was in his ability to co-opt public funds and to secure state protection for his enterprises which were not under formal state or bureaucratic control. Thus his Dah Sun Mill remained a privately run company.

A number of modern enterprises operated by official-entrepreneurs were therefore successful ventures. But the prospect of a sustained growth into a Rostowian "take-off" still eluded them. Chou Hsueh-hsi's associates were so few in number that, collectively, their resources were severely limited. Chang Chien's official connections helped him with official loans, but he acquired them with great difficulty. In any case, to depend on official funds would confront him with the same old problems that had confounded earlier official promoters: there was just not enough official money to go round. What was needed was a popular movement willing and ready to support private enterprise by means of both money and spirit.

Between 1906 and 1909, such an opportunity emerged. The success of the Rights Recovery Movement for a number of railways brought forth privately run and popularly supported provincial railway companies in Kwangtung, Chekiang, and Kiangsu. Officials who preferred building railways under state control were put on the defensive because they were seeking foreign loans to pay for their construction costs. By pointing out this link between state control and foreign concessions, advocates of private enterprise were able to transform their cause into popular politics. They also shrewdly lowered the value per share of railway company stocks until the average student or shop hand could afford them. The result was an astounding success. During 1906 and 1907, millions of taels were raised from tens of thousands of small but politicized contributors. And for the first time in China, a major private modern enterprise needed no official sponsors or managers to assure it of state protection.

But managerial malpractices and shareholder factionalism followed. By 1909, these private railway companies were in ruins. Soon thereafter, state control was reimposed in the form of the nationalization of railways.

The private railways were the first and last major experiment during the late Ch'ing to try to operate as modern enterprises without state control. That they too failed should be a reminder that state control was not the only force necessarily inhibiting to economic growth. In any case, there were categories of control connected with official power. Those categories which Chou Hsueh-hsi and Chang Chien exploited in fact proved to be highly beneficial. Where state controlled businesses stagnated or failed, the culprit was most likely not control itself but how control was exercised. In this sense, certain categories of state or bureaucratic control were bad because they were a symptom of some deeper social and political malaise, reflecting values antagonistic to the development of modern enterprise.

Thus, even though the scholar-official class, like the other social classes of politicized merchants, shop hands, and students, were generally committed to economic modernization as a national goal, there was precious little understanding that such a commitment required them not only to build factories according to some Western model, but also to alter drastically many of the values and institutions that made up the Chinese world. This lack of understanding, coupled with the frustrations of running operations which often seemed unmanageable, led most industrial managers and sponsors to prefer personal over public interests. For personal interests are always far more manageable. Besides, it was easy for a Chang Chih-tung or a Chou Hsueh-hsi to rationalize that what was good for him would ultimately be good for China.

Finally, there was the problem of long-term political stability. The Meiji leaders' successful efforts in the comparable field of modernization are often attributed to their foresight in selling government run and financed industry at bargain prices to private entrepreneurs. The Japanese bureaucrats had developed managerial and technical skills at great cost to the state; they then turned to private entrepreneurs as soon as the various enterprises were able to stand on their own feet. But the Japanese success was equally the result of a long and stable political order. If the Chinese after 1912 had enjoyed similar political stability, it is probable that such enterprises as those organized by Chou Hsueh-hsi, Chang Chien, the Jung brothers, and the managers of the private railway companies would have developed further by cross-fertilization into a successful model of economic modernization for China.

Even before the total collapse of central authority in Peking, the political context already had a disastrous effect on the development of a modern economy. Because of the nature of power relationships between the center and the provinces, practically all enterprises founded before 1900 were sponsored by senior provincial officials. This meant that their development took place regionally. There was poor coordination of policies, and there was a total absence of uniform principles. Since the provincial officials were subject to frequent reassignments, this injected disruptive elements into their sponsorship. Many a struggling company failed because a new mandarin put in charge would no longer support it. This was what happened to the Kweichow Mining and Ironworks. There were some exceptions. Chang Chih-tung, for example, was able to carry his cotton cloth mill from Canton to Wuhan, where his new assignment took him. But there were few men who had Chang's power and influence. Indeed Chang Chih-tung and Li Hung-chang were the two preeminent patrons and promoters of modern enterprises precisely because they each had a long and stable power base. Li was Governor-general of Chihli from 1870 to 1895. Similarly, Chang, with a few brief interruptions, was Governor-general of Hu-Kuang from 1889 to 1907.

Following the disastrous outcome of the Boxer uprising, the central government began to challenge the domination of the provinces by initiating a national policy of commerce and industry of its own. It carried out major institutional reforms. The Shang pu and its successor, the Nung-kung-shang pu, in turn promulgated a modern commercial law code, set up a number of specialized agencies, and tried to establish branch offices in the provinces. That last measure ran into strong resistance from the provincial hierarchy. The two ministries consequently did not succeed in setting up their own supporting bureaus, but had to accept some existing ones which were part of the provincial bureaucracy. Thus, they found that their directives and programs were given at best token compliance by provincial officials, who had their own interests as well as having been highly circumscribed by the power of local bureaucrats and gentry-merchants. Modern industry had become a major source of revenue to the provinces and the individual officials who controlled them.

The central government also tried to seek an alternate link with the local merchants by encouraging them to organize themselves into a national network of chambers of commerce. Merchant organizations had been undergoing much institutional change since the late Ming. These changes reflected corresponding changes in the merchants' economic functions and social commitments. By 1900, when the encouragement came from above to model their community-based chambers of commerce upon the West's, the merchants were ready and willing, for their more traditional guilds and charitable halls were developing along a parallel path.

Soon after chambers of commerce were established, the central government found that the major chambers, like those in Shanghai and Canton, became self-assertive and independent. Furthermore, local chambers realized that they had more in common with local government than with the central government. Thus, the legitimacy the central government unwittingly offered to the chambers of commerce resulted in greater local autonomy, for part of the independent power local governments enjoyed rested on the strength of their merchant communities. Consequently, the Shang pu and the Nung-kung-shang pu failed to establish reliable supporting institutions in the provinces. But after 1912, with the collapse of central authority, the competition between the center and the province for control over the nation's industry was no longer a meaningful issue, for the new political situation infused into the whole question of economic modernization a new set of problems.

ABBREVIATIONS USED IN THE NOTES
(See bibliography for full citations and characters)

CKKYSTL-I: Ch'en Chen, et al., comp., *Chung-kuo chin-tai kung-yeh shih tzu-liao, ti-i-chi.* 2 vols.

CKKYSTL-III: Ch'en Chen, et al., comp. *Chung-kuo chin-tai kung-yeh shih tzu-liao, ti-san-chi.* 2 vols.

HTJP: Hsiang-kang Hua-tzu jih-pao.

KYSTL-I: Sun Yü-t'ang, comp., *Chung-kuo chin-tai kung-yeh shih tzu-liao, ti-i-chi, 1840-1895 nien.* 2 vols.

KYSTL-II: Wang Ching-yü, comp., *Chung-kuo chin-tai kung-yeh shih tzu-liao, ti-erh-chi, 1895-1914 nien.* 2 vols.

NCH: North China Herald.

NKSPTCP-I: Nung-kung-shang pu t'ung-chi piao, ti-i-tz'u. 6 ts'e.

NKSPTCP-II: Nung-kung-shang pu t'ung-chi piao, ti-erh-tz'u. 5 ts'e.

PYKT: Pei-yang kung-tu lei-tsuan.

PYKTHP: Pei-yang kung-tu lei-tsuan hsu-pien.

SCMP: South China Morning Post.

SWKP: Shang-wu kuan-pao.

TFTC: Tung-fang tsa-chih.

THL/KH: Kuang-hsu-chao tung-hua lu.

NOTES

The word tael (Tl.) as used in this study refers to the standard unit of Chinese monetary currency. In the late Ch'ing, the value of the tael varied somewhat from place to place depending on its fineness of silver. The tael referred to here was usually the Shanghai or the "Haikwan" (Customs) tael. The dollar ($) throughout is the Mexican or Chinese silver dollar: $1 was equivalent to 0.72 taels. Both taels and dollars were used as units of accounts. Because the price of silver was falling in relation to gold during the period of this study, the dollar's exchange rate dropped more than 100 percent; from about 4 English shillings for $1 in the 1880s to about 2 shillings in the 1900s.

1. Introduction

1. Ta-chung Liu and Kung-chia Yeh, *The Economy of the Chinese Mainland: National Income and Economic Development 1933–1959* (Princeton, 1965), p. 89, and Hou Chi-ming, "Economic Dualism: The Case of China, 1840–1937," *Journal of Economic History,* 23.3:277–297 (1965).
2. My own understanding of the merchant's position in traditional China has been greatly benefited by a number of recent studies, esp. L. S. Yang, "Government Control of the Urban Merchant in Traditional China," *Tsing Hua Journal of Chinese Studies* (new ser.) 8.1-2:186-209 (1970); Thomas A. Metzger, "The State and Commerce in Imperial China," *Journal of Asian and African Studies* 6:23–46 (1970); P'eng Tse-i, "Shih-chiu shih-chi hou-ch'i Chung-kuo ch'eng-shih shou-kung-yeh shang-yeh hsing-hui ti chung-chien ho tso-yung," *Li-shih yen-chiu* 1:71–102 (1965); Thomas G. Rawski, "Chinese Dominance of Treaty Port Commerce and Its Implications, 1860–1875," *Explorations in Economic History* 7.4: 451–473 (1970); Yen-p'ing Hao, *The Comprador in Nineteenth Century China* (Cambridge, Mass., 1970); W. E. Willmott, ed., *Economic Organization in Chinese Society* (Stanford, 1972); Fu I-ling, *Ming-Ch'ing shih-tai shang-jen chi shang-yeh tzu-pen* (Peking, 1956) and Joseph P. C. Jiang, "Towards a Theory of Parish Entrepreneurship," in Gerhan Wijeyewardene, ed., *Leadership and Authority* (Singapore, 1968), pp. 147–162.
3. E.g. see Mark Elvin's "The High-Level Equilibrium Trap: The Causes of the Decline of Invention in the Traditional Chinese Textile Industries," in W. E. Willmott, ed., *Economic Organization in Chinese Society* for an ingenious hypothesis explaining the great spurts of technological and economic activity in one industry, only to be followed by stagnation.
4. Saeki Tomi, *Shindai ensei no kenkyū* (Kyoto, 1956), p. 205.

5. Dwight H. Perkins, *Agricultural Development in China, 1368-1968* (Chicago, 1969), p. 33; also see Yeh-chien Wang, *Land Taxation in Imperial China, 1750-1911* (Cambridge, Mass., 1973), pp. 6-7 for slight modifications of some of Perkins's grain yield figures.
6. Rhoads Murphey, "The Treaty Ports and China's Modernization," in Mark Elvin and G. William Skinner, eds., *The Chinese City Between Two Worlds* (Stanford, 1974), pp. 17-71, esp. pp. 40-47.
7. Carl Riskin, "Surplus and Stagnation in Modern China," in Dwight H. Perkins, *China's Modern Economy in Historical Perspective* (Stanford, 1975), pp. 49-84, esp. p. 72.
8. Wang, *Land Taxation in Imperial China,* p. 133. The Japanese figure is from E. Sydney Crawcour, "The Tokugawa Heritage," in W. W. Lockwood, ed., *The State and Economic Enterprise in Japan* (Princeton, 1965), pp. 31-32. Wang also observes that "12 percent may be taken as fairly typical of low-income countries." (p. 151, n. 4)
9. The term "modern" is used broadly throughout to include all enterprises whose organizational structure, mode of production, or nature of business followed some Western model. Modern enterprises also appeared, at least on paper, to subscribe to a rationalization of business practices, even though they might not adhere to it in fact. Because this study deals with the early phase of China's modern industrial development, the industries to be discussed generally refer to the primary type–i.e., textiles, railways, mining, etc.–and they all used some form of power-driven machinery for their operation. On the subject of "modernization" referred to several times in the text, the literature is too voluminous to cite here other than to call attention to C. E. Black, *The Dynamics of Modernization* (New York, 1966).
10. For an example of the usual statement about Chinese rigidity, see Alexander Eckstein's "Individualism and the Role of the State in Economic Growth," in Galy D. Ness, ed., *The Sociology of Economic Development* (New York, 1970), p. 420. On the other hand, Thomas A. Metzger's "The Organizational Capabilities of the Ch'ing State in the Field of Commerce: The Liang-huai Salt Monopoly, 1740-1840," in W. E. Willmott, ed., *Economic Organization in Chinese Society* (Stanford, 1972), pp. 9-45, shows how the organizational flexibility of the Liang-huai salt administration was matched by the manipulative skills and nonconformist behavior of its administrators.
11. Thomas C. Smith, *Political Change and Industrial Development in Japan: Government Enterprise 1868-1880* (Stanford, 1965), passim, but especially Chapter 1.
12. Ibid., Chapters 7 and 8.
13. See Dwight H. Perkins, "Introduction: The Persistence of the Past," in

Perkins, ed., *China's Modern Economy,* pp. 1-18, for an analysis of how contemporary China's economic development is influenced by the unique experiences of her own past.

2. Merchants, Commerce, and the State

1. Cheng Hsing-sun, *Chung-kuo shang-yeh shih* (Shanghai, 1932), pp. 36-38.
2. *The I-ching or Book of Changes,* tr. into German by R. Wilhelm, English tr. by C. F. Baynes (New York, 1961), II. 129.
3. James Legge, tr., *The Chinese Classics* (Hong Kong, 1960), III, 327.
4. Cf. Cho-yun Hsu, *Ancient China in Transition* (Stanford, 1965), pp. 11-12, 128-130.
5. "Only men of education (*shih*) are able to maintain a fixed heart without a certain livelihood. As for the people, if they have not a certain livelihood, it follows that they will not have a fixed heart" (*Mencius,* I, 7:20).
6. See Esson M. Gale, *Discourses on Salt and Iron* (Leiden, 1931).
7. Metzger, "State and Commerce."
8. Cheng Hsing-sun, pp. 45-46.
9. Jiang, "Theory of Parish Entrepreneurship;" also see Gideon Sjoberg, *The Preindustrial City* (New York, 1960), pp. 136, 183-187.
10. Jiang, "Theory of Pariah Entrepreneurship," p. 147.
11. L. S. Yang, "Notes on Dr. Swann's *Food and Money* in Ancient China," *Harvard Journal of Asiatic Studies* 13:526 (1950).
12. L. S. Yang, "Government Control of the Urban Merchants."
13. Cited in Wm. T. de Bary, et al., eds. *Sources of Chinese Tradition* (New York, 1960), pp. 231-232.
14. Ying-shih Yü, *Trade and Expansion in Han China* (Berkeley and Los Angeles, 1967), pp. 17-18.
15. Ping-ti Ho, *The Ladder of Success in Imperial China* (New York, 1964), p. 81. Professor Ho's interpretation that these officials could "engage" in trade is probably too liberal. As the following pages will show, most officials with business interest hired "front men" as managers to run their business.
16. Ibid., pp. 81-86.
17. T'ao Hsi-sheng, *Chung-kuo cheng-chih ssu-hsiang shih* (Chungking, 1942), IV, 203-204.
18. Ch'üan Han-sheng, "Sung-tai kuan-shih chin ssu-ying shang-yeh," *Bulletin of the Institute of History and Philology* (Academia Sinica) 7.2:199-253 (1936).
19. See L. S. Yang, "Government Control of Urban Merchants," p. 191; Ping-ti Ho, *The Ladder of Success*, p. 50; Fu I-ling, *Ming-Ch'ing Shang-jen*, pp. 41-44.

20. Chang Chung-li, *The Income of the Chinese Gentry* (Seattle, 1962), pp. 181–188, 280–287.
21. *Wu-chung Yeh-shih tsu-p'u,* 2:12a. Cited in Chang Chung-li, *Income,* pp. 154–155.
22. Marian J. Levy Jr. and Shih Kuo-heng, *The Rise of the Modern Chinese Business Class* (New York, 1949), pp. 5, 13; also E. Balazs, *Chinese Civilization and Bureaucracy* (New Haven, 1964), p. 42. The quote is taken from Bernard Barber, *Social Stratification: A Comparative Analysis of Structure and Process* (New York, 1957), p. 4.
23. Wu Chien-jen, *Erh-shih-nien mu-tu kuai-hsien-chuang* (Hong Kong, 1969), I, 190. The novel first appeared in serial form in 1902 and was then published as a book between 1907 and 1909. For a critique of its sociological value, see Ch'ien Hsiang-ts'un (pseud. Ah-ying), *Wan-Ch'ing hsiao-shuo shih* (Hong Kong, 1966), pp. 16-20.
24. Wu Chien-jen, *Erh-shih-nien,* I, 106, 156.
25. The most important of these works still in existence is Wu Chung-fu's *Shang-chia pien-lan,* with a preface dated 1792. A second volume from the same period is *Chiang-hu ch'ih-tu fen-yun* by Yü Hsueh-pu and Wan Ch'i-shih. Earlier ones from the Ming period include *Shang-ch'eng i-lan* by T'ao Ch'eng-ch'ing; *Pao-hua pien-i*; and *Chiang-hu pi-tu*. The Oki Bunko Collection at Tokyo University has some of this literature. See E. P. Wilkinson, "Chinese Merchant Manuals and Route Books," *Ch'ing-shih wen-t'i* 2.1 (1972); Chü Ch'ing-yuan, "Ch'ing kai-kuo ch'ien-hou ti san-pu shang-jen chu-tso," in Li Ting-i, et al., eds., *Chung-kuo chin-tai-shih lun-ts'ung,* 2nd coll., vol. 2 (Taipei, 1958); and Hsueh-ch'i, "Ch'ing-ch'u ti shang-li chih-nan," *Ming-pao wan-pao,* 4/25/1970.
26. Ch'ü Tung-tsu, "Chinese Class Structure and Its Ideology," in John K. Fairbank, ed. *Chinese Thought and Institutions* (Chicago, 1957), p. 248; Jiang, "Theory of Pariah Entrepreneurship," pp. 157-158.
27. See Li Ch'en Shun-ping, "Wan-Ch'ing ti chung-shang chu-i," *Chung-yang yen-chiu yuan chin-tai shih yen-chiu-so chi-kan* 3.1:207–221 (1972).
28. *THL/KH* 29/3, pp. 27–28.
29. "Chiang-li Hua-shang kung-ssu chang-ch'eng," in *Nung-kung-shang pu hsien-hsing chang-ch'eng* (Peking, 1909); also *KYSTL-II,* I, 461.
30. Chang Hsin-pao, *Commissioner Lin and the Opium War* (Cambridge, Mass., 1964), pp. 95–96.
31. Albert Feuerwerker, *The Chinese Economy, ca. 1870–1911* (Ann Arbor, 1969), p. 50.
32. After the 1902 publication of Yen Fu's translation of Adam Smith's *Wealth of Nations* and Yen's general subscription to a free trade theory, Chinese intellectuals began to discuss the various components that went

into making up a national capital deficit or surplus. Liang Ch'i-ch'ao gave a far more sophisticated discussion of this issue in 1902 when he published his "Sheng-chi-hsueh hsueh-shuo yen-ke hsiao-shih." For Yen Fu's discussion, see Chao Feng-t'ien, *Wan Ch'ing wu-shih-nien ching-chi ssu-hsiang shih* (Peking, 1939), pp. 135-141.

33. Feuerwerker, *Chinese Economy,* pp. 48-51.
34. Hsueh Fu-ch'eng, "Ch'ou-yang ch'u-i," in *Wu-hsu pien-fa,* eds. Chieng Po-tsan, et al. (Shanghai, 1953), I, 154-156.
35. Ibid., I. 163-164; also see Chao Feng-t'ien, pp. 95-99.
36. As Ma Chien-chung explained it, "Wealth and power are the bases of political control over a state. In order to be powerful, the state must first enrich itself." Ibid., I, 163.
37. Chang T'ing-chü, "Wu-hsu cheng-pien shih-ch'i wan-ku p'ai chih ching-chi ssu-hsiang," *Chung-kuo ching-chi* 4.6:141-147 (June 1936).
38. Ibid., pp. 145-146.
39. Mary C. Wright, *The Last Stand of Chinese Conservatism: The T'ung-chih Restoration* (Stanford, 1957).
40. Lloyd Eastman, "Political Reformism in China before the Sino-Japanese War," *Journal of Asian Studies* 27.4:695-710 (1968); Benjamin Schwartz, *In Search of Wealth and Power: Yen Fu and the West* (Cambridge, Mass., 1964), pp. 6-19.
41. For a discussion on this kind of writings, see Chao Fen-t'ien, *Ch'ing-chi ssu-hsiang shih,* pp. 41-146.
42. See, e.g., Mou An-shih, *Yang-wu yun-tung* (Shanghai, 1956), p. 128.
43. Liang Ch'i-ch'ao, "Shih-chi huo-chih lieh-chuan chih-i" in his *Yin-ping-shih wen-chi* (Shanghai, 1926), ts'e 1:10b.
44. Liang Ch'i-ch'ao, "Nung-hui pao-hsu," in ibid., ts'e 4:11b.
45. Liang Ch'i-ch'ao, "Shih-chi huo-chih," in ibid., ts'e 1:1b-11.
46. Liang Ch'i-ch'ao, "Shang-hui i," in ibid., ts'e 28:32b-38; "Lun shang-yeh hui-i-so chih-i," in ibid., ts'e 28:38-41; "Lun nei-ti tsa-chu yü shang-wu kuan-shih," in ibid., ts'e 28:42b-47.
47. Ibid., ts'e 28:41a.
48. Ibid., ts'e 11:17a.
49. Ibid., ts'e 11:17a.
50. Liang Ch'i-ch'ao, "Nung-hui pao-hsu," in ibid., ts'e 4:11b.
51. Liang Ch'i-ch'ao, "Sheng-chi-hsueh," in ibid., ts'e 11:34-47b.
52. Ibid., ts'e 11:47b.
53. Liang Ch'i-ch'ao, "Erh-shih shih-chi chih chü-ling: t'o-la-ssu," in ibid., ts'e 23:33a-b, 52b.
54. Liang Ch'i-ch'ao, "Shuo ch'ün hsu," in ibid., ts'e 3:45a-b; Also see Hao Chang, *Liang Ch'i-ch'ao and Intellectual Transition in China, 1890-1907*

(Cambridge, Mass., 1971) for an extensive discussion of Liang's ideas about "grouping" and its relation to his central concept of the "new citizen."

55. Liang Ch'i-ch'ao, "Shuo ch'ün shu," ts'e 51a–b; "Erh-shih shih-chi," ts'e 23:51a–b.
56. Ibid., ts'e 23:53a, 33a.
57. Ibid., ts'e 23:53a.
58. Yen Chung-p'ing, *Chung-kuo mien-fang-chih shih-kuo* (Peking, 1955), p. 84. P'eng was probably a comprador.
59. In recent decades, *kung-yeh* and *shih-yeh* are interchangeable; in fact, *kung-yeh* is more frequently used to mean modern industry.
60. Chao Feng-t'ien, *Ch'ing-chi ssu-hsiang shih*, pp. 74-86.
61. "Lun Chung-kuo shang-yeh pu fa-ta chih yuan-yin," in *Hsin-hai ko-min ch'ien-shih-nien chien shih-lun hsuan-chi* (Peking, 1960), I.1:467.
62. Cited in Chang Chung-li, *Income,* pp. 153–154.
63. *THL/KH* 23/2, pp. 9–10.
64. Until very recent times, any Chinese who could lay claim to any education or worldly success had at least one or two names (usually one courtesy name [*tzu*] and one or more style names [*hao*] other than his personal name [*ming*]). Thus an official who wanted to adopt another personal name in order to assume a different identity or role could simply take on a new name and minimize his psychological unease by assuming that it was in the same category as another *tzu* or *hao*. In this way, I believe that the use of a second or third name as "assumed" names must have been culturally less unnerving for a Chinese than for an Indian or a Westerner.
65. See Chang Chung-li, *Income*, pp. 164-165.
66. Art. 5 of "Shang-jen t'ung-li" in *Ta-Ch'ing Kuang-hsu hsin fa-ling* (Shanghai, 1910), ts'e 16:1b.
67. See Articles 3 and 18 of "Company Registration Laws," in ibid., ts'e 16:26b–28b; *TFTC,* 4.1: Shang-wu, p. 30 (1907).
68. Cheng Kuan-ying, *Sheng-shih wei-yen hou-pien* (Shanghai, 1910), 8: 34b–35.
69. *HTJP,* 3/16/1909.
70. *HTJP,* 1909: 3/20, 4/3.

3. Changes in the Merchant's Roles, Composition, and Status

1. Schwartz, *Wealth and Power,* p. 123.
2. Professor Rhoads Murphey, in his provocative study, "The Treaty Ports and China's Modernization," has emphasized that neither the treaty ports nor foreign trade had a significant impact on the Chinese scene as a whole. While this was no doubt true, the fact remains that very many

individual merchants and literati inside and outside the treaty ports (and they included a sizeable portion of the articulate part of the population) felt the impact of the treaty port experience. At least among this group, the merchant's social breakthrough was very real indeed.

3. Marie-Claire Bergère has characterized Chinese merchants of this period as "closed in," "creating small islands of security" for themselves, and believing that "China's revival could be achieved by nonpolitical means, i.e. by practical actions which had no need of an accompanying ideology." See her "The Role of the Bourgeoisie," in Mary C. Wright, ed., *China in Revolution: The First Phase 1900–1913* (New Haven, 1968), p. 246.
4. Cheng Kuan-ying, *Sheng-shih wei-yen* (n.p., 1895), 3:4a–9b. This work, the most famous of Cheng's works, was collected and published for the first time around 1893. It was expanded from an earlier work entitled *I-yen* (Easy words), whose first edition went back to around 1873. *I-yen,* in turn, was an improved version of his earliest volume *Chiu-shih chieh-yao.* For the different editions of Cheng's works, see Yen-p'ing Hao, "Cheng Kuan-ying: The Comprador as Reformer," *Journal of Asian Studies* 24.1:15-22 (1969).
5. Cheng Kuan-ying, *Hou-pien* 15:9–10.
6. Cheng Kuan-ying, *Sheng-shih wei-yen,* 3:10–18b.
7. Ho Ch'i and Hu Li-yuan, *Hsin-cheng chen-ch'üan* (Hong Kong, 1895); see also Eastman, "Political Reformism in China," where he credited Ho for ideas and Hu for putting them down in classical Chinese in their collaborated essays.
8. For Ho's biography, see Arnold Wright and H. A. Cartwright, eds., *Twentieth Century Impressions of Hong Kong, Shanghai and other Treaty Ports of China* (London, 1908), p. 109.
9. For Hu's biography, see Lu Ting-ch'ang "Hu I-nan hsien-sheng shih-k'o," in *Hu I-nan hsien-sheng ch'üan-chi* (Hong Kong, 1920), ch'üan 1.
10. See Ho Ch'i and Hu Li-yuan "Hsin-cheng lun-i," in *Hsin-cheng chen-ch'üan,* ts'e 2, passim.
11. Ping-ti Ho, "The Salt Merchants of Yang-chou: A Study of Commercial Capitalism in Eighteenth Century China," *Harvard Journal of Asiatic Studies* 17:13–68 (1954).
12. Liang Chia-pin, *Kuang-tung shih-san-hang k'ao* (Shanghai, 1937); William C. Hunter, *The 'Fan Kwae' at Canton before Treaty Days, 1825–1844* (Shanghai, 1911).
13. Chang Peng, "Distribution of Provincial Merchant Groups in China, 1842–1911" (Unpublished Ph.D. thesis, University of Washington, Seattle, 1958); Fu I-ling, *Ming-Ch'ing shang-jen,* pp. 39–41; Peng Tse-i, "Shih-chiu shih-chi hou-ch'i."
14. Ibid.

15. Charles J. Stanley, *Late Ch'ing Finance: Hu Kuang-yung as an Innovator* (Cambridge, Mass., 1961), p. 2.
16. John K. Fairbank, *Trade and Diplomacy on the China Coast: The Opening of the Treaty Ports, 1842–1854* (Cambridge, Mass., 1964).
17. See Liang Chia-pin, *Kuang-tung shih-san-hang k'ao,* pp. 11, 169.
18. Ibid., p. 325.
19. *HTJP,* 8/23/1901.
20. Yen-p'ing Hao, *Comprador,* passim, esp. pp. 45–54; Rawski, "Chinese Dominance of Treaty Port Commerce."
21. *Pei-ching Jui-fu-hsiang* (Peking, 1959), pp. 2–3, 6–9.
22. Ibid., p. 4.
23. Ibid., p. 6.
24. Ch'en Ch'i-t'ien, *Shan-hsi p'iao-chuang k'ao-lueh* (Shanghai, 1937); L. S. Yang, *Money and Credit in China: A Short History* (Cambridge, Mass., 1952), pp. 81–84.
25. *Shang-hai ch'ien-chuang shih-liao* (Shanghai, 1960), pp. 13–29; Susan M. Jones, "Finance in Ningpo: The 'Ch'ien Chuang,' 1750–1880," in W. E. Willmott, ed., *Economic Organization in Chinese Society* (Stanford, 1972), pp. 47–77.
26. Marie-Claire Bergère, *Une crise financière à Shanghai à la fin de l'ancien regime* (Paris, 1964).
27. Stanley's *Late Ch'ing Finance,* which gives the only lengthy study in English on Hu Kuang-yung, shows how he successfully combined his private entrepreneurial activities with his advice and management of public finance.
28. See Kenneth E. Folsom, *Friends, Guests and Colleagues: The Mu-fu system in the late Ch'ing Period* (Berkeley and Los Angeles, 1968) for a discussion of the greatly expanded functions of the *mu-yu* from the early 1850s, esp. pp. 58–77.
29. Stanley, *Late Ch'ing Finance,* pp. 8–13. Several sketches on Hu exist in Chinese. See Yü-tzu, "Tsai-t'an Hang-chou ti hung-ting shang-jen," in his *Chang-ku man-t'an* (Hong Kong, 1974), for the range of types (from entries in contemporary diaries to folklore) and their credibility.
30. For Ch'ien Hsing-ts'un's critique, see his *Wan-Ch'ing hsiao-shuo shih,* pp. 67–70. Published in Tokyo (n.d.), Ohashi's novel is unavailable. Recently, Kao Yang's *Hu Hsueh-yen* (Taipei, 1973), in 3 volumes, deals with Hu's rise to prosperity around 1851–52, for, according to this account, Fu-k'ang was founded in about 1852 when Wang Yu-ling was only a prefect. From internal evidence, it appears that Mr. Kao bases his work upon the older novel. It is from this modern version that I draw the above conclusions.
31. On Hu's investment in the modern textile industry, see Edward LeFevour,

Western Enterprise in Late Ch'ing China (Cambridge, Mass., 1968), pp. 41, 46; and Nakamura Tadashi, "Shimmatsu seiji to Kanryō shihon—Sei Sen-kai no yakuwari o megutte" in *Chūgoku kinkaida no shakai kōzō* (Tokyo, 1960), pp. 21-44.

32. *Pei-ching Jui-fu-hsiang,* pp. 6-8, 11-16.
33. Albert Feuerwerker, *China's Early Industrialization: Sheng Hsuan-huai (1844-1916) and Mandarin Enterprise* (Cambridge, Mass., 1958), pp. 110-113.
34. The standard work on Sheng's involvements in modern enterprise is Feuerwerker's *China's Early Industrialization* just cited. A more recent study, and in Chinese, is by Hsieh Shih-chia, *Sheng Hsuan-huai yü t'a so ch'uang-pan ti ch'i-yeh* (Taipei, 1971).
35. See, e.g., Feuerwerker, *China's Early Industrialization,* pp. 73-78, 100.
36. For Yen Hsin-hou's biographies, see *Shang-hai tsung-shang-hui yueh-pao*, 1.1: Chuan-chi, p. 1 (July, 1921) and 2.3: Chuan-chi, p. 1; *KYSTL-II*, II, 929-930.
37. For a biography of Chang in English which gives an excellent assessment of Chang as a modernizer, see Samuel Chu, *Reformer in Modern China: Chang Chien, 1853-1926* (New York, 1965). Chang Chien's most extensive biography is in Chinese and is written by his son: Chang Hsiao-jo, *Nan-t'ung Chang Chi-chih hsien-sheng chuan-chi* (Taipei, 1965). See V, 480 for the reference to the family business.
38. Ibid., I, 15.
39. Cf. Samuel Chu, *Reformer in Modern China,* pp. 8-9.
40. Chang Hsiao-jo, *Nan-t'ung Chang Chi-chih*, I, 68.
41. Ibid., I, 69; II, 90.
42. See Chapter 6 below.
43. Nieh Tseng Chi-fen, *Ch'ung-te lao-jen pa-shih tzu-ting nien-p'u* (Shanghai, 1933), pp. 12b, 13b, and 16b-17, gives very candid accounts of Nieh's entry and promotions in the official world through the wife's family connections.
44. Ibid.
45. Ibid., p. 23a; *CKKYSTL-III,* I, 397-401.
46. *Ch'ung-te lao-jen,* p. 16b.
47. *KYSTL-II,* I, 474-475, cited from an article in the *Shih-pao* dated 3/4/1913.
48. Wu Chien-jen, *Erh-shih-nien,* I, 209-218.
49. Chang Hsiao-jo, *Nan-t'ung Chang Chi-chih,* I, 68.
50. See Nieh Tseng Chi-fen, *Ch'ung-te lao-jen,* p. 23a.
51. According to the authoritative Japanese study, *Shina keizai zencho* (Osaka and Tokyo, 1907-1908), which gives a broader interpretation to the term *shen-shang,* it should also include retired officials, heirs

of officials, and officials. It agreed, however, on the diffusiveness of its component groups, stating that "sometimes it is difficult to distinguish whether they are merchants or officials. Although on the surface they are seen as an official, yet they are carrying on business activities in secret" (I, 175).

52. Fei Hsiao-t'ung, "Peasantry and Gentry: An Interpretation of Chinese Social Structure and its Changes," *American Journal of Sociology* 52.1: 1-17 (1946). Rentals at roughly 50% of crop yields are generally agreed upon by different authorities to show how profitable land investments could be.
53. Chang Chung-li, *Income*, pp. 138-139.
54. Chang Chung-li has estimated that no appreciable change in ownership distribution occurred between the 1880s and 1920s. See his *Income*, p. 145. It is, however, very difficult to be accurate about who the gentry were at any given time. Many merchants who purchased land could be entered as gentry owing to their purchased official titles or secondary gentry functions.
55. Muramatsu Yuji, "A documentary study of Chinese Landlordism in the late Ch'ing and the Early Republican Kiangnan," *Bulletin of the School of Oriental and African Studies* 29.3:566-599 (1966). Muramatsu concludes that many of the absentee landowners were actually merchants because a high percentage of owners used *hao* (company) names. He also assumes that the fewer owners using *t'ang* (hall) names were gentry and officials (p. 572). In fact, while *hao* almost invariably represented merchant ownership, *t'ang* could also be used by some merchants if they represented joint investments by different merchant members of an extended family, or if they were owned by merchants of gentry status.
56. Chang Chung-li, *Income*, pp. 127-147.
57. Cf. Kwang-ching Liu, "Nineteenth Century China: The Disintegration of the Old Order and the Impact of the West," in Ping-ti Ho and Tang Tsou, eds., *China in Crisis* (Chicago, 1968), I, 1:170-171.
58. Chang Chung-li has commented that "what one might call big [traditional] business in nineteenth century China was concentrated largely in the hands of gentry members or was carried on with their backing." See his *Income*, p. 126. For the smaller business, Chang saw many lower gentry in competition with the small merchants.
59. Yen Chung-p'ing, *Chung-kuo mien-fang-chih*, p. 139.
60. *CKKYSTL-I*, I, 247-256.
61. See the discussions on gentry and merchants by the various contributors in Mary C. Wright, ed., *China in Revolution*, esp. the article by Marie-Claire Bergère "The Role of the Bourgeoisie" already cited.
62. Even Bergère's carefully narrow definition for the emergence of a class

of "commercial bourgeoisie" at this time made up of compradors, businessmen, bankers, industrialists, and overseas Chinese is probably unwarranted, if only for the reasons she herself has pointed out—that this new "class" of bourgeoisie was weak and divided (pp. 239-41). Also see Joseph W. Esherick, "1911: A Review," *Modern China* 2.2: 141-184 (1976) for a summary and a reassessment of the main literature on this subject.

4. From Merchant to Bureaucratic Management

1. See Thomas A. Metzger, "State and Commerce in Imperial China," pp. 35-38, for a study of the *wu-wei* and *yu-wei* theories as alternative policies and the difficulty of enforcing the former.
2. Francis X. Sutton, et al., *The American Business Creed* (New York, 1962), p. 188.
3. Ibid., pp. 171-172.
4. Ibid., pp. 67-74, 85.
5. See Feuerwerker, *China's Early Industrialization,* pp. 8-12 for the origin and an analysis of the term *kuan-tu shang-pan.*
6. E.g., K. C. Liu, in his "British-Chinese Steamship Rivalry in China, 1873-85," in C. D. Cowan, ed., *The Economic Development of China and Japan: Studies in Economic History and Political Economy* (London, 1964), argues that it should be translated as "merchant undertaking," and that, at the beginning at least, Li who had established the shipping company as a "chü" or "an *ad hoc* government agency," appointed an official, Chu Ch'i-ang, to run it (pp. 53-54). It appears, however, that Chu Ch'i-ang, like P'eng Ju-tsung, the promoter of the cotton cloth mill which came a few years later, were primarily merchants with the purchased official rank of expectant taotai. Chu's merchant background is discussed in Feuerwerker, *China's Early Industrialization,* p. 108; P'eng's, in Yen Chung-p'ing, *Chung-kuo mien-fang-chih,* p. 84. As for the term *chü* it indicates official affiliations, but does not preclude management by merchants; e.g. the merchant-run new Hua-hsin Spinning and Weaving Mill, to be discussed in Chapter 5 below, was also a *chü.* Terms like *chü, kuan-shang ho-pan, kuan-tu shang-pan* were all used loosely to meet the needs of specific cases. They had no legally definable limits.
7. See Metzger's "Organizational Capabilities" (pp. 19-27) for a study of the policy of co-optation.
8. *Shina keizai zensho,* I, 185-187.
9. Feuerwerker, *China's Early Industrialization*, pp. 99-100, 108-110, 208-213; Ellsworth C. Carlson, *The Kaiping Mines, 1877-1912* (Cambridge, Mass., 2nd ed. 1971), pp. 30-39; also see Yen Chung-p'ing, *Chung-kuo*

mien-fang-chih, pp. 87-89, for a discussion of the merchant background of Li's six appointees for the Shanghai Cotton Cloth Mill.

10. Feuerwerker, *China's Early Industrialization,* pp. 114, 212-214.
11. Ibid., pp. 154-157.
12. Chang Kuan-ying, *Hou-pien,* 11:26-32b.
13. On "pooling agreements," see K. C. Liu, "British-Chinese Steamship Rivalry," pp. 61-63.
14. Feuerwerker, *China's Early Industrialization,* pp. 213-225.
15. Carlson, *Kaiping Mines,* pp. 50-56.
16. Feuerwerker, *China's Early Industrialization,* p. 115; Carlson, *Kaiping Mines,* pp. 50-51.
17. Feuerwerker, *China's Early Industrialization,* pp. 124-125.
18. Carlson, *Kaiping Mines,* pp. 35-39.
19. Feuerwerker, *China's Early Industrialization,* p. 212.
20. Li Hung-chang, *Li Wen-chung-kung ch'üan-chi,* ed. Wu Ju-lun (Shanghai, 1921), Tsao-kao, 69:40-42b, provides a brief biography of Li Chin-yung. Li's memorial, dated KH16/11/16 (12/27/1890), was to announce Li Chin-yung's death on Oct. 17, 1890. See also ibid., 61:45-54 for the setting up of the Mo-ho mines.
21. Kung Chün, *Chung-kuo hsin kung-yeh fa-chiang-shih ta-kang* (Shanghai, 1933), pp. 36-43.
22. Feuerwerker, *China's Early Industrialization,* pp. 194-209.
23. "Wu-shih-nien lai Chung-kuo ching-chi," *Chung-kuo t'ung-shang yin-hang ch'uang-li wu-shih chou-nien chi-nien-ts'e* (Shanghai, 1947), pp. 3-4.
24. Chang Chih-tung, *Chang Wen-hsiang-kung chi,* ed., Hsu T'ung-hsin (Peiping, 1919-1921), Tsou-kao, 25:11b-13b.
25. *KYSTL-II,* I, 470-472.
26. Albert Feuerwerker, "China's Nineteenth Century Industrialization: the case of the Hanyehping Coal and Iron Company Limited," in C. D. Cowan, ed., *The Economic Development of China and Japan* (London, 1964), pp. 87-99; Ch'üan Han-sheng, "Ch'ing-mo Han-yang t'ieh-chang," *She-hui k'o-hsueh lun-ts'ung* 1:18-21 (1950); also see Sheng Hsuan-huai, *Sheng shang-shu Yü-chai ts'un-kuo ch'u-k'an,* ed. Lü Ching-tuan (Shanghai, 1939) 4:24-26 for his own acknowledgement that the "merchant shares" in these various enterprises were invested by the same men.
27. Cheng Kuan-ying, *Hou-pien,* 10:27a.
28. Feuerwerker, *China's Early Industrialization,* p. 180.
29. Hsu Jun, *Hsu Yü-chai tzu-hsu nien-p'u* (Hsiang-shan, 1927), p. 73b.
30. Cited in Li Kuo-ch'i, *Chung-kuo tsao-ch'i ti t'ieh-lu ching-ying* (Taipei, 1961), p. 131.
31. Feuerwerker, *China's Early Industrialization,* p. 218.

32. Hsu Jun, *Nien-p'u,* pp. 92b–93; Sheng Hsuan-huai, *Yü-chai ts'un-kao,* 5:41–43.
33. Cheng Kuan-ying, *Hou-pien,* 8:43–44.
34. Ibid., 10:100a–b, 12:4a.
35. Ibid., 8:56b–57.

5. The Illusions of Merchant Partnership

1. Ma Chien-chung, "T'ieh-lu lun," *Shih-k'o-chai chi-yen,* in *Hsi-cheng ts'ung-shu* (Shanghai, 1897), ts'e 27.
2. See Mou An-shih, *Yang-wu,* p. 160; *Chung-kuo chin-tai kuo-ming ching-chi-shih chiang-i* (Peking, 1958), p. 227; Immanuel C. Y. Hsu, *The Rise of Modern China* (New York, 1970), p. 347, relies on Mou, but incorrectly gives the date of founding as 1891, which was when the ironworks changed management and went out on a limb. The most extensive source material compiled on the Kweichow Mining and Ironworks may be found in *Yang-wu yun-tung* (8 vols., Shanghai, 1961), 7:169–198.
3. *Yang-wu yun-tung,* 7:171–174.
4. Ibid., 7:191–192, Tseng to P'an, undated.
5. Ibid., 7:177–195.
6. Ibid., 7:182–183.
7. Ibid., 7:182–187.
8. *KYSTL-II,* I, 535–536.
9. This mill should not be confused with Hua-hsin sha-ch'ang, founded in Tientsin in 1918 by Chou Hsueh-hsi.
10. Materials from the company archives, managers' "confessions," and old workers' reminiscences have been collected and published as *Heng-feng sha-chang ti fa-sheng fa-cha yü kai-tsao* (Shanghai, 1958); also see *CKKYSTL-I,* I:33, 397; Mou An-shih, *Yang-wu,* pp. 153–155.
11. *Heng-feng sha-chang,* pp. 2–5. Mou An-shih gives another set of figures: 7,000 spindles in 1891, 9,024 by 1892, and 50 looms in 1894. See his *Yang-wu,* pp. 153–155.
12. *Heng-feng sha-chang* suggests that part of the capital came in originally as government shares or loans, but that none remained by the 1900s (p. 10). More likely, the original transfers of public funds came under the name of official loans, but as they remained in the individual officials' private accounts, they gradually lost their official identity.
13. *Heng-feng sha-chang,* pp. 2–5; Nieh Tseng Chi-fen, *Ch'ung-te lao-jen,* pp. 17a, 22b–23; Yen Chung-p'ing, *Chung-kuo mien-fang-chih,* pp. 139–140, 328.
14. That this monopoly was in force is shown by Chang Chih-tung's inquiry to Li Hung-chang in 1888 seeking his opinion on whether the monopoly

extended to Canton. Li's reply stated that Canton, being so far away, would be all right, thus implying that he would block competitors in Shanghai (see note 20 below).

15. Cf. Wu Ch'eng-lo, *Chih-shih Chung-kuo shih-yeh t'ung-chih* (Shanghai, 1929), II, 106; Kung Chün, *Chung-kuo hsin-kung-yeh,* p. 47, n. 8.
16. *Heng-feng sha-chang,* p. 5; Yen Chung-p'ing, *Chung-kuo mien-fang-chih,* p. 328; Li Hung-chang, Tsao-kao, 78:10.
17. *Heng-feng sha-chang,* pp. 6–12; Nieh Tseng Chi-fen, *Ch'ung-te lao-jen,* pp. 22b–23.
18. Feuerwerker, *China's Early Industrialization,* p. 224.
19. Chang Chih-tung, Tsou-kao, 17:24–26, memorial dated KH15/8/6 (8/31/1889). His other memorial proposing the Hanyang Ironworks was written twenty days later; see Ibid., 17:42b–44b; Yen Chung-p'ing, *Chung-kuo mien-fang-chih,* pp. 93–98.
20. Chang Chih-tung, Tsou-kao, 10:12, Chang to Li KH14/10/9 (11/12/1888); Li Hung-chang, Tsou-kao, 10:20, 37, Li to Kung, KH14/11/1, (12/3/1888), Li to Chang, KH14/11/3 (12/5/1888).
21. Among the Chinese, stories about the incorrigible Cantonese gambler are still legendary. The *wei-hsing* lottery was only one of the more quaint forms of gambling in the late Ch'ing period. For details about the *wei-hsing* lottery, see *Fo-shan chung-i hsiang-chih,* ed. Hsi Pao-kan (Canton, 1922), chüan 4.
22. *Yang-wu yun-tung,* 7:503, Grand Council to Chang, KH15/10/15 (11/7/1889).
23. Chang Chih-tung, Tsao-kao, 19:3b–6, memorial dated KH16/interc. 2/4 (3/24/1890).
24. Ibid.
25. Ibid.
26. Ibid., 21:9/10, KH19/6/4 (7/16/1893).
27. From the incomplete papers of Governor-general Jui-fang's Archives. Included in *KYSTL-II,* I, 572. These accounts are undated, but since Jui-fang's term of office in Wuchang as governor and then as acting governor-general lasted from 1901 to 1904, these figures probably reflected its total loans up to 1902.
28. For the text of Chang's 1894 prospectus inviting merchant shares, see ibid., I, 573–574.
29. Chang Chih-tung, Tsao-kao, 22:22b-23b, memorial dated KH20/10/3 (10/31/1894); Yen Chung-p'ing, *Chung-kuo mien-fang-chih,* pp. 96–97.
30. Chang Chih-tung, Tsao-kao, 21:1–5b memorial dated KH19/2/25 (4/11/1893).
31. Ibid., 29:30a–31b, memorial dated KH24/interc. 3/13 (5/3/1898).
32. *KYSTL-II,* I, 578.

33. Chang Chih-tung, Tsao-kao, 22:22b-23b, memorial dated KH20/10/3 (10/31/1894); *KYSTL-I,* II:936-948.
34. Chang Chih-tung, Tsao-kao, 22:22b-23b.
35. Ibid., 27:1-3b.
36. Chang Chih-tung, Kung-tu 12:15b-16b, Chang to Hupei Cotton Spinning Mill, KH23/6/15 (7/14/1897).
37. Ibid.
38. Ibid.
39. For a study of this highly complex economic phenomenon, see *KYSTL-II,* II, 1011-1015.
40. Yen Chung-p'ing, *Chung-kuo mien-fang-chih,* p. 98.
41. Chang Chien, *Chang Chi-tzu chih-lu,* ed. Chang Hsiao-jo (Shanghai, 1931), Shih-yeh lu, 1:14.
42. *KYSTL-II,* II, 579-591.
43. Cited in *KYSTL-II,* I, 613-614, letter dated KH31/4/12 (5/15/1905).
44. Ibid.; *HTJP,* 1905: 6/2, 6/20.
45. *KYSTL-II,* I, 592.
46. *HTJP,* 4/23/1908.
47. *KYSTL-II,* I, 614-620.
48. *PYKT,* 20:30b-33.
49. Ibid., 20:33-34.
50. Cited in Ch'üan Han-sheng, "Ch'ing-mo Han-yang t'ieh-ch'ang," p. 16.

6. State Control and the Official-Entrepreneur

1. For a contrary interpretation of Sheng's priorities, see Nakamura, "Shimmatsu seiji to kanryō shihon," esp. p. 34.
2. For Chou's biography, see Howard Boorman, ed. *Biographical Dictionary of Republican China* (New York, 1967-1971), I, 409-413; Chou Shu-chen, *Chou Chih-an hsien-sheng pieh-chuan* (Taipei, 1966); *KYSTL-II,* 1021; Chou's career as an entrepreneur is also discussed in Wellington K. K. Chan, "Bureaucratic Capital and Chou Hsueh-hsi in Late Ch'ing China," *Modern Asian Studies* (forthcoming).
3. *PYKT,* chüan 16, 17, 18 passim.
4. See Carlson, *Kaiping Mines,* pp. 84-106.
5. Ibid., pp. 108-109.
6. *PYKT,* 19:37-39b.
7. See *CKKYSTL-I,* I, 222-226.
8. *PYKTHP,* 19:29-31.
9. *PYKT,* 19:36-37.
10. *PYKTHP,* 19:38-39b.
11. Ibid., *PYKT,* 19:39. Carlson, in *Kaiping Mines* (p. 113), errs in thinking

that the requirements were 50, 100, and 500 shares respectively. Article 5 of the company regulations, referring to this subject, gives 50, and 500 *ling-ku* or fractional shares, each of which was valued at 10% of the full share. See *PYKTHP*, 19:38b.

12. *PYKTHP,* 19:39b-41.
13. *CKKYSTL-I,* I, 300; Chou Shu-chen, *Chou-chin-an,* pp. 33-40.
14. On Sun To-shen, see ibid. I, 474-476; on Kung Hsin-chan, see ibid. I, 302-303; also Chia Shih-i, *Min-kuo ch'u-nien ti chi-jen t'sai-cheng tsung-ch'ang* (Taipei, 1967), pp. 83-86; on Li Shih-wei, see ibid. 94-95; also *Who's Who in China,* 3rd ed. (Shanghai, 1926), pp. 477-478.
15. See the biographical data included in A. Feuerwerker, "Industrial Enterprise in Twentieth-Century China. The Chee Hsin Cement Company," in his, et al., eds., *Approaches to Modern Chinese History* (Berkeley and Los Angeles, 1967), pp. 334-335; also table in *CKKYSTL-I,* I, 302; and *Ch'i-hsin yang-hui kung-ssu shih-liao* (Peking, 1963), pp. 42-43.
16. The primary sources on Chee Hsin are the compilation of the company archives published under the title *Ch'i-hsin yang-hui kung-ssu shih-liao,* already cited, and some correspondence relating to it in *PYKT* and *PYKTHP.* A recent study in English is by Feuerwerker, "Industrial Enterprise in Twentieth-Century China," also cited above.
17. *Ch'i-hsin yang-hui,* pp. 24-35.
18. Ibid., pp. 38-40; 90-91.
19. *PYKTHP,* 19:48b.
20. *Ch'i-hsin yang-hui,* p. 41.
21. *Ch'i-hsin yang-hui,* pp. 257-258, 260-261.
22. *PYKTHP,* 19:48b-50b.
23. Ibid., 19:51b-52b.
24. *Ch'i-hsin yang-hui,* p. 90-91.
25. Ibid., 93-96.
26. Ibid., p. 175.
27. Feuerwerker, "Industrial Enterprise in Twentieth-Century China," pp. 334-335; *CKKYSTL-I,* I, 302.
28. *Ch'i-hsin yang-hui,* p. 260.
29. Feuerwerker, *China's Early Industrialization,* pp. 186-188.
30. Feuerwerker, "Industrial Enterprise in Twentieth-Century China."
31. Boorman, ed., *Biographical Dictionary,* I, 412; *CKKYSTL-I,* I, 303.
32. Chang Chih-tung, Tsou-kao, 27:18-19; Yen Chung-p'ing, *Chung-kuo mien-fang-chih,* pp. 105, 121.
33. There are various accounts available on the founding of the Dah Sun (Ta-sheng) Cotton Spinning Mill. Chang Chien's own accounts are found in his *T'ung-chou hsing-pan shih-yeh chih li-shih: Ta-sheng sha-ch'ang* (Nan-t'ung, 1910) and *Chang Chi-tzu chiu-lu,* Shih-yeh lu, 1:14-18.

Chang Hsiao-jo's *Nan-t'ung Chang Chi-chih* has also devoted some space to it (I, 68-75). Excerpts from the above sources may be found in *CKKYSTL-I,* I, 348-365. One recent study in English is by Samuel C. Chu, "Chang Chien and the Founding of Dah Sun," *Tsing Hua Journal of Chinese Studies* (new ser.) 2.1:310-314 (1960).

34. *CKKYSTL-I,* I, 352.
35. Ibid., I, 355.
36. Ibid., I, 353.
37. Cf. Feuerwerker, *China's Early Industrialization,* pp. 222-223.
38. *CKKYSTL-I,* I, 354.
39. Ibid., I, 353.
40. Ibid.
41. Ibid., I, 353-354.
42. Feuerwerker, *China's Early Industrialization,* pp. 223-224.
43. *CKKYSTL-I,* I, 354-355.
44. Samuel Chu, "Founding of Dah Sun," pp. 305-310.
45. Shen Hsieh-chün was the only scholar-gentry out of all of the original directors. He probably had never been a merchant before. See Chang Hsiao-jo, *Nan-t'ung Chang Chi-chih,* V, 471-472.
46. Cited in *CKKYSTL-I,* I, 355.
47. Chang Hsiao-jo, *Nan-t'ung Chang Chi-chih,* I, 72.
48. Chang Chien, *Chiu-lu,* Shih-yeh lu, 1:15b.

7. Merchant and Gentry in Private Enterprise

1. *NCH,* 2/23/1906, pp. 396-397, 427.
2. Edward J. M. Rhoads, *China's Republican Revolution: The Case of Kwangtung, 1895-1913* (Cambridge, Mass., 1975), pp. 131-132, 148-152.
3. Chang Ts'un-wu, *Chung-Mei kung-yueh fang-chiao* (Taipei, 1965); Margaret Field, "The Chinese Boycott of 1905," *Papers on China* 11:63-98 (1957).
4. Wright and Cartwright, eds., *Twentieth Century Impressions*, pp. 423-424; *NCH*, 7/27/06, pp. 181-182, 6/25/1907, pp. 153-154; *Shang-hai tsung-shang-hui yueh-pao*, Chi-lu, 4.6:9-10 (1924).
5. Mary C. Wright, "Introduction: The Rising Tide of Change," in her ed., *China in Revolution: The First Phase, 1900-1913* (New Haven, 1968), pp. 1-63.
6. On the Shanghai-Woosung Railway, see Cheng Lin, *The Chinese Railways Past and Present* (Shanghai, 1937), pp. 2-8; On Kaiping's railway from T'ang-shan to Hsu-ko-chuang, see *Chung-kuo chin-tai t'ieh-lu shih tzu-liao, 1863-1911,* comp. Mi Ju-ch'eng (Peking, 1963), I, 121. Despite the

protests of some court officials, an engine was substituted the following year.

7. Li Kuo-ch'i, *T'ieh-lu ching-ying,* pp. 84-85.
8. *THL/KH* 21/10, p. 154.
9. Sheng Hsuan-huai, *Yü-chai ts'un-kao,* 24:23b-24.
10. Ibid., 24:23a, 25:7b-8a.
11. Chang Chih-tung, Tsao-kao, 27:1-3b.
12. Michael R. Godley, "Chang Pi-shih and Nanyang Chinese Involvement in South China's Railroads, 1896-1911," *Journal of Southeast Asian Studies* 4.1:16-30 (1973).
13. Chang Chia-ao, *China's Struggle for Railway Development* (New York, 1943), p. 35.
14. Sheng Hsuan-huai, *Yü-chai ts'un-kao,* 21:9-10.
15. *SCMP,* 1904:8/5, 10/19, 10/24, 10/26; *HTJP,* 1904:10/7, 10/15, 10/17, 10/25.
16. Cheng Kuan-ying, *Hou-pien,* 9:8-10, 13b-14b.
17. For a contemporary foreign reporter's view of the changing mood among the Chinese, see *SCMP,* 1/12/1906.
18. For examples of merchant interests in feeder lines, see *SCMP,* 10/21/1904; 6/21/1905.
19. E-tu Zen Sun, *Chinese Railways and British Interests, 1898-1911* (New York, 1954), pp. 73-84.
20. *SCMP,* 11/1/1904.
21. Shang Ping-ho, *Hsin-jen ch'un-chiu* (n.p., 1924) ts'e 2:1a-b.
22. E-tu Zen Sun, *Chinese Railways,* pp. 90-96.
23. *TFTC,* Chiao-tung, 4.7:132-142, 4.8:165-167 (1907); *TFTC,* Tsou-tu, 6.10:95 (1909).
24. *HTJP,* 1906:1/9, 1/15; *SCMP,* 1906:1/12, 1/15, 1/18. Only sketchy official documentations of these dramatic conflicts among officials, gentry, and merchants exist, e.g. the collection in *Chung-kuo chin-tai t'ieh-lu shih tzu-liao,* III, 1045-1055. Governor-general Ts'en Ch'un-hsuan wrote nothing about this episode in his autobiography, *Lo-chai man-ch'i,* published some years later, although it contributed to the loss of his office in 1907. Much of the available record can be gleaned only from two contemporary newspapers, the *Hua-tzu jih-pao* and the *South China Morning Post,* both published in Hong Kong.
25. *SCMP,* 1906:1/18, 1/19, 1/22, 2/1.
26. *SCMP,* 1906:1/23, 2/1; *HTJP,* 2/3/1906.
27. *SCMP,* 1906:1/27, 2/1, 2/16; *HTJP,* 1906:2/2, 2/5, 2/6, 2/17, 2/20.
28. *SCMP,* 2/21/1906; *HTJP,* 1906:2/17, 4/3; *NCH,* 2/21/1906.
29. *SCMP,* 1905:8/14, 8/17, 8/26; *HTJP,* 8/17/1905.
30. *HTJP,* 1906:2/6, 2/7.

31. Cheng Kuan-ying, *Hou-pien,* 9:14b-15b; *HTJP,* 8/18/1905, 1906:1/12, 2/1.
32. *SCMP,* 3/2/1906.
33. *SCMP,* 1906:3/4, 3/7, 3/10, 4/14; *HTJP,* 1906:3/3, 3/5, 3/10, 3/19.
34. *HTJP,* 1906:3/17, 3/28, 4/12, 5/1, 5/12, 5/22.
35. *TFTC,* Chiao-tung, 4.12:235-236 (1907).
36. *Chung-kuo chin-tai t'ieh-lu shih tzu-liao,* III, 1055 shows that the total receipt might have been about $1 million less. Its somewhat higher figure for tracks built (106 km.), however, includes those portions completed by the American company prior to recovery by the Chinese.
37. *TFTC,* Tsa-tsu, 3.4:31-33 (1906); Cheng Kuan-ying, *Hou-pien,* 9:44a-b, 65-67; *SCMP,* 1906:6/19, 6/22, 6/26; *HTJP,* 1906:5/2, 5/18.
38. *SCMP,* 1906:5/26, 6/19; *HTJP,* 1906:2/18, 2/21.
39. *SCMP,* 7/13/1907.
40. *HTJP,* 1906:3/28, 3/29, 4/2; *SCMP,* 8/14/1906.
41. *SCMP,* 1906:8/15, 9/1, 9/5.
42. *SCMP,* 9/27/1907; *HTJP,* 10/16/1907, 1909:8/11, 12/2; *TFTC,* Chi-tsai, 7.1:13-15 (1910); Cheng Kuan-ying, *Hou-pien,* 3:23.
43. *TFTC,* Chi-tsai, 7.3:72-75 (1910).
44. *HTJP,* 1906:11/26, 12/1, 12/6, 12/11, 12/31.
45. *HTJP,* 1907:5/7, 5/11, 5/13; *SCMP,* 1907:5/13, 6/21.
46. On the original decentralized structure and its results, see Cheng Kuan-ying, *Hou-pien,* 9:46b-47, 61a-b, 74a-b.
47. *TFTC,* Chi-shih, 6.4:38, 43, 48 (1909); *SCMP,* 1908:4/29, 5/1, 6/27, 9/24, 12/28; 2/23/1909.
48. *SCMP,* 12/28/1908.
49. *Ch'ing-chi hsin-she chih-kuan nien-p'iao,* comp. Ch'ien Shih-fu (Peking, 1961), p. 69.
50. *HTJP,* 1909:2/18, 3/4, 3/18, 3/19, 3/26, 3/27.
51. *Chung-hua min-kuo k'ai-kuo wu-shih-nien wen-hsien* (Taipei, 1962-1965), 1.16:652-658.
52. *TFTC,* Wen-chien, 7.1:1-8 (1910), Chi-tsai, 7.1:14-15, 7.2:43-44 (1910); *HTJP,* 1909:8/16, 8/20, 12/20, 12/21; *K'ai-kuo wu-shih-nien wen-hsien,* 1.16:640-652.
53. Ibid., 1.16:652-660.
54. Three studies in English dealing largely with the foreign interest aspects of this railway are: E-tu Zen Sun, "The Shanghai-Hangchow-Ningpo Railway Loan of 1908," *Far Eastern Quarterly* 10.2:136-150 (1950), later incorporated into her book, *Chinese Railways* already cited; Madeleine Chi, "Shanghai-Hangchow-Ningpo Railway Loan: A Case Study of the Rights Recovery Movement," *Modern Asian Studies* 7.1:85-106 (1973); and En-han Lee, "The Chekiang Gentry-Merchants

vs. the Peking Court Officials: China's Struggle for Recovery of the British Soochow-Hangchow-Ningpo Railway Concession, 1905-1911," *Chung-yang yen-chiu yuan chin-tai shih yen-chiu so chi-kan* 3.1:223-268 (1972). A Chinese collection, hastily compiled while the movement was still going on, is Mo Pei, ed., *Chiang-Che t'ieh-lu fang-ch'ao* (reprinted, Taipei, 1968). Also see *Chung-kuo chin-tai t'ieh-lu shih tzu-liao,* III, 999-1009.

55. *TFTC,* Chiao-tung, 4.10:207-210 (1907).
56. Mo Pei, ed., *Chiang-Che t'ieh-lu,* pp. 278-281, 370-371.
57. *Chung-kuo chin-tai t'ieh-lu shih tzu-liao,* III, 1008.
58. *TFTC,* Chi-shih, 6.7:192-196 (1909), 7.3:64-67, 7.6:129 (1910).
59. *TFTC,* Chi-shih, 6.9:227, 6.10:315-317 (1909).
60. Ibid.; *TFTC,* Chung-kuo ta-shih, 7.9:68, 7.10:78-79 (1910); *NCH,* 9/11/1909; also see Madeleine Chi, "Shanghai-Hangchow-Ningpo Railway Loan" on how the money was manipulated by the Yu-ch'uan pu.
61. *NCH,* 1/14/1910.
62. *TFTC,* Chi-tsai, 7.8:108-111 (1910); *K'ai-kuo wu-shih-nien wen-hsien,* 1.16:676-677.
63. See En-han Lee, "Chekiang Gentry-Merchants vs. Peking Court Officials," esp. pp. 267-268.
64. *NCH,* 1910:9/2, 9/14; *TFTC,* Chung-kuo ta-shih, 7.9:67-70, 7.10:75-77, 7.11:87, 94-95 (1910).
65. Ibid.
66. *TFTC,* Chung-kuo ta-shih, 7.12:107-108 (1910-11).
67. *Hsiang-kang Yung-an yu-hsien kung-ssu erh-shih-wu chou-nien chi-nien lu* (Hong Kong, 1932); *Hsien-shih kung-ssu erh-shih-wu chou-nien chi-nien ts'e* (Hong Kong, 1924-25).
68. *CKKYSTL-I,* I, 372-374.
69. Ibid.
70. *CKKYSTL-I,* I, 374-376.
71. "Wu-hsi Jung-shih ch'i-yeh-chia chia-tsu chi ch'i ch'i-chia ti mien-fan yeh," *Hsin shih-chieh* 9:19-25 (1944).
72. *CKKYSTL-I,* I, 374-376, 381-382.
73. *NKSPTCP-I,* ts'e 5:1b.
74. *CKKYSTL-I,* I, 374-376.
75. *KYSTL-I,* II, 1035-1037.
76. *CKKYSTL-I,* I, 374, 381.

8. The Founding of New Ministries

1. For discussion on the reform of the bureaucracy at this time, see Esther Morrison, "The Modernization of the Confucian Bureaucracy," (unpubl.

Ph.D. Thesis, Radcliffe College, 1959); also see Meribeth E. Cameron, *The Reform Movement in China 1898-1912* (New York, 1963); Wright, ed., *China in Revolution;* and Chang P'eng-yuan, *Li-hsien p'ai yü hsin-hai ko-ming* (Taipei, 1969) for studies on constitutional and other reforms.

2. *HTJP,* 12/12/1906.
3. See Metzger, "Organizational Capabilities," and Yeh-chien Wang, *Land Taxation,* pp. 12-15.
4. For a study of the Tsungli Yamen, see S. M. Meng, *The Tsungli Yamen: Its Organization and Functions* (Cambridge, Mass., 1962).
5. Cameron, *Reform Movement,* p. 59.
6. *HTJP,* 7/3/1901.
7. Cheng Kuan-ying, *Sheng-shih wei-yen,* 3:3a-b.
8. Ho Ch'i and Hu Li-yuan, *Hsin-cheng chen-ch'üan,* 2:21a.
9. Feuerwerker, *China's Early Industrialization,* pp. 73-77.
10. *HTJP,* 3/26/1902.
11. *HTJP,* 1901:7/24, 7/26.
12. *HTJP,* 8/1/1901.
13. When the Shang pu opened in 1903, Wu was a supernumerary department director in that ministry. For a while, he was in charge of the ministry's sponsored newspaper, the *Shang-wu pao.* See "Hui-pan shang-pan," File no. B-1-4 of *Wai-chiao tang-an,* Academia Sinica; also see *Ta-Ch'ing chin-shen ch'uan-shu* of this period for Wu's various assignments.
14. *HTJP,* 11/13/1901.
15. *HTJP,* 1902:3/26, 4/4, 12/5. Tsai-chen's initial interest in industry is recalled in Ts'ao Ju-lin, *I-sheng chih hui-i* (Taipei, 1964), pp. 5-6.
16. "Hui-pan shang-pan," File B-1-4, *Wai-chiao tang-an.*
17. *HTJP,* 1903:3/23, 5/7, 9/26, 10/10, 12/30.
18. *HTJP,* 1903:7/18, 8/3, 8/13, 9/10. It seems that at least part of the contribution was actually made. The *shih-lang* title was awarded him, but as a rank without official duties or office. During the first year or so, the Shang pu's official roster included his name.
19. *THL/KH* 29/3, pp. 27-28.
20. *HTJP,* 8/8/1903.
21. *Nung-kung-shang pu hsien-hsing chang-ch'eng* (Peking, 1908), ts'e 1:4-11b.
22. *HTJP,* 1903:10/13, 11/28; 10/24/1905; 1/21/1907. In 1903, the Shang pu still did not lose hope although the Hu pu had categorically rejected it. Tsai-chen ordered that special agents be sent to different provinces to investigate the Salt Administration to see how the transfer might best be done.
23. *HTJP,* 10/15/1903. In 1906, the Ts'ai-cheng ch'u merged with the old Ministry of Revenue to form the new Ministry of Finance (Tu-chih pu).

24. The office of the *shang-yao ta-chen* was created on February 23, 1902 to manage the specific task of commercial treaty negotiations. The first incumbents were Lu Hai-huan, president of the Ministry of Works, and Sheng Hsuan-huai.

    The *shang-wu ta-chen* office was created by an imperial decree dated November 24, 1899. It was given to Li Hung-chang. This apparently marked the return of imperial favor to Li, who, since 1895, had been in disgrace. Less than a month later, Li was, in addition, given the post of Acting Governor-general of Liang-Kuang. In July 1902, following Li's death, the title was transferred to Chang Chih-tung, Governor-general of Hu-Kuang. Three months later, Yuan Shik-k'ai, Governor-general of Chihli, was also appointed to the same office to hold it jointly with Chang. It is not clear how its functions varied with the original and much better known commissions of trade for the northern and southern ports (*Pei-yang* and *Nan-yang ta-chen*).

    The office of *t'ieh-lu ta-chen* was opened in 1895 with Hu Ch'ü-fen, a former judicial commissioner of Kweichow, in charge. Soon after that, the title was assigned to various officials all at once, each in control of one or two railways. See *Ch'ing-chi hsin-she chih-kuan nien-p'iao,* pp. 68, 71.
25. *HTJP,* 3/23/1903.
26. *HTJP,* 10/10/1903.
27. *HTJP,* 1904:2/9, 8/13.
28. *TFTC,* Chi-lu, 6.9:430 (1909).
29. *TFTC,* Chiao-yü, 1.3:52-53 (1904).
30. *HTJP,* 7/15/1904.
31. *HTJP,* 7/6/1904; 1905:2/24, 5/31.
32. *HTJP,* 9/26/1903 reports that the scale was finally pegged at 20% below the Wai-wu pu's.
33. *HTJP,* 9/24/1903. However, *HTJP* 10/20/1903 also gives conflicting reports of some officials from other ministries who declined to apply for fear of loss of seniority and reduced income.
34. *HTJP,* 10/31/1903.
35. *HTJP,* 1903:3/1, 12/30.
36. *HTJP,* 4/4/1903.
37. Ts'ao Ju-lin, *Hui-i,* pp. 5-7; *HTJP,* 10/13/1903.
38. *THL/KH* 32/7, pp. 97-98, 98-99; Cameron, *Reform Movement,* pp. 101-107.
39. *THL/KH* 32/9, pp. 111-114.
40. *TFTC,* Nei-wu, 4.2:59-66 (1907); for details of the structure of the Nung-kung-shang pu, see *Nung-kung-shang pu hsien-hsing chang-ch'eng.*

41. Not until May 30, 1911, did the Yu-ch'uan pu take over control of the postal services from the Maritime Customs Service. See *TFTC,* Ta-shih, 8.5:1 (1911).
42. One publicized clash between Peking and the provinces at this time was the confrontation between T'ieh-liang and Yuan shih-k'ai over the control of the New Army. T'ieh-liang, the first President of the Ministry of Army, insisted that Yuan should relinquish his command and turn his New Army into a national army. A compromise was finally concluded when an imperial edict ordered the transfer of the Second and Fourth Divisions of the New Army to T'ieh-liang's jurisdiction. Yuan, however, retained command over the First, Third, Fifth, and Sixth Divisions. See Hsiao I-shan, *Ch'ing-tai t'ung-shih*, 5 vols. (Taipei, 1963), IV, 2399-2403, 2455-2462.
43. En-han Lee, "Chekiang Gentry-Merchants vs. Peking Court Officials," esp. pp. 267-268.
44. See Stephen R. MacKinnon, "Liang Shih-i and the Communication Clique," *Journal of Asian Studies* 29.3:581-602 (1970).
45. Fei Hsing-chien, *Chin-tai ming-jen hsiao-chuan* (Taipei, 1967), pp. 137-138.
46. Ts'en Ch'un-hsuan, *Lo-chai man-ch'i.*
47. *TFTC,* Chi-lu, 5.10:93 (1908).
48. *HTJP,* 12/10/1907.
49. *HTJP,* 1907:4/1, 4/2.
50. Shen Yun-lung, "Chang-wo wan Ch'ing cheng-ping," II, 261-262; Hsiao I-shan, *T'ung-shih,* IV, 2457-2458.
51. *HTJP,* 1/15/10; also *TFTC,* Chi-lu, 5.10:92-93 (1908), regretted the popular Tsai-chen's departure, stating that he had true and sympathetic feelings for the industrial effort.
52. *TFTC,* Chi-lu, 6.9:43 (1909); *HTJP,* 10/16/1909 reported an alternative plan: out of the $10 million aimed for, $1 million would go to cash prizes, $8 million to set up an industrial corporation, $0.8 million for the Shang pu's administrative use, and $0.2 million as a contribution (*pao-hsiao*) to the state. Those who received no cash prizes would automatically become shareholders of the corporation, their shares being worth 80% of the face value of the tickets owned.
53. *HTJP,* 1909:10/8, 11/22; *TFTC,* Chi-lu, 6.13:443 (1909-1910), 7.1:10 (1910).
54. *HTJP,* 11/8/1909.
55. Indeed such a new hierarchy was suggested by the imperial commission which drew up the new bureaucratic structure for the central government. See *THL/KH* 32/9, p. 112.

9. Programs and Experiments at the Capital

1. *HTJP*, 3/15/1905.
2. See "An Economic Study of the Last 25 Years," in *Hsien-shih kung-ssu*, pp. 42-43; *HTJP*, 3/15/1905; 1906:4/5,4/21.
3. *TFTC*, Shih-yeh, 1.3:180-182 (1904).
4. *HTJP*, 7/8/1901.
5. *TFTC*, Shih-yeh, 1.3:180-182 (1904).
6. *HTJP*, 1904:7/9, 5/24; 1905:11/3, 10/28; 8/15/1906.
7. *HTJP*, 1903:10/3, 10/10, 11/14, 12/27. The first issue appeared on 12/28/1903.
8. *HTJP*, 10/12/1903; 1904:1/6, 1/28, 2/27.
9. *HTJP*, 3/3/1906.
10. A complete set of the *Commercial Gazette* from 1906 to 1912 is deposited at the Toyo Bunko in Tokyo, courtesy of the Peking office of the Mitsubishi Company. But no copy of its predecessor, the *Shang-wu pao*, can be located. On the *Gazette*'s brisk sales, see *SWKP*, No. 1 (1907).
11. The full text of the Company Law is found in *Nung-kung-shang pu hsien-hsing chang-ch'eng*.
12. Through the publication of two collections of statistics by the Nung-kung-shang pu, these five years are the only ones of which detailed records are available. The two publications are *NKSPTCP-I* and *NKSPTCP-II*.
13. Kung Chün, following a Japanese source, gives the number of "modern" industries registered with the ministry during the same period as 127, with a total capital of approximately $46,000,000. Of the 127, there were 98 joint-stock companies of limited liability, 17 partnerships of limited liability, 1 partnership of unlimited liability, and 11 sole proprietorships. See his *Chung-kuo hsin-kung-yeh*, pp. 69-71.
14. See Wang Ching-yü, "Shih-chiu shih-chi."
15. In 1907, the ministry required all pawnshops to register as companies of unlimited liability on the ground that their clients were mostly poor people who should be reimbursed to the full extent a bankrupt pawnshop owner could pay. It seems that a similar restriction had already been imposed upon local banks. See *Ta-Ch'ing Kuang-hsu hsin fa-ling*, ts'e 16:29b-30.
16. *NKSPTCP-I*, ts'e 5:6b-8.
17. *HTJP*, 10/18/1905; 5/8/1906.
18. *NKSPTCP-I*, ts'e 5:11b-13b; 15b-16. Five companies were registered on 1/20/1906; 5 on 1/24/1906; 2 on 3/17/1906; 1 on 5/23/1906; 2 on 6/29/1906; 1 on 7/3/1906.

19. *HTJP,* 1903:2/10, 3/4, 7/10, 10/5, 10/20.
20. *HTJP,* 2/7/1903.
21. *PYKT,* 20:7-9, 10-14b.
22. *HTJP,* 1905:2/28, 8/10, 10/14, 12/17/1906.
23. *HTJP,* 12/30/1907; 12/10/1908. *HTJP* 2/8 and 12/3 of 1909 report on preparations being made for another exhibition. But apparently nothing came of them.
24. *NKSPTCP-I,* ts'e 3:1-4b.
25. *HTJP,* 1904:7/11, 11/12; Sheng Hsuan-huai, *Yü-chai ts'un-kao,* 11:1-3b.
26. Chang Chih-tung, Kung-tu, 10:5b-6.
27. William Ayers, *Chang Chih-tung and Educational Reform in China* (Cambridge, Mass., 1971), p. 106. Chang had already opened the Industrial Arts School (Kung-i hsueh-t'ang) in 1898. Also see *HTJP,* 10/15/1902 for the editorial's view on the importance of proper commercial training.
28. *HTJP,* 4/16/1904.
29. Ch'en Ts'an and Mei Ju-mei, *Chung-kuo shang-yeh-shih kai-yo* (Taipei, 1965), p. 145.
30. *NKSPTCP-I,* ts'e 6:3-7, II ts'e 5:14a-b.
31. *SWKP,* 19:1-3 (1911).
32. *CKKYSTL-III,* I, 7.
33. *THL/KH* 24/5, pp. 112-114.
34. *KYSTL-II,* I, 640-641.
35. *THL/KH* 30/3, p. 18; *NKSPTCP-I,* ts'e 6:9a-b.
36. Ibid. The two officials were Yuan Shu-hsun, Provincial Judge of Kiangsu, and Ting Pao-ch'uan, taotai of Swatow.
37. Tsai Chih-li, comp., *Szu-ch'uan pao-lu yun-tung shih-liao* (Peking, 1959), p. 34.
38. *THL/KH* 32/8, pp. 107-108; *TFTC,* Shih-yeh, 3.11:223-225 (1906).
39. See Table 3 below for the differences. As a result of these revisions, Chang Chien, on January 26, 1908, was awarded the less exalted "advisor, first class" on the basis of other investments he had raised of over $1,000,000. The available document is vague as to whether he still retained his first class conselorship given to him in 1904. See *NKSPTCP-I,* ts'e 6:20b-21. This shows the general confusion which surrounded these various awards.
40. *TFTC,* Shih-yeh, 4.12:175 (1907-1908).
41. *TFTC,* Shang-wu, 2.1:2-3 (1905).
42. See Hsu Ta-ling, *Ch'ing-tai chüan-na chih-tu* (Peking, 1950).
43. Ibid., pp. 160-161.
44. *HTJP,* 9/10/1909.
45. H. S. Brunnert and V. V. Hagelstrom, *Present Day Political Organization of China* (Shanghai, 1912), pp. 500-504.

10. The Search For Supporting Institutions in the Provinces

1. Kwang-ching Liu, "The Limits of Regional Power in Late Ch'ing Period: A Reappraisal," *The Tsing Hua Journal of Chinese Studies* (new ser.) 10.2:176–223 (1974). On the growth of regionalism in general, see Mary C. Wright, *China in Revolution;* Stanley Spector, *Li Hung-chang and the Huai Army* (Seattle, 1964); and Philip A. Kuhn, *Rebellion and Its Enemies in Late Imperial China: Militarization and Social Structure 1796–1864* (Cambridge, Mass., 1970).
2. Chang Chien, *Chiu-lu,* Cheng-wen lu, 1:19a–b.
3. *THL/KH* 21/12, pp. 188–191.
4. Ibid.
5. *HTJP,* 1896:1/20, 1/25.
6. *KYSTL-II,* I, 592–593.
7. Ibid., I, 596–597.
8. Ibid., I, 597–598.
9. *HTJP,* 5/11/1901.
10. Cited in Wen Chung-chi, "The Nineteenth Century Imperial Chinese Consulates in the Straits Settlements" (unpublished M.A. thesis, University of Singapore, 1964), pp. 189–190.
11. Song Ong Siang, *One Hundred Years' History of the Chinese in Singapore* (Singapore, 1967), pp. 279, 281–282.
12. Wen Chung-chi, "Imperial Chinese Consulates," pp. 252–253.
13. *HTJP,* 11/30/1901.
14. *TFTC,* Shang-wu, 3.3:7 (1906); Ch'en Ts'an and Mei Ju-mei, *Shang-yeh shih,* p. 144; *HTJP,* 1901:3/19, 4/3, 7/6, 8/22.
15. *THL/KH* 29/2, pp. 15–16.
16. *The Fiftieth Anniversary Commemorative Issue of the Singapore Chinese Chamber of Commerce* (Singapore, 1954).
17. For example, the bureau head Hsiao Yung-sheng was the same person or brother of Hsiao Yung-hua, who was vice-president of the Swatow Chamber of Commerce when it was founded in 1906. See *NKSPTC-I,* ts'e 4:10b. On its cordial relations with the Shang pu, see "Shang-wu an," of *Wai-chiao tang-an,* II, 1 (File B-1-4).
18. Chou Shu-chen, *Pieh-chuan,* pp. 13–27; *SWKP,* Kung-tu, 20:6–7b (1907); *PYKT,* 16:7–14, 17:3–10b; *TFTC,* Shih-yeh, 1.10:175–177 (1904), 2.5:64–73 (1905).
19. *PYKT,* 16:2a–b, 18:29b–30, 31a.
20. *PYKT,* 16:2b–6.
21. *HTJP,* 12/6/1905.

22. Cheng Kuan-ying, *Hou-pien,* II, 799-807; 801-811; *HTJP,* 12/29/1905, 8/7/1906, 4/11/1908.
23. *HTJP,* 10/14/1902; 4/13/1904.
24. *HTJP,* 8/10/1904.
25. *THL/KH* 29/3, p. 26.
26. *HTJP,* 10/22/1903.
27. *Ta-Ch'ing Kuang-hsu hsin fa-ling*, 16:36-37; *TFTC*, Shang-wu, 2.11:135-137 (1905).
28. *NKSPTCP-I,* ts'e 1:26b-31, 6:10-14; *NKSPTCP-II,* ts'e 5:16a-b.
29. *HTJP,* 8/2/1904.
30. *HTJP,* 8/6/1904, 3/26/1906.
31. *NKSPTCP-I,* ts'e 6:13b-14b.
32. *TFTC,* Shang-wu, 1.11:119-120 (1904).
33. *SWKP,* 30:31 (1907); *P'an-yü hsien hsu-chih,* ed. Wang Chao-yung (n.p., 1931), 4:5a.
34. *Ta-Ch'ing Kuang-hsu hsin fa-ling,* 16:45a.
35. *TFTC,* Shang-wu, 2.9:88-90 (1905).
36. *TFTC,* Shang pu, 2.9:88-90 (1905).
37. Wang Yu-ling, "Shang pu chih tse-jen," *SWKP,* No. 7 (1906).
38. *SWKP,* 19:5-7 (1908).
39. See *NKSPTCP-II,* ts'e 5:17a-b.
40. See Chou Shan-p'ei, *Hsin-hai Szu-ch'uan cheng-lu ch'in-li chih* (Chungking, 1957).
41. Franz Schurmann, *Ideology and Organization in Communist China* (Berkeley and Los Angeles, 1968), pp. 188-194.

11. The Continuing Search: The Chamber of Commerce

1. Ch'üan Han-sheng, *Chung-kuo hang-hui chih-tu shih* (Shanghai, 1934), pp. 99-101; Peter J. Golas, "Early Ch'ing Gilds," unpublished paper delivered at the Conference on Urban Society in Traditional China, Wentworth-by-the-Sea, New Hampshire, Aug. 31-Sept. 7, 1968; Peng Chang, "Distribution of Provincial Merchant Groups in China, 1842-1911," pp. 51-55.
2. H. B. Morse, *The Gilds of China* (London, 1909), pp. 35-48; Ho P'ing-ti, *Chung-kuo hui-kuan shih-lun* (Taipei, 1966). The German terms like Landsmannschaften were first suggested by D. J. MacGowan, in his "Chinese Guilds or Chambers of Commerce and Trade Unions," *Journal of North-China Branch of the Royal Asiatic Society,* vol. 21 (1888-89). They are also used by Prof. Ho.
3. For a detailed account of the cemetery dispute, see Fang T'eng, "Yü

Hsia-ching lun," in *Tsa-chih Yueh-k'an* 12.2:46-51, 12.3:62-67, 12.4: 59-64 (1943-44). An English summary is found in Susan M. Jones, "The Ningpo *Pang* and Financial Power at Shanghai," in Mark Elvin and G. William Skinner, eds., *The Chinese City Between Two Worlds* (Stanford, 1974), pp. 86-88.

4. *T'ung-chih Shang-hai hsien-chih,* ed. Yü Yueh (n.p., preface 1871), 2:21-28; and Mark Elvin, "The Administration of Shanghai, 1905-1914," in Elvin and Skinner, eds., *Chinese City Between Two Worlds,* pp. 240-242.
5. *Nan-hai hsien-chih,* eds. Chang Feng-chieh, et al. (n.p., preface 1910), 6:10b-13. There were also some older, government supported charitable halls already in existence. But they seemed to be small and poorly run. See Edward J. M. Rhoads, "Merchant Associations in Canton, 1895-1911," in Elvin and Skinner, eds., *Chinese City Between Two Worlds,* p. 104.
6. They were Ai-yü, Kuang-chi, Kuang-jen, Ch'ung-cheng, Shu-shan, Ming-chan, Hui-hsing, Fang-pien, Jun-shen.
7. A. M. Kotenev, *Shanghai: Its Mixed Court and Council* (Shanghai, 1925), p. 253n.
8. Such a trend toward more integrated and community-wide organizations is discussed in Wellington K. K. Chan, "Merchant Organizations in Late Imperial China: Pattern of Change and Development," *Journal of the Hong Kong Branch of the Royal Asiatic Society,* vol. 15 (1975).
9. Mark Elvin, discussing a parallel development in local government in Shanghai, observes that "The 'modern' city government that emerged after 1905 was largely a fusion of indigenous institutions that had evolved very late in traditional times, though it was the challenge and example of the West that induced, and to some extent directed, this fusion," p. 13 of his "Introduction" in Elvin and Skinner, eds., *Chinese City Between Two Worlds*. Also see Mark Elvin, "The Gentry Democracy in Chinese Shanghai, 1905-14," in Jack Gray, ed., *Modern China's Search for Political Form* (Oxford, 1969).
10. For a similar observation regarding Shanghai, see Jones, "The Ningpo *Pang,*" esp. p. 89.
11. Chao Feng-t'ien, *Ching-chi ssu-hsiang shih,* pp. 109, 129-130; Hao Yen-p'ing, *Comprador,* p. 192; *Ou Chü-chia chuan,* pp. 111-127.
12. *Ta Ch'ing Kuang-hsu hsin fa-ling,* 16:30b-34b.
13. Ibid., 16:30a-b.
14. Sheng Hsuan-huai, *Yü-chai ts'un-kao,* 7:35-37.
15. *Shang-hai hsien hsu-chih,* ed. Yao Wen-nan (Shanghai, 1918), 2:51-52; *Shang-hai tsung-shang-hui yueh-pao,* Chuan-chi, 1.2:1 (1921), 2.3:1 (1922).

16. Feuerwerker, *China's Early Industrialization,* p. 21.
17. *TFTC,* Shang-wu, 1.5:58-59 (1904); *Shang-hai tsung-shang-hui yueh-pao,* Chuan-chi, 1.2:1 (1921).
18. Feuerwerker, *China's Early Industrialization,* pp. 21, 112-114, 116; Hsu Jun, *Nien-p'u,* pp. 36b-39b.
19. Ibid., p. 106a; *KYSTL-II,* II, 967.
20. Jones, "The Ningpo *Pang.*"
21. For Tseng's biography, see *KYSTL-II,* II, 956.
22. *Shang-hai tsung-shang-hui yueh-pao,* Chuan-chi, 1.2:1-2 (1921).
23. *CKKYSTL-I,* I, 474-476.
24. *The China Weekly Review* (Shanghai), 7/24/1926, pp. 188, 190; Marie-Claire Bergère, *Crise financière à Shanghai,* pp. 51, n. 10, n. 13; 58, n. 3.
25. *HTJP,* 1903:8/24, 9/8, 9/24, 10/21, 10/22, 10/24.
26. Cheng Kuan-ying, *Hou-pien,* 8:25-26b, 31; *HTJP,* 12/15/1904; 1905: 1/12, 1/25, 5/24.
27. Cheng Kuan-ying, *Hou-pien,* 8:22b. From 1907, the number was reduced to four. See *HTJP,* 10/10/1907; 10/28/1908.
28. Rhoads, "Merchant Associations in Canton," and Elvin, "Administration of Shanghai."
29. Rhoads, in his "Merchant Associations in Canton," argues that the leaders of the Canton Chamber of Commerce were wealthy "gentry-merchants" friendly to the government, while the guilds were more representative of the ordinary merchants (p. 108). Yet, as my discussion shows, the Canton guilds remained the dominant organization throughout the 1900s, while several prominent gentry-merchants such as Cheng Kuan-ying and Tso Tsung-fan were directors of the guilds.
30. P'eng Tse-i, "Shih-chiu shih-chi hou-ch'i," pp. 76-77; Sidney D. Gamble, *Peking: A Social Survey* (Oxford, 1921), pp. 168-170.
31. The figures are 97 chambers each with an average of 496 member firms for Shansi and 79 chambers each with an average of 333 member firms for Kiangsu. See Elvin, "Introduction," pp. 7-8. Presumably Shansi's members were small in relation to Kiangsu's.
32. Gamble, *Peking,* pp. 194-195.
33. *Ta-Ch'ing Kuang-hsu hsin fa-ling,* 16:12b-19. See esp. Arts. 9-16.
34. *TFTC,* Shang-wu, 2.9:109-110 (1905); *TFTC,* Chi-lu, 6.3:9-10 (1909); Kotenev, *Shanghai,* p. 256.
35. Many examples may be cited, e.g., see *China Maritime Customs Statistical Series, Decennial Reports, 1882-1891* (Shanghai, 1892), "Swatow," pp. 537-538.
36. *Ta-Ch'ing Kuang-hsu hsin fa-ling,* 16:35-36; *TFTC,* Shang-wu, 1.2:35 (1904).
37. Many studies on this decade's spirit of activism have recently appeared,

see esp. Mary C. Wright, *China in Revolution*; Michael Gasster, *Chinese Intellectuals and the Revolution of 1911: The Birth of Modern Chinese Radicalism* (Seattle, 1969); Mary B. Rankin, *Early Chinese Revolutionaries: Radical Intellectuals in Shanghai and Chekiang 1902-1911* (Cambridge, Mass., 1971).

38. *HTJP*, 10/8/1903.
39. *Ching-chung pao*, 6/2/1904, cited in *TFTC*, Shang-wu, 1.5:55-56 (1904).
40. Ibid., pp. 58–59; *HTJP*, 5/7/1906.
41. *TFTC*, Shang-wu, 2.7:73 (1905).
42. *NKSPTCP-I*, ts'e 1:16a–25b; 2:9–12b.
43. Chow Tse-tsung, *The May Fourth Movement: Intellectual Revolution in Modern China* (Cambridge, Mass., 1960), p. 380. After that, the number stabilized, e.g. the number of chambers around 1920 was 1,239 (see Elvin, "Introduction," p. 7).
44. The sources for the 1910 financial crisis in Shanghai are collected in *Shang-hai ch'ien-chuang shih-liao* (Shanghai, 1960), pp. 72-82. Marie-Claire Bergère has translated and written commentaries on many of its documents in her *Crise financière à Shanghai* already cited.
45. Ibid., p. 10.
46. Ibid., pp. 12, n. 13; 5.
47. Hou Yen-p'ing, *Comprador,* p. 189.
48. *NCH,* 1910:7/29, p. 268; 9/30, pp. 783-785; 10/14, p. 82.
49. *China Maritime Customs, Returns of Trade at the Treaty Ports of China: Trade Reports, 1910,* "Shanghai," p. 399.
50. Cheng Kuan-ying, *Hou-pien,* 8:50b–51.
51. *HTJP,* 1907:9/2, 11/9.
52. Feuerwerker, *China's Early Industrialization,* pp. 80–81; *Shang-hai tsung-shang-hui yueh-pao,* Chuan-chi, 1.2:2 (1921).
53. *China Maritime Customs, Returns of Trade, 1910,* "Hangchow," p. 499.
54. *Shang-hai ch'ien-chuang,* pp. 88–93; *NCH,* 1/9/1909; *HTJP,* 1/1/1909.
55. *NCH,* 1910:10/7, p. 42; 10/14, p. 81.
56. See Chapter 7 above.
57. Kotenev, *Shanghai,* p. 255.
58. See Shirley S. Garrett, "The Chamber of Commerce and the YMCA," (pp. 213–238) and the other articles by Elvin, Rhoads, and Jones already cited, all in Elvin and Skinner, *Chinese City Between Two Worlds.*
59. Cheng Kuan-ying, *Hou-pien,* 8:31b–33, 34b–37.
60. *TFTC,* Shang-wu, 1.12:154–157 (1904–1905).
61. Ibid.
62. *SWKP,* 6:18–19 (1907).

63. Wright and Cartwright, eds., *Twentieth Century Impressions,* pp. 67, 423-424; *Shang-hai hsien hsu-chih,* 12:11b-13b.
64. *HTJP,* 1907:7/16, 7/27, 7/29, 9/4, 9/6, 9/13.
65. Bergère, "Role of the Bourgeoisie"; Jones, "Ningpo *Pang*"; Elvin, "Gentry Democracy in Chinese Shanghai"; and Rhoads, "Merchant Associations in Canton."

BIBLIOGRAPHY

Arnold, Julian H., et al., eds. *Commercial Handbook of China.* 2 vols. Washington, U.S. Government Printing Office, 1919–1920.

Ayers, William. *Chang Chih-tung and Educational Reform in China.* Cambridge, Harvard University Press, 1971.

Balazs, Étienne. *Chinese Civilization and Bureaucracy.* New Haven, Yale University Press, 1964.

Barber, Bernard. *Social Stratification: A Comparative Analysis of Structure and Process.* New York, Harcourt, Brace & World, 1957.

Bergère, Marie-Claire. *Une crise financière à Shanghai à la fin de l'ancien régime.* Paris, Mouton & Cie., 1964.

———. "The Role of the Bourgeoisie," in Mary C. Wright, ed., *China in Revolution: The First Phase 1900–1913.* New Haven, Yale University Press, 1968.

Black, Cyril E. *The Dynamics of Modernization.* New York, Harper and Row, 1966.

Boorman, Howard. *Biographical Dictionary of Republican China.* 4 vols. New York, Columbia University Press, 1967–1971.

Brunnert, H. S. and V. V. Hagelstrom. *Present Day Political Organization in China,* tr. A. Beltchenko and E. E. Moran. Shanghai, Kelly and Walsh, 1912.

Cameron, Maribeth E. *The Reform Movement in China, 1898–1912.* 1st ed., 1931; photocopy, New York, Octagon Books, Inc., 1963.

Carlson, Ellsworth C. *The Kaiping Mines, 1877–1912.* 2nd ed. Cambridge, East Asian Research Center, Harvard University, 1971.

Chan, Wellington K. K. "Politics and Industrialization in Late Imperial China," *Occasional Paper No. 30.* Institute of Southeast Asian Studies, Singapore, 1975.

———. "Merchant Organizations in Late Imperial China: Pattern of Change and Development," *Journal of the Hong Kong Branch of the Royal Asiatic Society,* vol. 15 (1975).

———. "Bureaucratic Capital and Chou Hsueh-hsi in Late Ch'ing China," *Modern Asian Studies* (forthcoming).

Chang Chia-ao (Chang Kia-ngau). *China's Struggle for Railroad Development.* New York, The John Day Co., 1943.

Chang Chien 張謇. *T'ung-chou hsin-pan shih-yeh chih li-shih: Ta-sheng sha ch'ang* 通州新辦實業之歷史：大生紗廠 (The Dah Sun Mill: the history of a modern enterprise in T'ung-chou). Nan-t'ung, 1910.

———. *Chang Chi-tzu chiu-lu* 張季子九錄 (The nine records of Chang Chien), ed. Chang Hsiao-jo 張孝若. 80 chüan. Shanghai, 1931.

Chang Chih-tung 張之洞. *Chang Wen-hsiang-kung chi* 張文襄公集 (The papers of Chang Chih-tung), ed. Hsu T'ung-hsin 許同莘. 150 chüan in 65 ts'e. Peiping, 1919–1921. Includes drafts of memorials (*tsou-kao* 奏稿), 50 chüan; drafts of telegrams (*tien-kao* 電稿), 66 chüan; correspondence (*kung-tu* 公牘), 28 chüan; miscellaneous (*han-chung* 函種), 6 chüan.

Chang Chung-li. *The Income of the Chinese Gentry.* Seattle, University of Washington Press, 1962.

Chang Hao. *Liang Ch'i-ch'ao and Intellectual Transition in China, 1890–1907.* Cambridge, Harvard University Press, 1971.

Chang Hsiao-jo 張孝若. *Nan-t'ung Chang Chi-chih hsien-sheng chuan-chi* 南通張季直先生傳記 (A biography of Mr. Chang Chien of Nan-t'ung). Shanghai, 1929. Reprinted in 6 vols., Taipei, 1965.

Chang Hsin-pao. *Commissioner Lin and the Opium War.* Cambridge, Harvard University Press, 1964.

Chang Peng. "Distribution of Provincial Merchant Groups in China, 1842–1911." Unpublished Ph.D. thesis, University of Washington, Seattle, 1958.

Chang P'eng-yuan 張朋園. *Li-hsien p'ai yü hsin-hai ko-ming* 立憲派與辛亥革命 (The Constitutionalists and the Revolution of 1911). Taipei, 1969.

Chang T'ing-chü 張廷舉. "Wu-hsu cheng-pien shih-ch'i wan-ku p'ai chih ching-chi ssu-hsiang" 戊戌政變時期頑固派之經濟思想 (The economic thought of the reactionary clique during the reform of 1898), *Chung-kuo ching-chi* 中國經濟 (The Chinese economy) 4.6:141–147 (June 1936).

Chang Ts'un-wu 張存武. *Chung-Mei kung-yueh fang-chiao* 中美工約風潮 (Disputes over the Sino-American labor agreement). Taipei, 1965.

Chao Feng-t'ien 趙豐田. *Wan-Ch'ing wu-shih-nien ching-chi ssu-hsiang shih* 晚清五十年經濟思想史 (History of economic thought during the last fifty years of the Ch'ing period). Peking, Harvard-Yenching Institute, Yenching University, 1939.

Ch'en Chen, et al., comp. *Chung-kuo chin-tai kung-yeh shih tzu-liao, ti-i-chi,* see *CKKYSTL-I.*

———, et al., comp. *Chung-kuo chin-tai kung-yeh shih tzu-liao, ti-san-chi,* see *CKKYSTL-III.*

Ch'en Ch'i-t'ien 陳其田. *Shan-hsi p'iao-chuang k'ao-lueh* 山西票莊考略 (A brief study on the remittance banks of Shansi). Shanghai, 1937.

Ch'en Ts'an 陳燦 and Mei Ju-mei 梅汝玫. *Chung-kuo shang-yeh-shih kai-yo* 中國商業史概要 (An outline of the history of commerce in China). Taipei, 1965.

Cheng Hsing-sun 鄭行巽. *Chung-kuo shang-yeh shih* 中國商業史 (A commercial history of China). Shanghai, 1932.

Cheng Kuan-ying 鄭觀應. *Sheng-shih wei-yen* 盛世危言 (Warnings to a seemingly prosperous age). 14 chüan. Shanghai, first preface 1892, rev. and enlarged ed. 1895.

———. *Sheng-shih wei-yen hou-pien* 盛世危言後編 (Warnings to a seemingly prosperous age, second part). 15 chüan. First preface 1910. Reprinted in 3 vols., Taipei, 1969.

Cheng Lin. *The Chinese Railways Past and Present.* Shanghai, 1937.

Chi, Madeleine. "Shanghai-Hangchow-Ningpo Railway Loan: A Case Study of the Rights Recovery Movement," *Modern Asian Studies* 7.1:85–106 (1973).

Ch'i-hsin yang-hui kung-ssu shih-liao 啓新洋灰公司史料 (Historical materials on Chee Hsin Cement Company). Peking, 1963.

Chia Shih-i 賈士毅. *Min-kuo ch'u-nien ti chi-jen t'sai-cheng tsung-ch'ang* 民國初年的幾任財政總長 (The several finance ministers during the early years of the Republic). Taipei, 1967.

Chiang-Che t'ieh-lu fang-ch'ao 江浙鐵路風潮 (Storm over the Kiangsu-Chekiang railway), ed. Mo Pei 墨悲. Shanghai, 1907. Photo reprint Taipei, 1968.

Chiang-hu pi-tu 江湖必讀 (An essential guide for the [merchant] traveler). N.p., n.d.

"Chiang-li Hua-shang kung-ssu chang-ch'eng" 獎勵華商公司章程 (Regulations of awards for Chinese-owned companies), in *Nung-kung-shang pu hsien-hsing chang-ch'eng* 農工商部現行章程 (Regulations of the Ministry of Agriculture, Commerce, and Industry currently in use). 13 ts'e. Peking, 1909.

Ch'ien Hsing-ts'un 錢杏邨 (pseud. Ah-ying 阿英). *Wan-Ch'ing hsiao-shuo shih* 晚清小說史 (A history of the late Ch'ing novels). Hong Kong, 1966.

China, Imperial Maritime Customs. *Decennial Reports on the Trade,*

Navigation, Industries, etc., of the Ports Open to Foreign Commerce in China and on the Conditions and Development of the Treaty Port Provinces, 1882–1891. Shanghai, 1893.

———. *Returns of Trade at the Treaty Ports of China.* Shanghai, 1870–1912, annually.

China Weekly Review, The. Published originally under the name of *Millard's Review.* Shanghai, 1917–1937.

Ch'ing-chi hsin-she chih-kuan nien-p'iao 清季新設職官年表 (Chronological tables of the newly established offices of the late Ch'ing period). Comp. Ch'ien Shih-fu Peking, 1961.

Chou Shan-p'ei 周善培. *Hsin-hai Ssu-ch'uan cheng-lu ch'in-li chi* 辛亥四川爭路親歷記 (An eyewitness account of the fight for the Szechwan railway in 1911). Chungking, 1957.

Chou Shu-chen 周叔楨. *Chou Chih-an hsien-sheng pieh-chuan* 周止菴先生別傳 (An unofficial biography of Chou Hsueh-hsi). Preface 1948. Taipei reprint, 1966.

Chow Tse-tsung. *The May Fourth Movement: Intellectual Revolution in Modern China.* Cambridge, Harvard University Press, 1960.

Chu, Samuel C. "Chang Chien and the Founding of Dah Sun," *Tsing Hua Journal of Chinese Studies* (new series) 2.1:310–314 (May 1960).

———. *Reformer in Modern China: Chang Chien, 1853–1926.* New York, Columbia University Press, 1965.

Chü Ch'ing-yuan 鞠清遠. "Ch'ing k'ai-kuo ch'ien-hou ti san-pu shang-jen chu-tso" 清開國前後的三部商人著作 (Three merchant works written around the time of the Manchus' entry into China), in Li Ting-i 李定一 et al., eds., *Chung-kuo chin-tai-shih lun-ts'ung* 中國近代史論叢 (Collection of essays on modern history), 2nd coll., vol. 2. Taipei, 1958.

Ch'ü T'ung-tsu. "Chinese Class Structure and Its Ideology," in John K. Fairbank, ed., *Chinese Thought and Institutions.* Chicago, University of Chicago Press, 1957.

Ch'üan Han-sheng 全漢昇. *Chung-kuo hang-hui chih-tu shih* 中國行會制度史 (An institutional history of the Chinese guilds). Shanghai, 1934.

———. "Sung-tai kuan-shih chih ssu-ying shang-yeh" 宋代官吏之私營商業 (Private enterprises of the Sung officials), *Bulletin of the Institute of History and Philology* (Academia Sinica) 7.2:199–253 (1936).

———. "Ch'ing-mo Han-yang t'ieh-chang" 清末漢陽鐵廠 (The Hanyang Ironworks during the late Ch'ing), in *She-hui k'o-hsueh lun-ts'ung* 社會科學論叢 (Collected studies on the social sciences) 1:18–21 (April 1950).

Chung-hsu Hsi-hsien hui-kuan lu 重續歙縣會館錄 (A repeat edition of the continuation to the records of the Hsi-hsien Landsmannschaft). First preface, 1834.

Chung-hua min-kuo k'ai-kuo wu-shih nien wen-hsien 中華民國開國五十年文獻 (Documents on the fiftieth anniversary of the founding of the Republic of China). 1st. ser., 15 vols.; 2nd ser., 5 vols. Taipei, 1962–1965.

Chung-kuo chin-tai kuo-ming ching-chi-shih chiang-i 中國近代國民經濟史講義 (Lectures on the modern national economic history of China), ed. Hu-pei ta-hsueh cheng-chih ching-chi hsueh chiao-yen tsu 湖北大學政治經濟學教研組 (Committee on research and teaching of political economy, Hupei University). Peking, 1958.

Chung-kuo chin-tai t'ieh-lu shih tzu-liao, 1863–1911 中國近代鐵路史資料 (Source materials on the history of modern railways in China, 1863–1911), comp. Mi Ju-ch'eng 宓汝成. 3 vols. Peking, 1963.

CKKYSTL-I: Ch'en Chen 陳真, et al., comp. *Chung-kuo chin-tai kung-yeh shih tzu-liao, ti-i-chi,* 中國近代工業史資料第一輯 (Source materials on the history of modern industry in China, 1st collection). 2 vols. Peking, 1957.

CKKYSTL-III: Ch'en Chen, et al., comp. *Chung-kuo chin-tai kung-yeh shih tzu-liao, ti-san-chi* 中國近代工業史資料第三輯 (Source materials on the history of modern industry in China, 3rd collection). 2 vols. Peking, 1961.

Crawcour, E. Sydney. "The Tokugawa Heritage," in William W. Lockwood, ed., *The State and Economic Enterprise in Japan.* Princeton, Princeton University Press, 1965.

de Bary, Wm. Theodore, et al., eds. *Sources of Chinese Tradition.* New York, Columbia University Press, 1960.

Eastman, Lloyd. "Political Reformism in China before the Sino-Japanese War," *Journal of Asian Studies* 27.4:695–710 (1968).

Eckstein, Alexander. "Individualism and the Role of the State in Economic Growth," in Galy D. Ness, ed., *The Sociology of Economic Development.* New York, 1970.

Elvin, Mark. "The Gentry Democracy in Chinese Shanghai, 1905–14," in Jack Gray, ed., *Modern China's Search for Political Form.* Oxford, Oxford University Press, 1969.

———. "The High-Level Equilibrium Trap: The Causes of the Decline of Invention in the Traditional Chinese Textile Industries," in W. E. Willmott, ed., *Economic Organization in Chinese Society.* Stanford, Stanford University Press, 1972.

———. "Introduction," in Mark Elvin and G. William Skinner, eds., *The Chinese City Between Two Worlds.* Stanford, Stanford University Press, 1974.

———. "The Administration of Shanghai, 1905–1914," in Mark Elvin and G. William Skinner, eds., *The Chinese City Between Two Worlds.* Stanford, Stanford University Press, 1974.

Esherick, Joseph W. "1911: A Review," *Modern China* 2.2:141–184 (1976).

Fairbank, John K. *Trade and Diplomacy on the China Coast: The Opening of the Treaty Ports, 1842–1854.* Cambridge, Harvard University Press, 1964.

Fang T'eng 方騰. "Yü Hsia-ch'ing lun" 虞洽卿論 (On Yü Hsia-ch'ing), *Tsa-chih yueh-k'an* 雜誌月刊 (Monthly miscellany) 12.2:46–51 (Nov. 1943); 12.3:62–67 (Dec. 1943); 12.4:59–64 (Jan. 1944).

Fei Hsiao-t'ung. "Peasantry and Gentry: An Interpretation of Chinese Social Structure and its Changes," *American Journal of Sociology* 52.1:1–17 (July, 1946).

Fei Hsing-chien 費行簡. *Chin-tai ming-jen hsiao-chuan* 近代名人小傳 (Short biographies of famous persons in modern times). Taipei reprint, 1967.

Feuerwerker, Albert. *China's Early Industrialization: Sheng Hsuan-huai (1844–1916) and Mandarin Enterprise.* Cambridge, Harvard University Press, 1958.

———. "China's Nineteenth Century Industrialization: the Case of the Hanyehping Coal and Iron Company Limited," in C. D. Cowan, ed., *The Economic Development of China and Japan.* London, George Allen & Unwin Ltd., 1964.

———. "Industrial Enterprise in Twentieth-Century China: The Chee Hsin Cement Company," in his, et al., eds., *Approaches to Modern Chinese History.* Berkeley and Los Angeles, University of California Press, 1967.

———. *The Chinese Economy, ca. 1870–1911.* Ann Arbor, Michigan Papers in Chinese Studies No. 5. Center for Chinese Studies, The University of Michigan, 1969.

Field, Margaret. "The Chinese boycott of 1905," *Papers on China,* 11:63–98 (1957). East Asian Research Center, Harvard University.

Fo-shan chung-i hsiang-chih 佛山忠義鄉志. (Gazetteer of Fu-shan), ed. Hsi Pao-kan 洗宝幹. Canton, 1922.

Folsom, Kenneth E. *Friends, Guests and Colleagues: The Mu-fu System in the Late Ch'ing Period.* Berkeley and Los Angeles, University of California Press, 1968.

Fu I-ling 傅衣凌. *Ming-Ch'ing shih-tai shang-jen chi shang-yeh tzu-pen* 明清時代商人及商業資本 (Merchants and commercial capital during Ming-Ch'ing times). Peking, 1956.

Gale, Esson M. *Discourses on Salt and Iron.* Leiden, 1931.

Gamble, Sidney D. *Peking: A Social Survey.* Oxford, Oxford University Press, 1921.

Garrett, Shirley S. "The Chamber of Commerce and the YMCA," in Mark Elvin and G. William Skinner, eds., *The Chinese City Between Two Worlds.* Stanford, Stanford University Press, 1974.

Gasster, Michael. *Chinese Intellectuals and the Revolution of 1911: The Birth of Modern Chinese Radicalism.* Seattle, University of Washington Press, 1969.

Godley, Michael R. "Chang Pi-shih and Nanyang Chinese Involvement in South China's Railroads, 1896–1911," *Journal of Southeast Asian Studies* 4.1:16–30 (1973).

Golas, Peter J. "Early Ch'ing Gilds." Unpublished paper delivered at the Conference on Urban Society in Traditional China, Wentworth-by-the-Sea, New Hampshire, Aug. 31–Sept. 7, 1968.

Hao Yen-p'ing. "Cheng Kuan-ying: The Comprador as Reformer," *Journal of Asian Studies* 29.1:15–22 (Nov. 1969).

———. *The Comprador in Nineteenth Century Chind: Bridge between East and West.* Cambridge, Harvard University Press, 1970.

Heng-feng sha-ch'ang ti fa-sheng fa-chan yü kai-tsao 恒丰紗厂的发生发展与改造 (The origin, growth, and reconstruction of the Heng-feng Spinning Mill). Shanghai, 1958.

Ho Ch'i 何啓 and Hu Li-yuan 胡禮垣. *Hsin-cheng chen-ch'üan* 新政真詮 (The true meaning of new government). Hong Kong, 1895. The essay cited in the notes from this book is "Hsin-cheng lun-i" 新政論議 (Proposals on the new government).

Ho Ping-ti. "The Salt Merchants of Yang-chou: A Study of Commercial Capitalism in Eighteenth Century China," *Harvard Journal of Asiatic Studies* 17:13–68 (1954).

———. *The Ladder of Success in Imperial China: Aspects of Social Mobility, 1368–1911.* New York, John Wiley & Sons, Inc., 1964.

——— 何炳棣. *Chung-kuo hui-kuan shih-lun* 中國會館史論 (A historical survey of Landsmannschaften in China). Taipei, 1966.

———. "Salient Aspects of China's Heritage," in his and Tang Tsou, eds., *China in Crisis: Volume One, China's Heritage and the Communist Political System.* 2 bks. Chicago, The University of Chicago Press, 1968.

Hou Chi-ming. "Economic Dualism: The Case of China, 1840–1937," *Journal of Economic History* 23.3:277–297 (1965).

Hsiang-kang Hua-tzu jih-pao, see *HTJP.*

Hsiang-kang Yung-an yu-hsien kung-ssu erh-shih-wu chou-nien chi-nien lu 香港永安有限公司廿五週年紀念錄 (The Wing On Co. Ltd. of Hongkong. In commemoration of the twenty-fifth anniversary, 1907–1932). Preface 1932. Hong Kong.

Hsiang-shan hsien-chih hsu-pien 香山縣志續編 (A continuation of the gazetteer of Hsiang-shan County), ed. Li Shih-chin 厲式金. 1923.

Hsiao I-shan 蕭一山. *Ch'ing-tai t'ung-shih* 清代通史 (A general history of the Ch'ing dynasty). 5 vols. Taipei. 1963.

Hsieh Shih-chia. 謝世佳. *Sheng Hsuan-huai yü t'a so ch'uang-pan ti ch'i-yeh* 盛宣懷与他所創辦的企業 (Sheng Hsuan-huai and the enterprises he founded). Taipei, 1971.

Hsien-shih kung-ssu erh-shih-wu chou-nien chi-nien ts'e 先施公司廿五週年紀念册 (The Sincere Company: twenty-fifth anniversary). Preface, winter of 1924–1925. Hong Kong.

Hsu Cho-yun. *Ancient China in Transition: An Analysis of Social Mobility, 722–222 B.C.* Stanford, Stanford University Press, 1965.

Hsu, Immanuel C. Y. *The Rise of Modern China.* New York, Oxford University Press, 1970.

Hsu Jun 徐潤. *Hsu Yü-chai tzu-hsu nien-p'u,* 徐愚齋自叙年譜 (Chronological autobiography). Hsiang-shan, 1927.

Hsu Ta-ling 許大齡. *Ch'ing-tai chüan-na chih-tu* 清代捐納制度 (The institution of purchasing office by contributions during the Ch'ing period). Peking, Yenching University, 1950.

Hsueh-ch'i 學計. "Ch'ing-ch'u ti shang-li chih-nan" 清初的商旅指南 (Guides for traveling merchants during the early Ch'ing), *Ming-pao wan-pao* 明報晚報 (Ming-pao Evening Newspaper), April 25, 1970.

Hsueh Fu-ch'eng, 薛福成. "Ch'ou-yang ch'u-i" 筹洋芻議 (Preliminary proposals on the management of foreign affairs), in *Wu-hsu pien-fa* 戊戌變法 (The reform of 1898), eds. Chien Po-tsan 翦伯贊 et al. 4 vols. Shanghai, 1953

HTJP: Hsiang-kang Hua-tzu jih-pao 香港華字日報 (Chinese mail). Hong Kong. Available at the Feng P'ing-shan Library, University of Hong Kong, Hong Kong.

"Hu I-nan hsien-sheng shih-lueh" 胡翼南先生事略 (A brief account of Mr. Hu Li-yuan), in *Hu I-nan hsien-sheng ch'üan-chi* 胡翼南先生全集 (The complete works of Mr. Hu Li-yuan). 60 chüan. Hong Kong, 1920.

Hunter, William C. *The 'Fan Kwae' at Canton before Treaty Days, 1825–1844, by an Old Resident.* Shanghai, 1911.

I-Ching or the Book of Changes, The, tr. into German by R. Wilhelm. English tr. by C. F. Baynes. 2 vols. New York, Bollingen-Pantheon, 1961.

Jiang, Joseph P. C. "Towards a Theory of Pariah Entrepreneurship," in Gerhan Wijeyewardene, ed., *Leadership and Authority.* Singapore, 1968.

Jones, Susan Mann. "Finance in Ningpo: the 'Ch'ien Chuang,' 1750–1880," in W. E. Willmott, ed., *Economic Organization in Chinese Society.* Stanford, Stanford University Press, 1972.

———. "The Ningpo *Pang* and Financial Power at Shanghai," in Mark Elvin and G. William Skinner, eds., *The Chinese City Between Two Worlds.* Stanford, Stanford University Press, 1974.

Kao Yang 高陽. *Hu Hsueh-yen* 胡雪巖. 3 vols. Taipei, 1973. First appeared in serial form in *Lien-ho pao* 聯合報 (United Daily Press [Taipei]) and the *Ming-pao wan-pao* 明報晚報 (the Ming-pao Evening Newspaper [Hong Kong]) from 1969 to 1972.

Kotenev, A. M. *Shanghai: Its Mixed Court and Council.* Shanghai, 1925.

Kuang-hsu-chao tung-hua lu, see *THL/KH.*

Kuhn, Philip A. *Rebellion and Its Enemies in Late Imperial China: Militarization and Social Structure, 1796–1864.* Cambridge, Harvard University Press, 1970.

Kung Chün 龔駿. *Chung-kuo hsin kung-yeh fa-chiang-shih ta-kang* 中國新工業發展史大綱 (An outline history of the Chinese modern industrial development). Shanghai, 1933.

KYSTL-I: Sun Yü-t'ang 孫毓棠, comp. *Chung-kuo chin-tai kung-yeh shih tzu-liao, ti-i-chi, 1840–1895 nien* 中國近代工業史資料第一輯 *1840–1895* (Source materials on the history of modern industry in China, first collection, 1840–1895). 2 vols. Peking, 1957.

KYSTL-II: Wang Ching-yü 汪敬虞, comp. *Chung-kuo chin-tai kung-yeh shih tzu-liao, ti-erh-chi, 1895–1914 nien* 中國近代工業史資料第二輯 *1895–1914* (Source materials on the history of modern industry in China, second collection, 1895–1914). 2 vols. Peking, 1957.

Lee, En-han. "The Chekiang Gentry-Merchants vs. the Peking Court Officials: China's Struggle for Recovery of the British Soochow-Hangchow-Ningpo Railway Concession, 1905–1911," *Chung-yang yen-chiu yuan chin-tai shih yen-chiu-so chi-kan* 中央研究院近代史研究所集刊 (Bulletin of the Institute of Modern History, Academia Sinica) 3.1:223–268 (1972).

LeFevour, Edward. *Western Enterprise in Late Ch'ing China: A Selective Survey of Jardine, Matheson & Company's Operations, 1842–1895.* Cambridge, East Asian Research Center, Harvard University, 1968.

Legge, James, tr. *The Chinese Classics.* 3rd ed. Hong Kong, University of Hong Kong Press, 1960.

Levy, Marion J. Jr. and Shih Kuo-heng. *The Rise of the Modern Chinese Business Class.* New York, Institute of Pacific Relations, 1949.

Li Ch'en Shun-ping (Mabel Lee) 李陳順妍. "Wan-Ch'ing ti chung-shang chu-i" 晚清的重商主義 (The "exalt commerce" movement of the late Ch'ing) *Chung-yang yen-chiu yuan chin-tai shih yen-chiu-so chi-kan* 中央研究院近代史研究所集刊 (Bulletin of the Institute of Modern History, Academia Sinica) 3.1:207–221 (1972).

Li Hung-chang 李鴻章. *Li Wen-chung-kung ch'üan-chi* 李文忠公全集 (Complete papers of Li Hung-chang), ed. Wu Ju-lun 吳汝綸. 100 ts'e. Photolithograph of the original ed. Shanghai, 1921.

Li Kuo-ch'i 李國祁. *Chung-kuo tsao-ch'i ti t'ieh-lu ching-ying* 中國早期的鐵路經營 (The early period of railway management in China). Taipei, 1961.

Liang Ch'i-ch'ao 梁啟超. *Yin-ping-shih wen-chi* 飲冰室全集 (Collected essays of the Ice-drinkers' Studio [Liang Ch'i-ch'ao]). 80 ts'e. Shanghai, Chung-hua shu-chü edition, 1926. The essays cited in the notes from this book are:

"Erh-shih shih-chi chih chü-ling: t'o-la-ssu" 二十世紀之巨靈:托辣斯 (Trusts: the great spirit of the twentieth century), ts'e 23:33–53;

"Lun nei-ti tsa-chu yü shang-wu kuan-shih" 論內地雜居與商務關係 (On the relationship between foreign merchants living in the interior and commercial affairs), ts'e 28:42b–47;

"Lun shang-yeh hui-i-so chih-i" 論商業會議所之益 (On the advantages of commercial consultative associations), ts'e 28:38–41;

"Nung-hui pao-hsu" 農會報序 (Preface to the periodical of the Agricultural Society), ts'e 4:11–12b;

"Shang-hui i" 商會議 (On chambers of commerce), ts'e 28:32b–38;

"Sheng-chi-hsueh hsueh-shuo yen-ke hsiao-shih" 生計學學說沿革小史 (A short history of the development of economics), ts'e 11:1–47b;

"Shih-chi huo-chih lieh-chuan chin-i" 史記貨殖列傳今義 (The present-day meaning of the 'Sketches of the Rich' in the *Historical Memoirs*), ts'e 1:1b–11;

"Shuo ch'ün hsu" 說羣序 (A preface on "grouping"), ts'e 3:45a–b.

Liang Chia-pin 梁嘉彬. *Kuang-tung shih-san-hang k'ao* 廣東十三行考 (A study of the thirteen Co-hong companies of Kwangtung). Shanghai, 1937.

Liu Kwang-ching. "British-Chinese Steamship Rivalry in China, 1873–85," in C. D. Cowan, ed., *The Economic Development of China and Japan: Studies in Economic History and Political Economy.* London, 1964.

———. "Nineteenth-Century China: The Disintegration of the Old Order and the Impact of the West," in Ping-ti Ho and Tang Tsou, eds., *China in Crisis: Volume One, China's Heritage and the Communist Political System.* 2 bks. Chicago, The University of Chicago Press, 1968.

———. "The Limits of Regional Power in Late Ch'ing Period: A Reappraisal," *The Tsing Hua Journal of Chinese Studies* (new series) 10.2:176-223 (1974).

Liu Ta-chung and Kung-chia Yeh. *The Economy of the Chinese Mainland, 1933–1959.* Princeton, Princeton University Press, 1965.

"Lun Chung-kuo shang-yeh pu fa-ta chih yuan-yin" 論中國商業不發達原因 (A discussion on the reasons for the lack of development of commerce in China), in *Hsin-hai ko-min ch'ien-shih-nien chien shih-lun hsuan-chi* 辛亥革命前十年間時論選集 (Selected essays on current events written during the ten years prior to the Revolution of 1911), eds. Chang Nan 張枬 and Wang Jen-chih 王忍之. 2 ser. in 4 vols. Peking, 1960, 1962.

Ma Chien-chung 馬建忠. "T'ieh-lu lun" 鐵路論 (On railways), in *Shih-k'o-chai chi-yen* 適可齋記言 (Records and sayings from the Shih-k'o studio), as ts'e 27 of *Hsi-cheng ts'ung-shu* 西政叢書 (A collection of books on the management of foreign affairs). 32 ts'e. Shanghai, 1897.

———. "Fu-min shuo" 富民說 (Discussion on the wealth of the

people), in *Wu-hsu pien-fa* 戊戌變法 (The reform of 1898), eds. Chien Po-tsan 翦伯贊 et al. 4 vols. Shanghai, 1953.

Ma Hui-ch'ing 馬惠卿. "Chin-shih shang-hui ti yen-ke" 津市商會沿革 (A survey of the Tientsin Chambers of Commerce), in *CKKYSTL-I*.

MacGowan, D. J. "Chinese Guilds or Chambers of Commerce and Trade Unions," *Journal of North-China Branch of the Royal Asiatic Society.* Vol. 21 (1888–89).

MacKinnon, Stephen R. "Liang Shih-i and the Communications Clique," *Journal of Asian Studies* 29.3:581–602 (1970).

Meng, S. M. *The Tsungli Yamen: Its Organization and Functions.* Cambridge, East Asian Research Center, Harvard University, 1962.

Metzger, Thomas A. "The State and Commerce in Imperial China," *Journal of Asian and African Studies* 6:23–46 (1970).

———. "The Organizational Capabilities of the Ch'ing State in the Field of Commerce: The Liang-huai Salt Monopoly, 1740–1840," in W. E. Willmott, ed., *Economic Organization in Chinese Society.* Stanford, Stanford University Press, 1972.

Morrison, Esther. "The Modernization of the Confucian Bureaucracy." Unpublished Ph.D. thesis, Radcliffe College, 1959.

Morse, Hosea Ballou. *The Gilds of China: with an Account of the Gild Merchants or Co-Hong of Canton.* London, Longmans, Green & Co., 1909.

Mou An-shih 牟安世. *Yang-wu yun-tung* 洋務運動 (The "foreign affairs" movement). Shanghai, 1956.

Muramatsu Yuji. "A Documentary Study of Chinese Landlordism in Late Ch'ing and Early Republican Kiangnan," *Bulletin of the School of Oriental and African Studies* 29.3:566–599 (1966).

Murphey, Rhoads. "The Treaty Ports and China's Modernization," in Mark Elvin and G. William Skinner, eds., *The Chinese City Between Two Worlds.* Stanford, Stanford University Press, 1974.

Nakamura Tadashi 中村義. "Shimmatsu seiji to kanryō shihon –Sei Sen-kai no yakuwari o megutte" 清末政治と官僚資本:盛宣懷の役割をめぐって (Late Ch'ing politics and bureaucratic capital: with reference to Sheng Hsuan-huai's role), in *Chūgoku kinkaida no shakai kōzō* 中国近代化の社会構造 (The social structure of China's modernization). Tokyo, 1960.

Nan-hai hsien-chih 南海縣志 (Gazetteer of Nan-hai County), eds. Chang Feng-chieh 張鳳喈, et al. Preface 1910.

NCH: North-China Herald and Supreme Court and Consular Gazette. Shanghai.

Nieh Tseng Chi-fen 聶曾紀芬. *Ch'ung-te lao-jen pa-shih tzu-ting nien-p'u* 崇德老人八十自訂年譜 (Chronological autobiography of Ch'ung-te lao-jen at eighty years of age). Shanghai, 1933.

NKSPTCP-I: Nung-kung-shang pu t'ung-chi piao, ti-i-tz'u 農工商部統計表第一次 (Statistical tables of the Ministry of Agriculture, Industry, and Commerce, first collection). 6 ts'e. Peking, 1909.

NKSPTCP-II: Nung-kung-shang pu t'ung-chi piao, ti-erh-tz'u 農工商部統計表第二次 (Statistical tables of the Ministry of Agriculture, Industry, and Commerce, second collection). 5 ts'e. Peking, 1910.

North-China Herald, see NCH.

Nung-kung-shang pu hsien-hsing chang-ch'eng 農工商部現行章程 (Current regulations of the Ministry of Agriculture, Industry, and Commerce). 13 ts'e. Peking, 1908.

Nung-kung-shang pu t'ung-chi piao, ti-i-tz'u, see *NKSPTCP-I.*

Nung-kung-shang pu t'ung-chi piao, ti-erh-tz'u, see *NKSPTCP-II*.

Ou Chü-chia 歐榘甲. *Ou Chü-chia chuan* 歐榘甲傳 (Autobiography). N.p., n.d.

P'an-yü hsien hsu-chih 番禺縣續志 (Continuation of the Gazetteer of the P'an-yü County), ed. Wang Chao-yung . N.p., 1931.

Pao-hua pien-i 寶貨辨疑 (How to distinguish forgeries in valuable goods). N.p., n.d.

Pei-ching Jui-fu-hsiang 北京瑞蚨祥 (The Jui-fu-hsiang Company of Peking). Peking, 1959.

Pei-yang kung-tu lei-tsuan, see *PYKT*.

Pei-yang kung-tu lei-tsuan hsu-pien, see *PYKTHP*.

P'eng Tse-i 彭澤益. "Shih-chiu shih-chi hou-ch'i Chung-kuo ch'eng-shih shou-kung-yeh shang-yeh hsing-hui ti chung-chien ho tso-yung" 十九世紀后期中國城市手工業商業行會的重建和作用 (The revival and function of urban handicraft and commercial organizations in late nineteenth-century China), *Li-shih yen-chiu* 歷史研究 (Historical studies) 1:71–102 (1965).

P'eng Yü-hsin 彭雨新. "Ch'ing-mo chung-yang yü ko-sheng ts'ai-cheng kuan-hsi" 清末中央與各省財政關係 (Fiscal relationships between the central government and the provinces during the last years of the Ch'ing dynasty), in *She-hui k'o-hsueh tsa-chih* 社會科學雜誌 (Journal of social sciences) 9.1:83–110 (June, 1947).

Perkins, Dwight H. *Agricultural Development in China, 1368–1968*. Chicago, Aldine Publishing Co., 1969.

———. "Introduction: The Persistence of the Past," in Dwight H. Perkins, ed., *China's Modern Economy in Historical Perspective*. Stanford, Stanford University Press, 1975.

PYKT: Pei-yang kung-tu lei-tsuan 北洋公牘類纂 (A categorized collection of official documents from the commission of trade for the northern ports), ed. Kan Hou-tz'u 甘厚慈. First preface 1907.

PYKTHP: Pei-yang kung-tu lei-tsuan hsu-pien 北洋公牘類纂續編 (Continuation of a categorized collection of official documents from the commission of trade for the northern ports), ed. Kan Hou-tz'u. First preface 1910.

Rankin, Mary B. *Early Chinese Revolutionaries: Radical Intellectuals in Shanghai and Chekiang, 1902–1911.* Cambridge, Harvard University Press, 1971.

Rawski, Thomas G. "Chinese Dominance of Treaty Port Commerce and Its Implications, 1860–1875," *Explorations in Economic History* 7.4:451–473 (1970).

Rhoads, Edward J. M. "Merchant Associations in Canton, 1895–1911," in Mark Elvin and G. William Skinner, eds., *The Chinese City Between Two Worlds.* Stanford, Stanford University Press, 1974.

———. *China's Republican Revolution: The Case of Kwangtung, 1895–1913.* Cambridge, Harvard University Press, 1975.

Riskin, Carl. "Surplus and Stagnation in Modern China," in Dwight H. Perkins, *China's Modern Economy in Historical Perspective.* Stanford, Stanford University Press, 1975.

Saeki Tomi 佐伯富. *Shindai ensei no kenkyū* 清代鹽政の研究 (A study of the Ch'ing dynasty's salt administration). Kyoto, 1956.

Schurmann, Franz. *Ideology and Organization in Communist China.* 2nd ed., enlarged. Berkeley and Los Angeles, University of California Press, 1968.

Schwartz, Benjamin. *In Search of Wealth and Power: Yen Fu and the West.* Cambridge, Harvard University Press, 1964.

SCMP: South China Morning Post. Hong Kong.

Shang-hai ch'ien-chuang shih-liao 上海錢莊史料 (Materials on the history of the local banks in Shanghai). Shanghai, 1960.

Shang-hai hsien hsu-chih 上海縣續志 (A continuation of the Gazetteer of Shanghai County), ed. Yao Wen-nan Shanghai, 1918.

Shang-hai tsung-shang-hui yueh-pao 上海總商會月報 (Journal of the [Chinese] General Chamber of Commerce of Shanghai). Published monthly between Jan. 1921 and Nov. 1927 (Vols. 1.1–7.11).

Shang Ping-ho 尚秉和. *Hsin-jen ch'un-chiu* 辛壬春秋 (1911 and 1912: a chronicle). 16 ts'e. N.p., 1924.

Shang-wu kuan-pao, see *SWKP.*

Shen Yun-lung 沈雲龍 "Chang-wo wan-Ch'ing cheng-ping ti I-k'uang" 掌握晚清政柄之奕劻 (Prince Ch'ing: wielder of political power in the late Ch'ing period), in his *Hsien-tai cheng-chih jen-wu shu-p'ing* 現代政治人物述評 (A critical review of some contemporary political personalities). 2 vols. Taipei, 1966.

Sheng Hsuan-huai 盛宣懷. *Sheng shang-shu Yü-chai ts'un-kao ch'u-k'an* 盛尚書愚齋存稿初刊 (Collected drafts of ministry president Sheng Hsuan-huai, first issue), ed. Lü Ching-tuan 呂景端. 101 chüan in 51 ts'e. Shanghai, 1939.

Shina keizai zensho 支那經濟全書 (Complete economic studies of China). Comp. Tō Dōbun Shoin 東亞同文書院 (East Asian Language School [of Shanghai]). 12 vols. Vols. 1-4, Osaka, 1907; vols. 5–12, Tokyo, 1908.

Singapore Chinese Chamber of Commerce, The: The Fiftieth Anniversary Commemorative Issue. Singapore, 1954.

Sjoberg, Gideon. *The Preindustrial City: Past and Present.* New York, The Free Press, 1960.

Skinner, George William. *Leadership and Power in the Chinese*

Community of Thailand. Ithaca, Cornell University Press, 1958.

Smith, Thomas C. *Political Changes and Industrial Development in Japan: Government Enterprise, 1868–1880.* Stanford, Stanford University Press, 1965.

Song Ong Siang. *One Hundred Years' History of the Chinese in Singapore.* Singapore, University of Malaya Press, 1967.

South China Morning Post. Hong Kong.

Spector, Stanley. *Li Hung-chang and the Huai Army.* Seattle, University of Washington Press, 1964.

Stanley, Charles J. *Late Ch'ing Finance: Hu Kuang-yung as an Innovator.* Cambridge, East Asian Research Center, Harvard University, 1961.

Sun, E-tu Zen. "The Board of Revenue in Nineteenth-Century China," *Harvard Journal of Asiatic Studies* 24:175–228 (1962–1963).

———. *Chinese Railways and British Interests, 1898–1911.* New York, King's Crown Press, 1954.

———. "The Shanghai-Hangchow-Ningpo Railway Loan of 1908," *Far Eastern Quarterly* 10.2:136–150 (1950).

Sun Yü-t'ang, comp. *Chung-kuo chin-tai kung-yeh shih tzu-liao, ti-i-chi, 1840–1895 nien,* see *KYSTL-I.*

Sutton, Francis X., et al. *The American Business Creed.* New York, Schocken Books, 1962.

SWKP: Shang-wu kuan-pao 商務官報 (The commercial gazette). Published three times each Chinese calendar month (5th, 15th, 25th) by the Shang-wu kuan-pao chü 商務官報局 (Bureau of the Commercial Gazette), Peking, April 1906– February 1912.

Ta-Ch'ing chin-shen ch'uan-shu 大清晉紳全書 (The complete directory of the Ch'ing officials and notables). Peking, issued quarterly.

Ta-Ch'ing Kuang-hsu hsin fa-ling 大清光緒新法令 (New ordinances promulgated during the Kuang-hsu reign of the Ch'ing dynasty). Shanghai, 1910.

T'ao Ch'eng-ch'ing 陶承慶. *Shang-ch'eng i-lan* 商程一覽 (A complete guide to the trade routes). N.p., n.d.

T'ao Hsi-sheng 陶希聖. *Chung-kuo cheng-chih ssu-hsiang shih* 中國政治思想史 (A history of Chinese political thought). 4 vols. Chungking, 1942.

Teng Ch'eng-hsiu 鄧承修 *Yü-ping ko tsou-i* 語冰閣奏議 (Memorials from the Yü-ping Pavilion). Taipei reprint, 1967.

TFTC: Tung-fang tsa-chih 東方雜誌 (Eastern miscellany).

THL/KH: Kuang-hsu chao tung-hua lu 光緒朝東華錄 (The tung-hua records of the Kuang-hsu reign), comp. Chu Shou-p'eng 朱壽朋. 5 vols. Peking, 1958.

Tsai Chih-li 戴執禮, comp. *Szu-ch'uan pao-lu yun-tung shih-liao* 四川保路運動史料 (Historical materials on the railway protection movement in Szechwan). Peking, 1959.

Ts'ao Ju-lin 曹汝霖. *I-sheng chih hui-i* 一生之回憶 (Reminiscences). Taipei, 1964.

Ts'en Ch'un-hsuan 岑春煊. *Lo-chai man-ch'i* 樂齋漫筆 (Autobiographical notes). Taipei reprint, 1962.

Tung-fang tsa-chih, see *TFTC.*

T'ung-chih Shang-hai hsien-chih 同治上海縣志 (Gazetteer of the Shanghai County for the T'ung-chih reign), ed. Yü Yueh 余樾. Preface 1871.

T'ung-chou hsing-pan shih-yeh chih li-shih: Ta-sheng sha-ch'ang 通州興辦實業之歷史：大生紗廠 (A history of the industries established at T'ung-chou: Dah Sun Cotton Spinning Mill). Nan-t'ung, 1910.

Wai-chiao tang-an 外交檔案 (Materials from the Foreign Affairs Ministry). Deposited at the Academia Sinica, Nan-kang, Taiwan. Files consulted and included in the notes are:

"Hui-pan shang-pan" 會辦商辦 (Assisting in commercial cases), File No. B-1-4.

"Shang-wu an" 商務案 (Commercial cases), Vols. 2 and 5, File No. B-1-4.

Wang Ching-yü, comp. *Chung-kuo chin-tai kung-yeh shih tzu-liao, ti-erh-chi, 1895–1914 nien,* see *KYSTL-II.*

———. 汪敬虞. *"Shih-chiu shih-chi wai-kuo ch'in Hua ch'i-yeh chung ti Hua-shang fu-ku huo-tung"* 十九世紀外國侵华企業中的华商附股活動 (Investment by Chinese merchants in the foreign firms that invaded China in the nineteenth century), *Li-shih yen-chiu* 歷史研究 (Historical studies) 4:39–74 (1965).

Wang, Y. C. *Chinese Intellectuals and the West, 1872–1949.* Chapel Hill, The University of North Carolina Press, 1966.

Wang Yeh-chien. *Land Taxation in Imperial China, 1750–1911.* Cambridge, Harvard University Press, 1973.

Wang Yu-ling 王有齡. "Shang-pu chih tse-jen" 商部之責任 (The responsibility of the Ministry of Commerce), in *SWKP,* No. 7 (1906).

Wen Chung-chi. "The Nineteenth Century Imperial Chinese Consulates in the Straits Settlements." Unpublished M.A. thesis, University of Singapore, 1964.

Who's Who in China. 3rd ed. Shanghai, 1936.

Wickberg, Edgar. *The Chinese in Philippine Life.* New Haven, Yale University Press, 1965.

Wilkinson, Endymion P. "Chinese Merchant Manuals and Route Books," *Ch'ing-shih wen-t'i* 2.1 (1972).

Willmott, W. E., ed. *Economic Organization in Chinese Society.* Stanford, Stanford University Press, 1972.

Wright, Arnold and H. A. Cartwright, eds. *Twentieth Century Impressions of Hong Kong, Shanghai, and other Treaty Ports of China: Their History, People, Commerce, Industries, and Re-*

sources. London, Lloyd's Greater Britain Publishing Co., Ltd., 1908.

Wright, Mary C. *The Last Stand of Chinese Conservatism: The T'ung-chih Restoration, 1862–1874.* Stanford, Stanford University Press, 1957.

———. "Introduction: The Rising Tide of Change," in her ed., *China in Revolution: The First Phase, 1900–1913.* New Haven, Yale University Press, 1968.

Wu Ch'eng-lo 吳承洛. *Chin-shih Chung-kuo shih-yeh t'ung-shih* 今世中國實業通志 (A survey of industries in contemporary China). 2 vols. Shanghai, 1929.

Wu Chien-jen 吳研人. *Erh-shih-nien mu-tu kuai-hsien-chuang* 二十年目睹怪現狀 (Strange happenings eyewitnessed during the last twenty years). 2 vols. Hong Kong, 1969.

Wu Chung-fu 吳中孚. *Shang-chia pien-lan* 商賈便覽 (A convenient guide for resident and itinerant merchants). First preface 1792.

"Wu-hsi Jung-shih ch'i-yeh-chia chia-tsu chi ch'i ch'i-chia ti mien-fan yeh" 無錫榮氏企業家家族及其起家的麵粉業 (The family of Mr. Jung, the industrialist of Wusih, and his first successful industry, the flour industry), in *Hsin shih-chieh* 新世界 (The new world, new series) 9:19–25 (November 1944).

"Wu-shih-nien lai Chung-kuo ching-chi" 五十年來中國經濟 (The Chinese economy during the last fifty years), in *Chung-kuo t'ung-shang yin-hang ch'uang-li wu-shih chou-nien chi-nien-ts'e* 中國通商銀行創立五十週年紀念冊 (A commemorative issue of the Commercial Bank of China on the occasion of its fiftieth anniversary). Shanghai, 1947.

Yang Lien-sheng. "Notes on Dr. Swann's *Food and Money* in Ancient China," *Harvard Journal of Asiatic Studies* 13:524-527 (1950).

———. *Money and credit in China: A Short History.* Cambridge, Harvard University Press, 1952.

———. "Government Control of the Urban Merchant in Traditional China," *Tsing Hua Journal of Chinese Studies* (new series) 8.1–2:186–209 (August 1970).

Yang-wu yun-tung 洋務運動 (The "foreign affairs" movement), comp. Chung-kuo shih-hsueh hui 中國史學會 (The society for Chinese historical studies). 8 vols. Shanghai, 1961.

Yen Chung-p'ing 嚴中平. *Chung-kuo mien-fang-chih shih-kuo, 1289–1937* 中國棉紡織史稿, 1289–1937 (Draft history of the Chinese cotton industry, 1289-1937). Rev. ed. Peking, 1955.

Yü Hsueh-pu 虞學圃 and Wan Ch'i-shih 温岐石. *Chiang-hu ch'ih-tu fen-yun* 江湖尺牘分韻 (Sample letter writings for the traveler arranged by rhymes). N.p., n.d.

Yü-tzu 餘子. "Tsai-t'an Hang-chou ti hung-ting shang-jen" 再談杭州的紅頂商人 (Speaking again on the titled merchants of Hangchow), in Yü-tzu, *Chang-ku man-t'an* 掌故漫談 (Casual talks on history). Hong Kong, 1974.

Yü Ying-shih. *Trade and Expansion in Han China: A Study in the Structure of Sino-Barbarian Economic Relations.* Berkeley and Los Angeles, University of California Press, 1967.

GLOSSARY

Ai-yü shan-t'ang 愛育善堂

Chang Ch'a 張謇
Chang Jen-chün 張人駿
Chang Pi-shih 張弼士
Chang Po-hsi 張百熙
Chang Yen-mou 張燕謀
Chao Ch'i-lin 趙啓霖
Chao Pin-yen 趙濱彥
chao-shang chu-kuan 招商助官
Chao Shu-ch'iao 趙舒翹
Ch'ao-chou (or Teo-chiu) 潮州
Chen-wu tsung-she 振武宗社
Ch'en Chih 陳熾
Ch'en I-fu 陳一甫
Ch'en Ming-yuan 陳明遠
Ch'en Pi 陳璧
Ch'en Wei-yung 陳維鏞
Cheng-wu ch'u 政務處
chi (company) 記
Ch'i-shih-erh-hang shang-pao 七十二行商報
Chiang Shu-chen 蔣書箴
Ch'iao Mou-hsuan 喬茂萱
Chien(s) (Kans) 簡
chien-sheng 監生
ch'ien-chuang 錢莊
Ch'ien Hsing-ts'un 錢杏邨
ching-shang 經商
ch'ing (court rank) 卿
Ch'ing, Prince 慶親王
ch'ing-chi lung-tuan 傾擠攏斷
Ch'ing-ch'i hsien 青谿縣
ch'ing-i 清議
chiu-sheng i-ssu 九生一死
Chiu-shih chieh-yao 救世揭要
Chiu-ta shan-t'ang 九大善堂
Chou Chin-chen 周金箴
Chou Chin-piao 周晉鑣
Chou Fu 周馥
Chou-li 周禮
Chou Lin-shu 周麟述
Chou Shan-p'ei 周善培
Chu Ch'i-ang 朱其昂
Chu Chung-fu 朱仲甫
Chu Pao-san 朱葆三
Chu Ta-ch'un 祝大椿
Chu Wen-p'ei 朱文沛
Ch'u Ch'eng-po 褚成博
chü (bureau) 局
Ch'ü Tsan-shen 區贊森
Ch'uan-kung ch'en-lieh so 勸工陳列所
ch'uan-yeh tao 勸業道
Ch'üan-kung-ch'ang 勸工廠
Ch'un, Prince 醇親王
ch'ün (grouping) 羣

Chung-hua hui-kuan 中華會館
Chung-kuo t'ung-shang yin-hang 中國通商銀行
Ch'ung-cheng shan-t'ang 崇正善堂
Ch'ung-wen Gate 崇文門
Cohong 公行

Fa-lü pien-tsuan-kuan 法律編纂館
Fa pu 法部
Fan Fen 樊芬
Fang Chiao-po 方椒伯
Fang-pien shan-t'ang 方便善堂
Fen-shang-hui 分商會
Feng Kuei-fen 馮桂芬
fu-ch'iang 富强
Fu-feng 阜豐
Fu Hsiao-an 傅筱庵
Fu-k'ang 阜康
Fu-kuo ts'e 富國策
Fu-min shuo 富民說
Fu-t'ai 復泰

Hai-men 海門
han-che 函摺
Han-yang t'ieh-ch'ang 漢陽鉄廠
hang-hui 行會
Hanyehping 漢冶萍
Ho Ch'i (Ho Kai) 何啟
ho-pan 合辦
Hsiao Yung-hua 蕭永華
Hsiao Yung-sheng 蕭永笙
hsieh-li 協理
Hsin-an 新安
hsin-chü 新局
Hsiu-ting fa-lü-kuan 修定法律館
Hsu-ko-chuang 胥各莊
Hsu Shih-ch'ang 徐世昌
Hsu T'ung 徐桐
Hsu Tzu-ching 徐子靜
Hsu Ying-hung 許應鴻
Hsu Ying-kuei 許應騤
Hsueh Fu-ch'eng 薛福成
Hu Ch'ü-fen 胡燏棻
Hu-Hang-Yung t'ieh-lu 滬杭甬鐵路
Hu Kuang-yung (Hsueh-yen) 胡光鏞(雪岩)
Hu Li-yuan 胡禮垣
Hu Lin-i 胡林翼
Hu-pei chih-pu kuan-chü 湖北織布官局
Hu-pei fang-sha kuan-chü 湖北紡紗官局
Hu pu 户部
Hua-ch'iao kung-hui 華僑公會
Hua-hsin fang-chih hsin chü 華新紡織新局
Hua-sheng fang-chih, tsung-ch'ang 華盛紡織總廠
Huai Army 淮軍
Huang Chin-ch'üan 黄晉荃
Huang Ching-t'ang 黄景棠

Huang Chung-hui 黄中慧
Huang Hou-ch'eng 黄厚成
Huang Shen-chih 黄慎之
Huang Tsun-hsien 黄遵憲
Hui-chi ssu 會計司
Hui-chou 徽州
Hui-hsing shan-t'ang 惠行善堂

hui-kuan 會館
hui-pan 會辦
hui-pan shang-wu ta-ch'en 會辦商務大臣
Hui-t'ung 惠通
huo 貨

i-kuan tso-shang 以官助商
I-t'u hsueh-t'ang 藝徒學堂
I-yen 易言
i-yuan 議員

Jih-sheng-ch'ang 日昇昌
Jui-ch'eng 瑞澂
Jui-fu-hsiang 瑞蚨祥
Jun-shen shan-t'ang 潤身善堂
Jung-lu 榮祿
Jung Pin-chih 榮秉之
Jung Teh-sheng 榮德生
Jung Tsung-ching 榮宗敬

K'ai-p'ing k'uang-wu chü 開平鑛務局
k'ai shang-chih 開商智
kan-she chu-i 干涉主義

Kao Li-ch'ing 高立卿
Kao-teng shih-yeh hsueh-t'ang 高等實業學堂
K'ao-cheng p'ai 考證派
k'e-ai 隔閡
ko 閣
ku-wen 顧問
kuan-ch'ih kung-ssu 官治公司
kuan-li 官利
kuan-pan 官辦
kuan-shang ho-pan 官商合辦
kuan-tu shang-pan 官督商辦
Kuan-tzu 管子
kuan-wei shang-ch'ang 官為商倡
kuan-wei tu-hsiao 官為督銷
Kuang-ch'ao kung-so 廣肇公所
Kuang-chi shan-t'ang 廣濟善堂
Kuang-jen shan-t'ang 廣仁善堂
Kuang-li (Kwong Lee) 廣利
Kuei-chou chi-ch'i k'uang-wu tsung-chü 貴州机器鑛務總局
Kuei Sung-ch'ing 桂嵩慶
kung (artisan) 工
kung (public) 公
Kung Chao-yuan 龔照瑗
Kung Hsin-chan 龔仙舟
Kung-i chü 工藝局
Kung pu 工部
kung-sheng 貢生
Kung Shou-t'u 龔壽圖

kung-so 公所
Kung-ssu chu-ts'e ch'u 公司註册處
Kung-ssu shang-lü 公司商律
Kung Yang-chü 龔仰遽
kung-yeh 工業
Kuo(s) 郭
Kuo Chuan (Philip Gockchin) 郭泉
kuo-ch'üan 國權
Kuo Hsun 郭勳
Kuo Lo (James Gocklock) 郭樂
Li Chin-yung 李金鏞
Li-fan yuan 理藩院
Li Han-chang 李瀚章
Li Hou-yu 李厚祐
Li Hung-tsao 李鴻藻
Li Kuo-lien 黎國廉
Li pu 禮部
Li Shih-chien 李士鑑
Li Shih-wei 李士偉
Li Sung-ch'en 李頌臣
Liang Ch'eng 梁誠
Liang Hsiao-shan 梁小山
Liang Shih-i 梁士詒
ling-ku 零股
Liu Chin-tsao 劉錦藻
Liu Kuei-hsing 劉桂馨
Liu K'un-i 劉坤一
Liu-pu 六部
Lu Chieh 盧傑
Lu Ch'uan-lin 鹿傳霖
Lu Jun-hsiang 陸潤庠
Lu Kuan-heng 盧觀恒
Lun-ch'uan chao-shang chü 輪船招商局
Lun Chung-kuo ch'iu fu-ch'iang i-ch'ou i-hsing chih fa 論中國求富强議籌易行之法

Meng Chin-hou 孟覲候
Meng Lo-ch'uan 孟洛川
Min-cheng pu 民政部
Ming-shan shan-t'ang 明善善堂
Mo-ho chin-k'uang chü 漠河金鑛局
mo-yeh 末業
mou-chi 某記
Mou-hsin mien-fen ch'ang 茂新麵粉廠
mu-fu 幕府
mu-yu 幕友

nan (baron) 男
nei-hang 内行
Nieh Ch'i-kuei 聶緝槼
Nieh Ch'i-chieh 聶其杰
Nieh Kuan-ch'en 聶管臣
nung 農
Nung-kung-shang pu 農工商部
Nung-kung-shang-wu chu 農工商務局
pa-cheng 八政

Pa-i hui-kuan 八邑會館
Pa-sheng hui-kuan 八省會館
P'an Chin-sheng 潘金甡
P'an Hua-mao 潘華茂
P'an Lu 潘露
P'an Wei 潘蔚
pang 幫
Pao-Chin kung-ssu 保晉公司

Pao-feng 保豐
pao-hsiao 報効
Pao-hui ssu 保惠司
Pao-shang chü 保商局
Pei-yang kung-i chü 北洋工藝局
Pei-yang Lan-chou kuan-k'uang yu-hsien kung-ssu 北洋灤州官礦有限公司
pen-yeh 本業
P'eng Ju-tsung 彭汝琮
p'iao-hao 票號
pin-tu 稟讀
P'ing-chün ssu 平均司
Po Leung Kuk (Pao-liang chü) 保良局
P'u-hsu 溥頊
P'u-yü t'ang 普育堂

sha-chu'an 沙船
Shan-hou chü 善後局
shan-t'ang 善堂
shang-chan 商戰
shang-cheng 商政
Shang-hai chi-ch'i chih-pu chü 上海机器織布局
Shang-hai shang-yeh hui-i kung-so 上海商業會議公所

shang-hsueh 商學
shang-hsun 商勳
shang-hui 商會
shang-jen 商人
"Shang-jen t'ung-li" 商人通例
Shang-lü kuan 商律館
Shang-pao kuan 商報館
Shang-piao chü 商標局
Shang pu 商部
shang-t'uan 商團
shang-tung 商董
shang-wu 商務
Shang-wu chü 商務局
Shang-wu hui 商務會
shang-wu i-yuan 商務議員
Shang-wu kuang-so 商務公所
Shang-wu pao 商務報
shang-wu ta-chen 商務大臣
shang-yao ta-chen 商約大臣
shang-yeh 商業
shang-yeh hui-i-so 商業會議所
Shen Chia-pen 沈家本
Shen Hsieh-chün 沈燮均

shen-shang 紳商
Shen-tu shang-pan 紳督商辦
shen-tung 紳董
Shen Yao 沈垚
Sheng Ch'un-i 盛春頤
sheng-yuan 生員
shih (food) 食
shih ("men of education") 士
shih-kuei 市儈
shih-lang 侍郎
shih-yeh 實業
shih-yeh chiao-yü 實業教育
Shu-shan shan-t'ang 述善善堂
Shun-t'ien fu 順天府
ssu (department) 司
Ssu-ming kung-so 四明公所
Su-lun 蘇倫
Sun Chia-nai 孫家鼐
Sun To-shen 孫多森
Sung Yun-tzu 宋芸子

Ta-sheng sha-ch'ang 大生紗廠
t'ai-p'ao 台炮
t'ang (hall) 堂
T'ang Kuei-sheng 湯癸生
T'ang-shan 唐山
T'ang Shao-i 唐紹儀
T'ang Shou-ch'ien 湯壽潛
T'ang Sung-yen 唐松岩
T'ang Tzu-chuang 湯子壯
T'ang Wei-chih 唐蔚之
ti-pao 地保
tien-hao 店號
T'ieh-liang 鐵良
T'ieh-lu kung-chü 鐵路公局
t'ieh-lu ta-chen 鐵路大臣
T'ien-chin kuan-yin-hao 天津官銀號
Ting Pao-ch'uan 丁寶銓
to-fang k'ai-tao 多方開導
Tong King-sing (T'ang T'ing-shu) 唐景星 (唐廷樞)
Tsai-chen 載振
Ts'ai(s) (Choys) 蔡
Ts'ai-cheng ch'u 財政處
Ts'ai Nai-huang 蔡乃煌
Ts'ao K'un 曹錕
Ts'en Ch'un-hsuan 岑春煊
Ts'en Yü-ying 岑毓英
Tseng Kuo-ch'üan 曾國荃
Tseng Kuo-fan 曾國藩
Tseng Lien 曾廉
Tseng Shao-ch'ing 曾少卿
Tseng Yen-ch'üan 曾彥銓
Tseng Yun 曾韞
tso-pan 坐辦
Tso Tsung-fan 左宗蕃
Tso Tsung-t'ang 左宗棠
tsu-chan 租棧
tsung-jen-fu fu-ch'eng 宗人府府丞

tsung-li 總理
tsung-pan 總辦
tsung-shang-hui 總商會
Tu-chih pu 度支部
tu-pan 督辦
Tu Yung-kuang 杜榮光
Tuan Chih-kuei 段芝貴
Tuan-fang 端方
t'ui-pu 退步
Tung-wah Hospital 東華醫院
T'ung-ch'ung-hai hua-yeh tsung-hui 通崇海花業總會

T'ung-i ssu 通藝司
t'ung-nien 同年
t'ung-p'an 通判
tzu (viscount) 子
Tzu-kung 子貢
Tz'u-ch'i 慈谿

wai-hang 外行
Wai-wu pu 外務部
Wang Ch'ang-ch'uan 王常川
Wang Chu-lin 王竹林
Wang Hsien-ch'ien 王先謙
Wang I-t'ang 王一亭
Wang K'ang-nien 汪康年
Wang P'eng-yun 王鵬運
Wang Ping-en 王秉恩
Wang Shao-lien 王劭廉
Wang Yu-ling 王有齡
wei-hsing 闈姓
Wei Ying-nan 韋應南
wei-yuan 委員
Wen-nien-feng 萬年豐
Wen-yü 文煜
Wu Chi-chih 吳繼之
Wu Ch'ung-yao 伍崇曜
Wu Fu-yuan 吳福元
Wu Mao-ting 吳懋鼎
Wu Shao-yung 伍紹榮
Wu T'ing-fang 伍廷芳
Wu T'ung-lin 吳桐林
Wu Yung-mou 伍永茂
wu-wei 無為

ya-hang 牙行
Yang-chi yuan 養濟院
Yang Shih-ch'i 楊士琦
Yang Shih-hsiang 楊士驤
Yao-hua 耀華
Yeh Kung-cho 葉恭綽
Yen Hsin-hou (Hsiao-fang) 嚴信厚（筱舫）
Yen I-pin (Tzu-chün) 嚴子均（義彬）
yin-hao 銀號
yin-yeh 淫業
Ying-ch'ang 應昌
Yu-ch'uan pu 郵傳部
Yu-pei li-hsien kung-hui 預備立憲公會
yu-wei 有為
Yü Hsi-sheng 郁熙繩

Yuan-ch'ang 源昌
Yuan Ko-ting 袁克定
Yuan Shih-k'ai 袁世凱
Yuan Shu-hsun 袁樹勛

Yueh-Han t'ieh-lu 粵漢鐵路
Yueh-shang tzu-chih hui 粵商自治會
Yun Hsin-yun 惲莘耘

INDEX

HARVARD EAST ASIAN MONOGRAPHS

1. Liang Fang-chung, *The Single-Whip Method of Taxation in China*
2. Harold C. Hinton, *The Grain Tribute System of China, 1845-1911*
3. Ellsworth C. Carlson, *The Kaiping Mines, 1877-1912*
4. Chao Kuo-chün, *Agrarian Policies of Mainland China: A Documentary Study, 1949-1956*
5. Edgar Snow, *Random Notes on Red China, 1936-1945*
6. Edwin George Beal, Jr., *The Origin of Likin, 1835-1864*
7. Chao Kuo-chün, *Economic Planning and Organization in Mainland China: A Documentary Study, 1949-1957*
8. John K. Fairbank, *Ch'ing Documents: An Introductory Syllabus*
9. Helen Yin and Yi-chang Yin, *Economic Statistics of Mainland China, 1949-1957*
10. Wolfgang Franke, *The Reform and Abolition of the Traditional Chinese Examination System*
11. Albert Feuerwerker and S. Cheng, *Chinese Communist Studies of Modern Chinese History*
12. C. John Stanley, *Late Ch'ing Finance: Hu Kuang-yung as an Innovator*
13. S. M. Meng, *The Tsungli Yamen: Its Organization and Functions*
14. Ssu-yü Teng, *Historiography of the Taiping Rebellion*
15. Chun-Jo Liu, *Controversies in Modern Chinese Intellectual History: An Analytic Bibliography of Periodical Articles, Mainly of the May Fourth and Post-May Fourth Era*
16. Edward J. M. Rhoads, *The Chinese Red Army, 1927-1963: An Annotated Bibliography*

17. Andrew J. Nathan, *A History of the China International Famine Relief Commission*

18. Frank H. H. King (ed.) and Prescott Clarke, *A Research Guide to China-Coast Newspapers, 1822-1911*

19. Ellis Joffe, *Party and Army: Professionalism and Political Control in the Chinese Officer Corps, 1949-1964*

20. Toshio G. Tsukahira, *Feudal Control in Tokugawa Japan: The Sankin Kōtai System*

21. Kwang-Ching Liu, ed., *American Missionaries in China: Papers from Harvard Seminars*

22. George Moseley, *A Sino-Soviet Cultural Frontier: The Ili Kazakh Autonomous Chou*

23. Carl F. Nathan, *Plague Prevention and Politics in Manchuria, 1910-1931*

24. Adrian Arthur Bennett, *John Fryer: The Introduction of Western Science and Technology into Nineteenth-Century China*

25. Donald J. Friedman, *The Road from Isolation: The Campaign of the American Committee for Non-Participation in Japanese Aggression, 1938-1941*

26. Edward Le Fevour, *Western Enterprise in Late Ch'ing China: A Selective Survey of Jardine, Matheson and Company's Operations, 1842-1895*

27. Charles Neuhauser, *Third World Politics: China and the Afro-Asian People's Solidarity Organization, 1957-1967*

28. Kungtu C. Sun, assisted by Ralph W. Huenemann, *The Economic Development of Manchuria in the First Half of the Twentieth Century*

29. Shahid Javed Burki, *A Study of Chinese Communes, 1965*

30. John Carter Vincent, *The Extraterritorial System in China: Final Phase*

31. Madeleine Chi, *China Diplomacy, 1914-1918*

32. Clifton Jackson Phillips, *Protestant America and the Pagan World: The First Half Century of the American Board of Commissioners for Foreign Missions, 1810-1860*

33. James Pusey, *Wu Han: Attacking the Present through the Past*
34. Ying-wan Cheng, *Postal Communication in China and Its Modernization, 1860-1896*
35. Tuvia Blumenthal, *Saving in Postwar Japan*
36. Peter Frost, *The Bakumatsu Currency Crisis*
37. Stephen C. Lockwood, *Augustine Heard and Company, 1858-1862*
38. Robert R. Campbell, *James Duncan Campbell: A Memoir by His Son*
39. Jerome Alan Cohen, ed., *The Dynamics of China's Foreign Relations*
40. V. V. Vishnyakova-Akimova, *Two Years in Revolutionary China, 1925-1927*, tr. Steven I. Levine
41. Meron Medzini, *French Policy in Japan during the Closing Years of the Tokugawa Regime*
42. *The Cultural Revolution in the Provinces*
43. Sidney A. Forsythe, *An American Missionary Community in China, 1895-1905*
44. Benjamin I. Schwartz, ed., *Reflections on the May Fourth Movement: A Symposium*
45. Ching Young Choe, *The Rule of the Taewŏn'gun, 1864-1873: Restoration in Yi Korea*
46. W. P. J. Hall, *A Bibliographical Guide to Japanese Research on the Chinese Economy, 1958-1970*
47. Jack J. Gerson, *Horatio Nelson Lay and Sino-British Relations, 1854-1864*
48. Paul Richard Bohr, *Famine and the Missionary: Timothy Richard as Relief Administrator and Advocate of National Reform*
49. Endymion Wilkinson, *The History of Imperial China: A Research Guide*
50. Britten Dean, *China and Great Britain: The Diplomacy of Commercial Relations, 1860-1864*

51. Ellsworth C. Carlson, *The Foochow Missionaries, 1847-1880*

52. Yeh-chien Wang, *An Estimate of the Land-Tax Collection in China, 1753 and 1908*

53. Richard M. Pfeffer, *Understanding Business Contracts in China, 1949-1963*

54. Han-sheng Chuan and Richard Kraus, *Mid-Ch'ing Rice Markets and Trade, An Essay in Price History*

55. Ranbir Vohra, *Lao She and the Chinese Revolution*

56. Liang-lin Hsiao, *China's Foreign Trade Statistics, 1864-1949*

57. Lee-hsia Hsu Ting, *Government Control of the Press in Modern China, 1900-1949*

58. Edward W. Wagner, *The Literati Purges: Political Conflict in Early Yi Korea*

59. Joungwon A. Kim, *Divided Korea: The Politics of Development, 1945-1972*

60. Noriko Kamachi, John K. Fairbank, and Chūzō Ichiko, *Japanese Studies of Modern China Since 1953: A Bibliographical Guide to Historical and Social-Science Research on the Nineteenth and Twentieth Centuries, Supplementary Volume for 1953-1969*

61. Donald A. Gibbs and Yun-chen Li, *A Bibliography of Studies and Translations of Modern Chinese Literature, 1918-1942*

62. Robert H. Silin, *Leadership and Values: The Organization of Large-Scale Taiwanese Enterprises*

63. David Pong, *A Critical Guide to the Kwangtung Provincial Archives Deposited at the Public Record Office of London*

64. Fred W. Drake, *China Charts the World: Hsu Chi-yü and His Geography of 1848*

65. William A. Brown and Urgunge Onon, translators and annotators, *History of the Mongolian People's Republic*

66. Edward L. Farmer, *Early Ming Government: The Evolution of Dual Capitals*

67. Ralph C. Croizier, *Koxinga and Chinese Nationalism: History, Myth, and the Hero*

68. William J. Tyler, tr., *The Psychological World of Natsumi Sōseki*, by Doi Takeo

69. Eric Widmer, *The Russian Ecclesiastical Mission in Peking during the Eighteenth Century*

70. Charlton M. Lewis, *Prologue to the Chinese Revolution: The Transformation of Ideas and Institutions in Hunan Province, 1891-1907*

71. Preston Torbert, *The Ch'ing Imperial Household Department: A Study of its Organization and Principal Functions, 1662-1796*

72. Paul A. Cohen and John E. Schrecker, eds., *Reform in Nineteenth-Century China*

73. Jon Sigurdson, *Rural Industrialization in China*

74. Kang Chao, *The Development of Cotton Textile Production in China*

75. Valentin Rabe, *The Home Base of American China Missions, 1880-1920*

76. Sarasin Viraphol, *Sino-Siamese Trade, 1652-1853*

77. Ch'i-ch'ing Hsiao, *The Military Establishment of the Yuan Dynasty*

78. Meishi Tsai, *Contemporary Chinese Novels and Short Stories, 1949-1972: An Annotated Bibliography*

79. Wellington K. K. Chan, *Merchants, Mandarins, and Modern Enterprise in Late Ch'ing China*